MACHINE POLITICS
A Study of Albany's O'Connells

Frank S. Robinson

Transaction Books
New Brunswick, New Jersey

To My Parents

Library of Congress Catalog Number: 76-3785.
ISBN: 0-87855-147-6.
Printed in the United States of America.

Library of Congress Cataloging in Publication Data
Robinson, Frank S.
    Machine politics.

    Reprint of the 1973 ed. published by Washington Park Spirit, Albany, under title: Albany's O'Connell machine.
    Includes index.
    1. Albany—Politics and government.   2. O'Connell, Daniel Peter, 1885-   I. Title.
JS512.R6 1976   329'.0211   76-3785
ISBN 0-87855-147-6

CONTENTS

Illustrations

PREFACE

THIS IS a book about an American institution known as the political machine. Most cities have had a machine at one time or another; a good many still do, but the phenomenon has been gradually dying out over the last forty years. It was a phenomenon substantially unique to this country and its form of democracy. A direct outgrowth of the democratization of our body politic, the machine was, to some extent, a perversion of it. Yet it must be remembered that for all their seemingly undemocratic attributes, most machines most of the time thrived on voter satisfaction.

This book examines one particular machine, exploring its antecedents, genesis, history, character, methodology and evolution. The subject machine happens to be the one running the city in which I live. It is a small city; all of it is hardly bigger than one of Chicago's fifty wards. But there is nothing that happens in Chicago that doesn't also happen in my microcosm. And the political machine here is the best textbook example presently operating anywhere, a rare survivor from another era. While by virtue of this fact, the O'Connell machine fails to be truly typical, much that can be said about it can be said not only about machines in general, but about politics in general as well.

When the book was nearly finished, I happened to comment to a friend of Dan O'Connell that it isn't really true that Republicans here get higher tax assessments, and that it is also untrue that the machine knows how everyone votes.

"Oh brother," he said, "have you got a lot to learn!"

In fact, I had learned a great deal, and not all of it confirmed my first assumptions or the myths of Albany politics. In a few areas the machine proved worse than I'd expected, in a few areas, better —and in those latter areas, it proved slyer than expected.

The writing of this book was prompted by the fact that nothing comprehensive had ever been published about Albany's machine. However, the local newspapers proved to be extremely helpful. They are independent of O'Connell (in fact, usually antagonistic) and while their bias had to be taken into account, many solid facts and valuable insights were gleaned from clippings files. Some of the points crystallized from there and out of other published materials, while some, such as the area of tax assessments, required probing. Personal interviews were of somewhat restricted value because those most interested in talking frankly about the machine are generally those not taken into its confidence. By and large, interviews helped to round out the picture on subject matter otherwise researched.°

I am especially indebted to the caretakers of the Harmanus Bleecker Library's Albany Room for a vast file of newspaper clippings related to the subject, and to Professor James A. Riedel of the State University of New York Graduate School of Public Affairs, who provided a wealth of student papers on machine topics. Most of these papers may be consulted at the University's Pierce Library. Gratitude must be expressed to their authors—who did much of the legwork for me.

Others consulted in the course of the work, or providing useful materials, include Professor Francis Anderson, Samuel E. Aronowitz, Harold E. Blodgett, John E. Boos, K. Scott Christianson, Professor Leon S. Cohen, Thomas D. Conole, Theresa B. Cooke, Mayor Erastus Corning, 2d, William Crotty, James A. Farley, Rocco Ferran, Robert G. Fichenberg, Morris Gerber, George W. Harder, Peter Jones, Thomas W. Keegan, Martin Kenny, Victor Lord, William Loudon, Donald L. Lynch, James MacDonough, Jane Maxwell, Thomas Maxwell, William Pauquette, Arnold W. Proskin, Francis Rivett, Father Joseph Romano, Professor William E. Rowley, James Ryan, Lewis Rubenstein, Robert J. Shillinglaw, Ralph Smith, Edward Swietnicki, Michael V. Tepedino, John Wolcott, and several others who requested that their names not be mentioned.

Generous use of photographs has been allowed by the Morris Gerber collection and the Capital newspapers' morgue.

° Dan O'Connell had agreed to be interviewed and was visited, but for various reasons, including his health, a full interview never took place. Such an interview would undoubtedly have added some color, but probably little light.

AMERICAN POLITICS
AND THE MACHINE

» »

POLITICS is the clash of people's divergent interests, ambitions and ideals, in the choice of their government, and in its operations.

In that clash, it is natural for those with similar views to band together to promote them. Such a grouping, when its objective is not merely to influence but to control the government, is a political party.

America has had a long tradition of two main parties contending for power: Tories and Whigs during colonial days, Federalists and Democratic-Republicans, then Whigs against Jackson's Democrats, and finally, Democrats against Republicans. The issues and even the underlying philosophies of the parties have evolved through the years; perhaps overall it can be said that the prime question dividing them has been who will rule the country.

A political party has a dual nature. Its philosophy and program will attract idealists and the body of its support among the people, which may be selfishly motivated. Government policies affect people's lives, and their support of a party that will do them good is legitimate—since conflicting interests will at the same time be clamoring for advancement.

The other facet of a political party is its organizational side. This will attract people whose ambitions are purely personal rather than class-oriented, that is, politicians. Their needs and the party's are complementary, since the party must win elections, and that takes organization and work. The politician takes care of that, and in return gains office or wealth or power.

Political organization dates back to ancient times, and flourished in colonial America. In Massachusetts, for example, clubs of revolutionists that named candidates were called "caucuses." In time, these caucuses became more and more open, and evolved into the convention system. Informality gave way to explicit rules for the selection of delegates and for the holding of conventions to choose candidates.

Nominations only mark the opening of a political contest, so caucuses and conventions would name campaign committees to take over from there. Committee structures became increasingly complex, and soon America had fully developed national, state, county and district organizations.

Such organizations for getting votes, especially on the local level, have come to be called political machines.

The first noteworthy machine in America was New York's Tammany Hall, beginning in the 1790's. One of its early leaders was Aaron Burr, who organized the campaign, ward by ward, in New York City. At that time one had to own property to vote, so Burr parceled out small shares in a single building to all of his supporters.

Then came the Clintons in New York. Their most effective tool was unprecedented use of patronage—the appointment of their followers to government jobs. This "spoils system" became nationwide during the Jackson era, and has remained part of our political life.

The next leader on the New York scene was "the little magician," Martin Van Buren, who started as a disciple of the Clintons. He soon headed a machine far surpassing theirs; known as the Albany Regency, it dominated the state for a quarter century. The Regency had an influential organ in the *Albany Argus* newspaper, and lieutenants in every county and town to keep the leaders attuned to popular sentiment. In the City of Albany itself, the Regency set the pattern for the machine-type rule which has prevailed for most of its subsequent history.

The business boom following the Civil War spurred the proliferation of political organization. Corporations had to be chartered by government, and depended on government for favorable treatment. Collusion between businessmen and politicians was the logical outgrowth, and scandals rocked Congress and the White House.

Venality was rife on the local scene too. Cities were expanding their services and public works, all of which was subject to favoritism and grafting. The alliance between the political machine and the business interests would extend to influencing elections. Big business could put the thumb on small business, through the banks upon whom firms depended for loans; and small businesses could pressure their employees to vote "right."

Republican bosses specialized in controlling state legislatures; but it was in the Democratic cities that the classic form of the political machine developed. While the Republican machines did favors for businessmen who helped keep them in power, the Democrats took a different tack. Since businesses preferred to deal with Republicans, the Democrats built favor-getting machines for voters who could keep them in power—which forced businessmen to deal with them.

The most malleable voters were the immigrants. They came off the boats bewildered, usually unable even to speak English. But there would be a politician on hand who knew the language of the old country, who would find them places to live, give them free food and coal, and help them get jobs. Then at election time, the immigrants would be naturalized *en masse* and herded to the polls with their citizenship papers in one hand, and their ballots in the other.

At that time, each party provided its own premarked ballots. A voter didn't have to be literate in order to cast the ballot given him by a politician. Of course, voters were exploited, and there was rampant vote buying and fraud. Eventually this system was replaced by the "Australian ballot," with all the candidates on one government-supplied sheet, but even this was subject to widespread abuses. Today, in many areas, voting machines are used, which are virtually tamper-proof and guarantee secrecy.

Despite the fraud, support for the machine would be broad-based in the old days, because not just immigrants, but all citizens, were susceptible to its wiles. Machine favors were almost limitless. It could fix your taxes, jury summonses, fire or sanitary inspections, get you out of jail or provide a clubhouse lawyer for whatever legal problems you might have. It would take you on the political club's boat ride or picnic, it would pay a bill for you if you were strapped for cash, deliver coal and food, Christmas and Thanksgiving turkeys. It would be your entree to city hall and the wheels of government, and could get you a job if you needed one. The neighborhood politician knew you personally by name, and greeted you enthusiastically as a friend. He often seemed the only man in the great impersonal metropolis genuinely concerned about you and your welfare. The poor were his constant constituency. The only thing he wanted in return for all this was your vote once a year, which seemed little enough, since you hardly cared which gang of thieves ran city hall. And worse come to worst, he would pay you for your vote.

Taxes might have been high to cover the grafting that was needed to finance this system. But taxes were paid by business. The man on the street saw the machine as making his life a little bit better.

We have noted the beginning of that paragon of machines, New York's Tammany Hall, which became almost a synonym for corruption. Its Board of Aldermen in 1851 was called "The Forty Thieves," and one of the forty was a young man named William Marcy Tweed.

Tweed climbed slowly to the top of the organization ladder. Once he got there, Tammany had never been ruled with such an iron hand. Tweed put his lackeys into office as mayor and even governor, and controlled the judges and the legislature as well. Then he and his ring commenced to steal—hundreds of millions of dollars. This was accomplished largely through padding the bills for city contracting work with outrageous liberality.

Tweed and his confreres were immortalized by Thomas Nast's biting cartoons; at the time, they may have hurt the boss more than anything else. Many of the voters couldn't read, he lamented, "but they can look at the damn pictures."

When the newspapers discovered the plundering of the city treasury, Tweed asked the people, "Well, what are you going to do about it?" The ring marked the city comptroller to play the scapegoat, but he rebelled and gave his records to a grand jury, and then fled to Europe. The boss went to prison; on his arrival there, he listed his occupation as "Statesman."

That was the end of Tweed, but not of Tammany. Still entrenched by virtue of its vast network of ward leaders and neighborhood committeemen who had done millions of favors, the machine continued to flourish. It was later weakened by the stanching of the immigrant flow, and by further corruption revelations during the Depression. When people are hungry, they are not very tolerant of graft.

In the present era, civil service reform has penetrated state and local governments, but there are still plenty of jobs for the political hacks. While a machine today can deliver a job, other changes in the total environment have brought about its gradual weakening. A general rise in the standard of living has reduced the effectiveness of the machine's welfare-style largesse, and the welfare function *per se* has been taken over by government altogether. There are fewer favors for which a citizen has to go to a politician. More rigorous election procedures have eliminated some of the shadier means by which machines had been able to perpetuate themselves in power. Tightening laws make grafting between politicians and businessmen ever more delicate to consummate and conceal. The decline in voter loyalty to the national parties has brought with it a greater willingness to abandon the party line at the local level. The electorate is slowly becoming more sophisticated, and dislikes being taken for granted by a machine.

So, across the nation, the old-style political machine is dying out. There are places where it has managed to adapt, and survive. And there are even places where the trend has been defied, where the machine plods on in the time-worn manner, and still reigns. One of the few and most effective such machines in an important city is Albany's O'Connell machine.

Daniel P. O'Connell in his eighties (*Washington Park Spirit*)

» »

CHAPTER 1

Billy Barnes, Boy Boss

ALBANY is the capital of New York State. Its location on the west bank of the Hudson River, 145 miles north of New York City, makes it the hub of the region bounded by New York, Boston and Montreal. It is also the seat of Albany County, containing today a little over forty percent of the county's population. Dotting the rest of the county are two small cities, Cohoes and Watervliet, and a number of townships.

Albany is one of the oldest American cities; the first permanent colonization there by Dutch Walloons occurred in 1624. Forty years later, the city was surrendered to the English, but its Dutch antecedents are still reflected in street and park names, and in the Dutch ancestry of many of the city's leading families. Architecture harking back to its earliest days is observable in many parts of Albany, and the layout of steep, narrow streets winding up from the river has hardly changed in three centuries.

Because of its strategic location, Albany has always been the commercial center for a large agricultural area. The city's key role in commerce was enlarged with the opening of the Erie canal and the birth of railroads in the 1820's, linking Albany to the great lakes. During the Civil War era, the city was a center for the lumber industry; later years saw diversification into papermaking, manufacture of felts and other textiles, printing, stationery and other paper products, drugs, foods, steel, foundry and other industries.

However, because of Albany's small size, being the state capital has been the chief determinant of its character. Certainly today, government is the major industry of Albany, employing far more of its citizens than any other.

For the first half of its history, Albany was a hamlet of only a few thousand people. By 1850, the population reached fifty thousand, and it doubled by the end of the century. There the growth stopped, and during the present century, Albany's population has remained fairly static in the 120,000 to 130,000 range. Its dominant ethnic strain is Irish Catholic, with German Catholic in second place. The city today is about half Catholic, a proportion down considerably from that of earlier periods.

Albany has a long history of oligarchical rule, starting with the commercially powerful Dutch traders and landholders. While in later periods, the financial interests have shared power with politicians, the domination of the city by a coterie of wealthy old families has never fully given way. Political rule of the city has also been concentrated in a few hands, since the days of Martin Van Buren's Albany Regency.

Albany in the 1890's was ruled by an entrenched Democratic political machine. Such is the case today, but the modern organization is not the lineal descendant of the earlier one. The tale of Albany's conversion from one Democratic machine to another is the tale of a Republican boss.

His name was William F. Barnes, Jr., and he was known, inevitably, as "Billy."

The grandson of Thurlow Weed, a longtime grey eminence of New York State politics, Barnes was born in 1866. When he returned to Albany from Harvard University, he took charge of the *Evening Journal*, a popular newspaper Weed had founded. With the paper as his influential base, it was easy for Barnes to move into the role of political operative.

Barnes entered politics as a Republican in a Democratic stronghold. The Albany G.O.P. at this time was in a sorry state of disorganization and factional bickering, too weak to elect the proverbial dogcatcher. William Barnes, by the sheer force of his personality, surmounted the party's internal difficulties and whipped it

William F. Barnes, the "Boy Leader" of Albany Republicans
(*Courtesy of the Times-Union*)

into fighting trim. Fresh from college, he was barely twenty-five, and was being called "The Boy Leader."

At first, Barnes found his party so dominated and corrupted by the reigning Democrats that many Republican votes were not even being counted because of the party's laxity. Thus the demand for honest elections became the Barnes campaign theme for years, and it continued to be used as a bugaboo against the Democrats long after they had lost out. Galvanized by Barnes and his militancy, the Republicans began to see to it that their ballots were counted, and they began to win an office here and there.

A split in the Democratic party in 1899 finally propelled Barnes into power. This party feud would continue to smolder for many years, and would even play a role in the ascent of the O'Connells, two decades later.

The feud began over the nomination for mayor. The elderly incumbent, Thomas J. Van Alstyne, had ostensibly agreed to step down and support John Bowe, a young man who had long been a prominent party leader of the South End, Albany's poor district. At the last minute, however, Van Alstyne's renomination was pushed through by the party boss, Judge D-Cady Herrick. Many Democrats were incensed at this move, and Bowe opposed the nominee in a primary. This was challenging the leadership of Herrick.

Van Alstyne won the primary, but the Democrats were hopelessly split. One of the ward leaders who had supported Bowe, Patrick E. McCabe, went to see Barnes. Out of this meeting came a deal to form a secret coalition for the election, with Barnes promising a share in patronage if his man won.° Barnes' candidate, James H. Blessing, was elected mayor.

Afterwards, charges were rife of collusion between Barnes and the Bowe-McCabe faction. It was found that in four Bowe-McCabe wards, the Republican vote had increased dramatically since the prior election. However, this revelation of party treachery did not daunt the Bowe-McCabe faction's war against Herrick. In 1900, bolstered no doubt by the patronage Barnes was throwing his way, Patrick E. McCabe gained control of the party and replaced Herrick as the Albany County leader.

The factional split resulted in the purging of many loyal Democrats from the organization and from their jobs. The recriminations weakened the party throughout McCabe's years at the

° John Piczak, *The O'Connell Machines: 1921-Present*, unpublished paper, State University of New York Graduate School of Public Affairs, undated, pp. 2–3.

helm. That McCabe proved so ineffective, in fact, gave rise to many suspicions that he was in cahoots with Barnes throughout two decades. (However, Dan O'Connell denies that McCabe made any deal with Barnes except the first one.)

Barnes had fully exploited the Democratic split in 1899, and continued to do so for many years by seducing Democratic politicians into his own organization. It was said that a roster of the Republican ward leaders of one era was about the same as the roster of the Democrats of a somewhat earlier time. In this Barnes was an avid utilizer of the patronage system, dispensing jobs on the public payroll to all and sundry, gaining their loyalty. The jibe was that "every door-knob in the State Capitol had a Barnes man hanging to it."

Barnes' leadership of the Republican party was ironclad. He refused to share his power with anyone, and even avoided putting strong men in public office, where they might be able to create their own followings. Instead, Barnes elevated unknowns to high office, and then demoted them if they got too popular. It was a cardinal principle that no one ought to keep any post for very long.

Through his two decades in power, Barnes himself never held any local office. Nor was he ever Republican chairman of Albany, preferring a state committee seat, with trusted henchmen as county leaders. Barnes sometimes used this plum to keep peace in the party, by giving it to younger men.

William Barnes' political importance extended beyond the limits of Albany early in his career. The boss of the state was Thomas C. Platt, and Barnes became one of Platt's chief lieutenants. When in the opening years of the twentieth century, the aging Platt let loose the reins, Barnes came into his own as the pre-eminent Republican party leader in New York State. His power was national in scope, and he gained the title "President-maker" for his successful effort to renominate William H. Taft and defeat Theodore Roosevelt in 1912.

Barnes' feud with Roosevelt dated back to 1900 when, as a Platt lackey, he had helped engineer Roosevelt's supposed side-tracking to the vice presidency. This had been designed to oust "the Roughrider" from the New York governorship, but it backfired when President McKinley was assassinated and Roosevelt inherited the presidency. While Roosevelt was in the White House, Barnes nursed his enmity; then in 1912, the former President sought a comeback, and the Albany boss rallied the old guard Re-

publican forces to beat him. During that campaign, Roosevelt denounced Barnes as a "corrupt boss," and Barnes sued for slander.
Roosevelt was held not liable, but ordered to pay court costs.

Meanwhile in New York State, Barnes supported the gubernatorial candidacy of Charles Evans Hughes in 1906. Hughes was
not long in office before Barnes started feuding with him, and this
tiff, like the one with Roosevelt, became heated. After Hughes
went on to the Supreme Court, the Republicans nominated Henry
Stimson for governor. Stimson, who had been backed by Theodore
Roosevelt, ran a suspiciously poor race in Barnes' upstate turf, and
the state fell into the hands of the Democrats. It is not unlikely
that Barnes connived the defeat of his own party—for with no Republican governor to get in the way, he was able to take full control. He served as state chairman in 1911–1914, and also as national committeeman 1912–1916. This was the zenith of his power.

The election of 1910 produced a Democratic state legislature,
which promptly set up a committee to investigate Republican
Albany. Uncovered were numerous irregularities, but the gravest
revelations concerned open vice and gambling, and the levying
of tribute by politicians on saloons and brothels.

Despite its lurid findings, the investigation failed to dislodge
Barnes; in the following city elections, his slate won with an increased vote.*

In 1914, Barnes nominated and elected Governor Charles S.
Whitman, as well as Senator James W. Wadsworth. Running true
to form, the Albany boss soon fell to quarreling with the Governor.
Barnes' importance waned.

Another reason for the decline in his influence was the reac-
tionary political opinions which Barnes expressed. He was most
noted for his vociferous opposition to prohibition and woman suf-
frage, and his basic philosophy might have been summed up by
the epigram, "Those who know must rule." He did not recognize
any right of ordinary people to participate in political decisions.
Thus did Barnes oppose, for example, the direct primary law. Such
postures were not calculated to endear him to the masses.

---

* The public basically regards all politicians as rogues—so that to throw
one out risks his replacement by an even worse rogue. The more that politicians are revealed as corrupt, the firmer becomes the public conviction of corruption's universality. This in turn lessens the vulnerability of the particular
politicians who are implicated, and raises the level of miscreancy required for
their expulsion from office.

In 1920, Barnes was reputed to be one of those who met in the "smoke-filled room" to pick Warren Harding for president. But by this time, his controversial views were making him increasingly unpopular. In a last bid for supremacy, he tried to have Albany State Senator Henry Sage nominated for governor. Sage was a strong candidate, but was handicapped by his link to Barnes. As the aging "Boy Leader" himself lamented: "If I were dead tonight, the convention would nominate Senator Sage tomorrow."

Barnes did not die and Sage was not nominated.

William Barnes was the boss of Albany for more than twenty years. At last, a confluence of adversities arose to topple him. Thus, where a Democratic machine had flourished, a Democratic machine arose again. Barnes retired to Mount Kisco, where he died in 1930.

The story of the fall of Barnes is the story of the rise of the O'Connells, which follows.

» »

CHAPTER 2

1919 and the
Soldier-Sailor Campaign

As THE political season of 1919 opened, ominous straws in the wind threatened William Barnes' Republican organization. A general postwar malaise was altering voter attitudes, spurred by labor unrest and the vague desire for a change. While new blood was invigorating the Democratic party, bad blood was brewing among Barnes' own henchmen.

Barnes had kept a lid on party dissension for many years, but he began spending less time in Albany. Now under his umbrella there coalesced two antagonistic camps, the old guard and another, more independent group.° In 1918 there had been a primary fight, and while Barnes had put across his slate, he looked uneasily at the large vote for the opposition. Divisive primaries are rarely helpful to a party's prospects, or to a boss's.

In 1919, then, with Mayor James R. Watt seeking a second two-year term, the Barnes machine was faltering and vulnerable to attack. The previous year, "the Happy Warrior," Alfred E. Smith, won the governorship for the Democrats, bolstering the party

---

° Personifying the old guard was City Corporation Counsel Arthur L. Andrews. The independent leaders were Judge William Woollard and Charities Commissioner Alwin C. Quentel, a Republican ward leader.

throughout the state. The longtime Democratic county leader, Patrick E. McCabe, was at last ready to mount a real challenge. Such prominent names as Gerrit Y. Lansing, Peter G. Ten Eyck and banker William S. Hackett were said to be under consideration for the mayoral nomination.

None of these men were willing to undertake the difficult campaign, and the nomination ultimately went to a war veteran, Captain Reynolds King Townsend. At 35, he was the grandson of an earlier mayor, and had served as military secretary to Governor Martin H. Glynn. Barnes' *Albany Evening Journal* suggested that McCabe chose Townsend because he would be popular as a soldier candidate, and that Townsend agreed to run because he owed it to the party for the good job he'd held under Governor Glynn.

Reporting on the rest of the Democratic slate, the *Evening Journal* indicated on July 25 that Edward J. O'Connell, a young lawyer, had been selected to run for district attorney. Meanwhile, his older brother—misidentified as "Daniel J. O'Connell" at this time by two of Albany's papers—was said to have been offered a prominent place on the ticket, that for state assemblyman. Supposedly too, Daniel O'Connell had expressed a willingness to run for that office.

Neither of these endorsements materialized at the convention held August first at 57 North Pearl Street. The nomination for district attorney was given to John Boyd Thacher, 2d, who promptly spurned it. In place of Thacher, Joseph L. Delaney was named for D.A., and as for the Assembly nomination supposedly lined up for Daniel O'Connell, that went to Ralph Santosuosso.

Those candidates for D.A. and assemblyman would suffer crushing defeats in November, and a similar fate probably would have befallen an O'Connell running for either office. The O'Connell boys of the South End, a fast rising clan of four brothers, were too canny to be enticed into running just for the exercise.

They were, however, going to run. The ticket as finally unveiled included the name of Daniel P. O'Connell for the unglamorous tax assessing board. Dan many years later explained that McCabe had simply asked him to take the assessor nomination, and that was all there was to it. Yet in sending brother Dan out for this lowly office, it is conceivable that the O'Connells knew exactly what they were doing. In any event, slating this particular man for this particular race was the crucial move on the political chessboard that would determine Albany's history for half a century and more.

Right: Mayor James R. Watt (*Morris Gerber Collection*)

Left: Patrick E. McCabe, Albany Democratic Leader (*Albany Evening Journal*)

The Albany O'Connell family was not an immigrant one newly arrived from Ireland. They had been in the city for several generations. Early in the nineteenth century, great-grandfather John O'Connell farmed land in Albany near what is now Second Avenue. The next John O'Connell, his son, was a prominent enough South Ender that O'Connell Street was named after him.

His son, John "Black Jack" O'Connell, married Margaret Doyle, and the couple produced five children, four boys and a girl. "My father," Dan recalls, "was a Republican. He was a farmer in Albany and then sold some property of his. It was where O'Connell Street and Ann Street are. He got into some difficulty, though. He had children. He had to make a living, and he opened a saloon in the South End. I always believed he should never have gotten into the saloon business." * It would seem, though, that the saloon business put John O'Connell into a comfortable financial state, and that Dan could have gone to college like his brother Ed, if he'd wanted to.

Despite his expressed aversion to the family business, young Dan along with his brothers tended bar and frequented the saloon. A neighborhood meeting place in that era of scarce diversions, men gathered there to discuss sports, politics and the state of the world. This strategic position of the saloon as the center of community affairs caused saloon keepers to gravitate toward politics, and made them natural political leaders. Most urban party machines of the nineteenth and early twentieth centuries sported saloon keepers as ward bosses and legislators.

"Black Jack" O'Connell's five children were Patrick, John, Daniel, Edward and Maud, later a school teacher. Of the sons, all but John J. "Solly" O'Connell went into politics. "Solly," in fact, was a Republican. Although he did help during the 1919 campaign, he was chiefly occupied with other interests such as prize fight promoting, nightclubbing, and gambling. He was the playboy of the family, but does not seem to have been regarded as a black sheep. Charged during his career with crimes ranging from rape to shooting, he was never convicted. "Solly" O'Connell died in 1953 at the age of 69.

The eldest of the brothers was Patrick H. O'Connell, who became Democratic leader of the South End's First Ward. "Packy" was known widely as a benefactor of the many poor families in

---

* Albany *Knickerbocker News*, November 12, 1970.

Daniel P. O'Connell, about 1920 (*Courtesy of Erastus Corning, 2d*)

Edward J. O'Connell, about 1920 (*Courtesy of Erastus Corning, 2d*)

that part of the city, the anonymous angel of multitudinous kind deeds and charities.*

Edward J. O'Connell, the youngest of the brothers, was born in 1887. He was a graduate of Albany Normal High School, Holy Cross Academy, and then Union College in Schenectady, where he earned a bachelor of philosophy degree. Finally came Albany Law School and admission to the bar in 1914.

While still a student, Ed O'Connell began working as a clerk in the law office of Neile F. Towner, a prominent attorney and later for many years president of the Albany Board of Education. Ed stayed with Towner after becoming an attorney himself, and often worked at night and into the small hours of the morning preparing cases. Towner was counsel for the municipal gas company, and O'Connell's work on a gas rate case brought him recognition as a rising member of the bar. Another of his noteworthy cases during these years was the contest over the estate of Anthony N. Brady, a multimillionaire utilities magnate linked with Republican boss William Barnes. Edward O'Connell was appointed special guardian over all of the minor Brady heirs, and eventually won the imbroglio by defeating all attempts to contest the will.

After several years with Towner, Ed opened his own office. This was before the O'Connell name meant much in Albany, and clients did not beat a path to his door. He soon bumped into his ex-employer on the street, and Towner asked how things were going. "They could be better," Ed admitted, whereupon Towner invited him back into the firm, and the offer was accepted.

Ed O'Connell's fortunes could not have been all bad during this stage of his career, though. In 1919, besides playing an important role in the campaign of his brother Dan, Ed contributed $500 to the Democratic war chest.

Daniel Peter O'Connell was born on Friday, the thirteenth of November, 1885. He had scant formal education, attending nothing beyond the tenth grade, and this was by his own choice. Dan in his early years was something of a vagabond, pursuing a variety of different occupations, and no particular career. Old city directories list his trade at various times as "clerk," "truckman," or just plain "saloon." He also worked in a Ravena bakery.

This latter experience may have been what caused his assign-

---

* In this, Packy was like many wardheelers of the era, whose benefactions were typically described as "anonymous." Yet plainly a politician hoped that gratitude for his charity would take the form of votes. He must have made sure that despite his "anonymity," people would know whom to thank.

ment as a cook, when he enlisted in the navy upon American entry into World War I. Dan served on the U.S.S. Prairie, a supply ship which made several ocean crossings during the war but which mostly cruised near the Azores. It was the mother ship of a fleet of four, a converted vessel of the Spanish-American War era.

Dan had been involved in politics, along with brothers Packy and Ed, even before the war. He became a Democratic precinct committeeman about 1913 in the Pearl Street area, in the heart of the poor South End. Embracing the Democrats was a break from the family's faith, and from the prevailing power in Albany, the Barnes machine. Perhaps the O'Connell brothers felt that there would be little opportunity for them to rise in the smug, aristocratic Republican organization. As energetic wardheelers in the South End, the brothers attracted a modest band of followers.

In 1919 Dan was thirty-three years old, just out of the navy, and now listing his address as 515 Pearl Street, still in a poor section of town. Nominating him for assessor that year was shrewd politics, balancing Captain Townsend of the army, the mayoral candidate, with a navy man. The *Times-Union* would later have occasion to note, with enthusiasm if not good grammar, that "as eagerly as are the soldiers to rally around the standard of Captain Townsend are the boys of the navy to rally round their shipmate, Dan O'Connell."

Political campaigns of that era had a different character than modern ones. Entertainment alternatives were few—there was no television nor even radio—and for most people, life was rather drab. Everyone looked to politics for color and excitement. Political orators, speaking on street corners or from the backs of trucks and wagons, were avidly heard, and heckled. Rallies were frequent and well attended, since they were almost literally the only show in town. During the campaign season everyone, small children included, was caught up in the spirit of active democracy.

A Daniel O'Connell Boosters Club was opened at 357 South Pearl Street where, as the *Times-Union* reported on one occasion, the "South End welcomed Democratic candidates with opened arms." The entire ticket, including mayoral hopeful Reynolds K. Townsend and O'Connell himself," were getting off real hot stuff in the South End and the headquarters on South Pearl Street were filled to their utmost capacity."

This was the kind of show that was expected and had to be given. Beyond that, O'Connell's election techniques were analyzed after the campaign by the *Evening Journal*. He "conducted a far

different campaign than the other nominees of his party. He did
not take kindly to the jazz stuff and did not hesitate in saying so.
The O'Connell boosters were organized and they went to work
with a will. O'Connell worked along quietly in his own way." It
was recognized that the function of hoopla is not to sway voters to
the candidate's side, but to bolster the enthusiasm of those who already support him. And the real work is the nitty gritty job of win-
nowing the electorate to identify one's supporters, and then to
make sure those supporters vote on election day.

But publicity doesn't hurt, and the Democratic *Times-Union*
was generous to Dan. On one occasion, that newspaper featured a
photo of the young man in his sailor suit, which he wore throughout his campaign. The accompanying story was about the support
he was receiving from his former shipmates on the U.S.S. Prairie. A
letter had been received from the ship, at sea, signed by a welter
of crewmembers, addressed to the citizens of Albany, lauding Dan.

O'Connell was pulling out all stops to get himself elected, not
content to rely on the play he was receiving gratuitously in the
Times-Union. Alone among his ticket-mates, he took a prominent
advertisement of his own, headed "Voters, At-tenshun!" Addressed
to the ladies of the City Club of Albany, the public letter made
four pledges:

FIRST—To lower the tax rate.

SECOND—To assess property at its fair value.

THIRD—To keep politics out of the Board of Assessors.

FOURTH—To assess corporations on the value of their property without regard for the political influence of the corporation.

If the foregoing pledges sound noncontroversial, they were not
without materiality to the situation in 1919. Dan was accusing the
Republicans of tax manipulation, and his ad elaborated:

> The present high tax rate is caused by the great number of
> office holders on the city pay-roll. A private corporation would
> conduct the business of the city of Albany in a business like
> and competent manner with not more than one-quarter of the
> present force of help. It does not seem to me that it would cost
> the city of Albany one dollar more than it would cost a pri-
> vate corporation to conduct the same amount of business. I be-
> lieve that the business of the city of Albany should be con-
> ducted along strict business lines.
>
> Under the present mode of assessment, property is not
> assessed at its fair value. The large property holders are given

an assessment lower than the value of their property warrants, because of political favoritism. The result is that the small property owner must make up the deficit caused thereby.

Politics has entered into and formed a part of the work of the Board of Assessors for the past twenty years. The method used in past years has been this: The Board of Assessors place an assessment upon a piece of property far in excess of a fair assessment. The owner then is compelled to see his ward leader in order to have the assessment reduced. Consequently, for any reduction he receives, the property owner is obligated to someone of the Board of Assessors and the latter expects the obligation to be met on election day. The householder should not be compelled each year to see his ward leader, in order to have his assessment reduced to a fair valuation.

At present the large interests in Albany are not assessed on the value of their property, but each corporation is assessed in accordance with the size of the campaign contribution it makes the Republican Organization. THE LARGER THE CONTRIBUTION, THE LOWER THE ASSESSMENT. I am firmly convinced that if corporations and large property owners were assessed for the fair value of their property, that the tax rate could be reduced.*

O'Connell's opponent in this race, John Franey, was no political greenhorn. Franey had held a gamut of public offices ranging from alderman to state athletic commissioner. He had started in politics in the South End in the early 1880's, and won his first election in 1897. A leading light of the Republican establishment, Franey had three times been elected county clerk, and had once unsuccessfully sought the mayoralty nomination. This race for assessor was the comeback bid at sixty of an old maestro.

Barnes had opposed Franey that time he had tried for mayor, but was now backing him. That mayoralty race had been an independent spree on Franey's part, so his organization support in the present battle was not enthusiastic. To complicate the ticklish entente between Franey and Barnes, there was conflict in Republican ranks in Franey's home Third Ward. The machine had tried to in-

---

* *Times-Union*, November 1, 1919. Present-day Albanians may find this campaign piece of peculiar interest. If Dan O'Connell learned anything from the assessorship contest, it was how tax assessments can be effectively used as a political instrument. In time, his own organization would come to ape the very practices he had once run against, making the politicization of assessments legendary in Albany.

cite a mutiny in "Franeyville" against Edward Dempsey, the leader there, but Franey had backed Dempsey and squelched the move. Even so, the machine threw a candidate into the primary for the aldermanic nomination, whom Dempsey easily trounced. As the *Times-Union* observed afterwards, "The Barnes men . . . are so angered over the nomination of Dempsey that they are already sharpening their knives to get vengeance on him and his backers."

Furthermore, the inconsistency of Barnes now supporting Franey after having once repudiated him was roundly ridiculed in the columns of the *Times-Union*. A front-page headline on October 23 jeered the boss' change of heart toward Franey.

That very same front page carried yet another article assailing Franey. Late in the campaign, the Prohibition Party had unveiled its slate, and it included John Franey's name. National prohibition had been enacted, and Albany was not the driest of towns in sentiment. Mayor Watt had spurned the Prohibition endorsement as being of doubtful value, and the Republicans were reported greatly surprised that the candidate for assessor had not done likewise. It may be observed, too, that Boss Barnes was outspoken in his opposition to prohibition. He could not have been pleased with Franey's newfound friends.

While Dan O'Connell was making his fight against Barnes henchman Franey, the campaign for the rest of the Democratic ticket was being waged with vigor as well.

Important in that campaign was the *Times-Union*, the creature of editor-publisher Martin H. Glynn, an Albanian who started in politics by licking Barnes' congressman. He was later state comptroller and lieutenant governor, and then briefly governor in 1913–14 following the impeachment of William Sulzer at the hands of Tammany Hall. Glynn remained a major figure in the New York State Democratic party. His newspaper, like Barnes', made no pretense of political objectivity, and its opinions were not confined to the editorial section.

Virtually every day of the campaign saw a *Times-Union* front page headlining the evil and consequent imminent demise of the Barnes machine. The newspaper likened the machine to "the vulture . . . continually soaring above the city and its activities, ready to swoop down upon its prey. It rules its satallites (sic) with an iron rod. It inspires them with the courage of desperation."

A front page cartoon in the classic mode was titled "THE SAME OLD GANG," and showed a sumptuous banquet table seat-ing William Barnes and his cronies. They look stonily self-satisfied while some tiny characters chitter about below, gathering crumbs and levelling criticisms.

As if all this was not partisan enough, modern newspaper readers would be surprised to see the daily stream of little articles in both parties' papers, each heralding one of their candidates for office, amounting to free advertisements in the guise of news stories. The headline would indicate that the candidate is certain of victory, and each article would feature a flattering photo of him.

These Democratic prophecies of victories were not as outlandish in 1919 as they had been in the past. The Republican machine could not keep even its own former stalwarts in line. One of them, William A. Bogart, an official of the machinists' union, bolted to join the Democratic ticket. "I have been a Republican all my life," he told a campaign rally, "but since the war I've been doing a lot of thinking. Something comes over me which is akin to the feeling one has when he hears the strains of the Star Spangled Banner played. To stick to the machine and its policies makes me feel as though I was 'yellow.' " Another prominent Republican, Assemblyman Clarence Welsh, had been denied renomination and was now stumping the campaign, blistering the Barnes machine and supporting the Democratic challengers.

Bogart's defection, noted above, was not the only sign of the crumbling alliance between organized labor and the political machine. The Building Trades Council went on record endorsing Townsend for mayor, and the President of the Central Federation of Labor denounced Mayor Watt for allowing city contracts to be fulfilled by outsiders.

It was not only tyranny over Albany for which the Barnes regime was castigated. Its opponents also hammered away on allegedly extravagant city government expenses. Underscored was the failure of the city to spend anything at all for garbage and ash collection. It was argued that while Albany's government was more expensive per capita than in comparable cities, the cost of salaries and administration was so high that nothing was left over for ash and garbage collection. Albany, it was pointed out, had a budget of $2,460,000, while nearby Schenectady, the same size, spent only $1,920,000.*

---

* This issue would crop up again; the usual excuse given by those in power is that Albany is more expensive to run by virtue of its being the state capital. Yet there is little evidence that this factor increases municipal expenses at all.

Right: Patrick O'Connell
(*N. Y. Mirror*)

Left: Former Governor
Martin H. Glynn, publisher
of the Times Union (*Morris Gerber Collection*)

As election day grew near, the issue of vote fraud exploded. A young man named Stephen Kaufman turned himself in after his having registered in two places was discovered. Then Frank Murphy, a Republican alderman, and William O'Connor, a ward worker and city employee, were arrested and charged with having induced Kaufman to register twice.

Naturally, the Democrats made much of the affair. The *Times-Union* boldly cartooned a grinning machine octopus, with tentacles ending in the heads of Barnes, Watt, Franey and others. The arm of the law is reaching for Kaufman, but the octopus beckons him, saying "It's all right, we'll take care of you"—which the implicated Republican officials had supposedly told him.

The charges were eventually dropped in police court, but the fat was kept in the fire by the threat of intercession by the Democratic state administration.

It began to look as though an upset were possible, and the Albany contest attracted interest throughout the state. Each side was charging the other with fraud before the fact. The Democrats alleged that Barnes was using vast sums of money to buy votes and that a corrupt election was his only hope of retaining power. Meanwhile, opposition leader Patrick McCabe was attacked for his plea to Democrats for campaign funds, the insinuation being that the money would go to foul purposes. The Republicans also warned that McCabe would import "New York 'Bulls'" to intimidate voters. Tammany Hall was still in its heyday in New York City, and was a name to strike terror and loathing into upstate Republican hearts; Tammany toughs were regarded as formidable characters.

On Election Day, November 4, 1919, the *Times-Union* triumphantly proclaimed CAPTAIN TOWNSEND ALBANY'S NEXT MAYOR before a single vote had been cast. It was reported that "the O'Connells were on the job in the Second Ward and in fact all the downtown wards, where there was every evidence of Republicans slashing John Franey."

Then the ballot boxes were opened, and the votes counted.

John J. "Solly" O'Connell (right) with Erastus C[
(*Courtesy of Capital Newspaper.*

» »

CHAPTER 3

"Hot Doings"

WHEN the 1919 count was complete, the Democrats' hopes were dashed. Despite all the hoopla and scandal, Albany was still run by an effective Republican political machine that could bring out the vote. Seriously imperiled for the first time in years, there was ample reason for the machine to turn all the screws.

It was a close election. Townsend lost by 23,553 votes to 22,-145; only two years before, Mayor Watt had swamped his challenger by a record breaking margin. The Democrats had come a long way in those two years, and had chalked up a moral victory.

Mayor Watt and the Republican organization carried in the rest of their ticket—they lost only three aldermen and four supervisors throughout the nineteen wards, and held onto every other city, county and state office.

All, that is, but one. One Democrat did eke out a victory.

On the front page, next to the photograph of loser Townsend, was a picture of that lucky lonesome winner. He wore a sailor suit.

In the race for assessor, John Franey polled 20,400 votes and Daniel P. O'Connell squeaked past him with 20,563. In his home Second Ward, O'Connell had piled up 1,535 votes to his opponent's 865, wherein lay his precarious citywide margin of 163.

But there was a slight complication to these results. According to the *Evening Journal's* figures, Franey had pulled through by 108.

In American elections, the government does not generally count the votes. The parties do, each of them supplying inspectors to oversee the conduct of the election in every precinct. Theoretically, each party watches the other, so that the result is an honest count. But where one party is much the stronger, there is no real check on it. In a machine controlled city, the machine counts the votes. Many candidates have won the votes, only to lose the count.

That was what Dan O'Connell faced in 1919. The Republicans had won every race but his, and seemed intent upon making it a clean sweep. They controlled the election board. Democrats feared chicanery, and the *Times-Union* warned that every safeguard would be taken to protect O'Connell against any "funny work" on the returns by the Barnes machine. Ironically, the Republicans likewise warned that McCabe was looking for a "loophole" through which O'Connell could be made the winner.*

The Republicans had a powerful motive to install Franey as assessor. Franey was an important leader with a large following, and he was threatening to quit the party if it couldn't bring his comeback bid to fruition.

Edward and John O'Connell, fearing trouble, watched over the official canvass of returns on Armistice Day. This count gave Dan 20,442 and Franey 20,297, a plurality of 145.

The machine still had some tricks up its sleeve. A few days later a State Supreme Court order was procured requiring the Board of Elections to open for inspection all protested, void and blank ballots. Through this move, the Republicans sought a basis for a judicial recount. Every void or blank paper ballot was to be scrutinized by the candidates and their attorneys. The painstaking examination began on November 14, attended by a crowd of inter-

---

* Even in claiming victory for Franey, the Republicans felt constrained to explain away on mechanical grounds his poor showing. Franey's name was at the bottom of the list of assessor candidates, and supposedly many voters had neglected him by oversight. (There were two assessorships up that year, but one was no real contest.) Franey's supporters also contended that many voters hadn't realized they could vote for two names.

Plainly many Republicans had indeed omitted voting for Franey—but that does not seem to have been wholly a result of negligence. Although O'Connell's campaign was vigorous, Franey would have won easily had he not been distasteful to many Republicans.

ested onlookers and formidable arrays of legal counsel for both sides; the Democrats' squad included Edward O'Connell and John Boyd Thacher, 2d.

Speculation bloomed over a possible grand jury investigation of the election. A G.O.P. lawyer contended that the irregularities charged to O'Connell's home Second Ward on Election Day were borne out now by the condition of the ballots. Many exhibited telltale erasures of crosses originally marked next to Franey's name, combined with suspicious looking crosses next to that of Dan O'Connell.*

Despite the allegations of fraud, On November 20, 1919, John Franey announced that he was dropping all claims to the assessorship. The canvass of void ballots had shown a possible 74 additional votes for him and 62 more for O'Connell. There was no way to overturn O'Connell's lead, and no evidence sufficient for carrying the case to the grand jury.

The day after Christmas, Dan O'Connell went to city hall to take his $2,750-a-year job. At thirty-four, he was the first Democrat elected to general city office in recent history.

He was sworn in by Mayor James Watt. Present at the ceremony were Corporation Counsel Arthur Andrews, Public Safety Commissioner J. Sheldon Frost, and City Engineer Frank Lanagan.

"I want to congratulate you, Mr. O'Connell," said the Mayor, shaking hands and smiling. "They came near to trimming you and they came near to trimming me."

"Yes," the young man answered, "we both weathered pretty heavy storms."

There were further storm clouds on the horizon for Dan O'Connell, but those clouds would bear silver linings.

After O'Connell's victory became known, the *Times-Union* carried a jubilant editorial lauding Dan as "an able, progressive and thoroughly competent public official." Yet the paper was not cuddling O'Connell to its breast. His success was a revolutionary development in Albany Democratic politics, long led by Packy

---

* It is an old trick of corrupt election inspectors to conceal a tiny pencil stub, or even just a bit of lead under a fingernail, to surreptitiously alter the ballots while counting them. Of course, Albany was in the clutches of a Republican machine, and whatever abuses may have been practiced by O'Connell's partisans, they were undoubtedly matched or surpassed by Republican abuses.

McCabe, who was allied with the *Times-Union*'s master-mind, ex-Governor Glynn. Dan O'Connell was a threat to that entrenched leadership, and he was to be soft-pedaled as a hero.

The above account of his installation comes not from the Democratic *Times-Union,* but from the Republican press, which carried the story and O'Connell's picture prominently on the front page. Glynn's paper gave the item a few inconspicuous lines. Of course, it was neither any sense of fairness nor newsworthiness that prompted the Republican organ. One of William Barnes' favorite techniques was to foster divisions among the opposition. Daniel O'Connell, simply by virtue of having been elected, gave promise of turning the Democratic party upside down. Thus, shortly after his victory, the *Evening Journal* portrayed O'Connell as ready and able to take over the party leadership.

Early in February, 1920, that newspaper appraisal was borne out, as the O'Connell camp launched its move to overthrow Patrick McCabe as county chairman. Dan himself refused comment, except to predict that there would be some "hot doings."

McCabe always had opponents within the party, unreconstructed remnants of the old Herrick crowd he had eclipsed two decades before. He was also handicapped by a record of unfavorable publicity, perhaps being a bit uncouth as leader, and therefore was thought no asset to his party. During the campaign, some had remarked that as long as McCabe remained leader, many people otherwise inclined to vote Democratic would be repelled from doing so.

The anti-McCabe sentiment, then, had long been smoldering, and it merely took the election of a man to city office to ignite it. McCabe had beaten his opponents before, but the O'Connells had their strength precisely where McCabe had been strong, in the city wards. The country wards had been perennially opposed to Packy's leadership. Without the firm city support to which he was accustomed, Packy couldn't win.

As the battle was joined, twenty-five prominent Democrats convened in the office of William T. Byrne (later state senator and congressman) and decided to put a full slate of rivals in the field against McCabe's men. Edwin Corning was proposed for chairman of the executive committee, the top leadership post. Edward J. O'Connell, Dan's younger brother, was entered as the choice for county committee chairman, and defeated mayoral candidate Reynolds K. Townsend for city committee chairman. The latter was a surprise, since Townsend had been thought a follower of McCabe and Glynn.

Edwin Corning, the candidate for leader, was a wealthy member of a prominent local family. The first Corning had arrived in America in the seventeenth century, and in 1812, the family had come to Albany. Edwin Corning's grandfather had been Erastus Corning, mayor of Albany 1834–37, as well as congressman and the first president of the New York Central Railroad.

The association between the Corning and the O'Connell families long antedates the political tie. John O'Connell, Dan and Ed's father, had been acquainted with the father of Edwin Corning, who had been known to stop by at the O'Connell saloon. As a boy, Dan O'Connell had attended cockfights at the Cornings' suburban Kenwood estate.

Born in 1883, Edwin Corning was educated at the Albany Boys' Academy and Groton School in Massachusetts. He graduated Yale University in 1906 and joined the Ludlum Steel Company (of which his father had been president), starting out as an iron puddler and working his way up to the presidency by 1910. He was also a director of several banks and treasurer of the Albany Felt Company. The latter enterprise had been started by his brother Parker Corning in 1895 at the age of twenty-one, and grew into a multimillion dollar concern.

As the *Evening Journal* reported the situation, "this idea of Corning being leader is all camouflage . . . Daniel P. O'Connell, known far and wide as 'Assessor Danny,' will be the real leader." The present mayor of Albany asserts that his father, Edwin Corning, was no figurehead at all, but had been for many years active and prominent in the Democratic party, having briefly served in fact as chairman a few years previously. The leadership of the insurgents, soon of the party, was actually a foursome consisting of the two Corning brothers and the two prominent O'Connell brothers. A third O'Connell, Patrick, was also quite influential. And if the real power rested with the O'Connells, as the newspaper account would have it, then it was probably more in Edward's hands than in Dan's.

The filling of 220 county committee seats was to be the battleground between the contending forces. McCabe had always succeeded in capturing the 131 city districts, a majority right there. Twenty in Colonie were also conceded to the incumbent leader. Cohoes started out as a no-man's-land, with its own local feud be-

Right: Edwin Corning (*Author's Collection*)

Left: Parker Corning (*Morris Gerber Collection*)

tween Michael T. Smith and former Mayor Michael J. Foley. Smith had been McCabe's henchman there and was thought to have great strength; he ultimately defected to O'Connell. All the other regions of the County of Albany were violently anti-McCabe.

The insurgents made camp in the Treadwell Building at the northeast corner of Orange and North Pearl Streets. To give assurance that their fight would be no "seven day wonder," the O'Connellcrats flourished a one-year lease on the place.

But it was obvious this time that McCabe's tormentors were in earnest. So on February 19, 1920, he issued a statement. "A primary contest now," said McCabe, "could serve no purpose other than make enemies out of friends and inflict wounds from which the party could not recover in years." To that party McCabe was "obligfied (sic) for the proud and treasured distinction of a leadership of 20 years." He had taken the reins of a party in defeat (which he had connived) and his fondest hope was to be able to put them down again in victory. But with the last election having come very close to fulfilling that dream, and to avoid a harmful schism, Patrick E. McCabe declared his retirement from the leadership.

The O'Connells, it seemed, had accomplished a bloodless coup.

Edwin Corning commented that McCabe's "many admirers among both his political friends and opponents recognize that his retirement is the end of the internal strife which has resulted in continuous defeat for our party."

This statement was not borne out by unfolding events. It was not a bloodless takeover after all; the wounds were merely slow to bleed.

The next chapter was a scuffle over the election of delegates to the Democratic state and national conventions. The First Assembly District selected a delegation dominated by Second Ward men and headed by Dan O'Connell, to the ominous grumbling of former McCabe partisans from other wards in the district. Shortly thereafter, the plot thickened at an unofficial state conclave at Odd Fellows' Hall, to designate delegates-at-large to the national convention. The women's caucus had endorsed Mrs. Elizabeth Colbert for one of these spots. She had built up the Albany Democratic women's ranks against the wishes of McCabe, and was now a leading O'Connell backer. Despite his ostensible retirement, McCabe showed up at the convention and went about instigating dissatisfaction over the Colbert choice. The women were reconvened, and they shifted their endorsement to Tammany's candidate. (The entire slate of delegates ultimately selected was in fact that of Tammany boss Charles F. Murphy.) In the end, Edwin Corning abandoned his threats of a floor fight in Mrs. Colbert's behalf, and the woman leader was mollified by Dan O'Connell's gallantry in yielding to her his own credentials as state convention delegate.

If the McCabe men had reason to resent the O'Connells, the O'Connells now had reason to resent McCabe.

On the night of February 27, the Albany Democratic County Committee met in what had been billed as a harmonizing session. But as the *Evening Journal* saw it, "Corning's dove of peace is a strange bird" which turned out to be a crow.

A new leadership was to be elected in the wake of McCabe's resignation. As a peacemaking move, it was predicted that McCabe follower Charles Friend would be made treasurer, and William F. Kearney, the organization's secretary and McCabe's right hand man, would be allowed to keep his job. Furthermore, the installation of Townsend as city chairman was to be put off for later.

But the new leaders of the party carried out a complete housecleaning. Edwin Corning and Edward O'Connell were elected executive committee and county committee chairmen respectively. Reynolds Townsend was made city chairman. Kearney was immediately booted out as secretary and replaced with John T. Delaney.

McCabe and his followers now declared war after all. The issue was delineated by them as fair play for loyal Democrats. McCabe himself served notice of his willingness to fight to prevent the humiliation of those who had stood behind him and the party, and swore to see the fall ticket destroyed should any of his former henchmen be made to suffer. There were indeed some who felt that the men who had done most of the work in the last campaign were being replaced by those who had done little. They recoiled at the broad-gauge purge being effected by the new leadership, and retaliated in kind.

Thus, the Tenth Ward kicked out its well known leader, Mike McAuliffe, who had defected to the O'Connells. The ouster was voted at a meeting held by candle light after McAuliffe, apprised of the impending move, had managed to shut off the electricity. Elsewhere, Patrick McDonald, dumped as county committee treasurer, was elected leader of a defiant Eighth Ward.

While the new leaders went about disparaging all stories of dissension, and asserting that harmony in fact prevailed, the primary petitions filed with the Election Board revealed a wide-ranging contest. Candidates were in the field against every county committeeman still aligned with McCabe.

The key contest being waged was that for state committeeman of the Second Assembly District, where John Bryce was vying with incumbent William V. Cooke. Cooke was a flowery orator in the tradition of William Jennings Bryan, whose talents were put to use in several gubernatorial nominating speeches. He was well experienced in politics, having served in the State Assembly, and would later be Albany's Commissioner of Public Safety. Cooke was supported by the O'Connells, and Bryce by the McCabe faction.

As the battle reached a crescendo, McCabe finally dropped all pretense of retirement and opened up a new headquarters in the Western Union Building on State Street. He issued a "fighting mad" statement, decrying the "nefarious attacks" being levelled at him by the O'Connell-Corning faction. They were accused of resorting to threats in order to compel harmony, with at least one employer approached to influence his men.*

Tuesday, April 6, 1920 was primary day for the election of party functionaries. Although the election—devoid of any contests in the dominant Republican party—was a quiet one, charges flew in typical fashion of dubious methods being used in Cooke's behalf. He was accused of using money freely and offering as high as $20 per vote. Given Albany's history in this regard, the charge may have been intended more to indict Cooke as extravagant than as corrupt. McCabe weighed in with a blast of his own, accusing Cooke of double dealing and betraying the organization. Rare for a political imbroglio, resort was had to Shakespeare: "I hate ingratitude more in a man than lying, vainness, babbling, drunkenness or any taint of vice, whose strong corruption inhabit our frail blood."

When the ballots were counted, one might have wondered what all the fighting was about. Cooke demolished Bryce, 2,006 votes to 593, and the Corning-O'Connell candidates won all of the district contests save two. They carried every ward but one with a

---

* In fact, McCabe was believed to retain recognition by the State Committee as the real leader of Albany, the State Committee being dominated by Tammany. Many patronage employees on the state payroll were hence afraid to go against McCabe.

safe margin, and prevailed in the committee contests in neighboring Cohoes, Green Island, Colonie and Bethlehem.

The fight for the Democratic party was over, and the O'Connells had won it.

Now, they began the fight for Albany.

» »

CHAPTER 4

*1921 and the Case
of the Missing Coal*

NINETEEN twenty-one was in Albany the year of coal.

Coal was a sore point throughout the year. Its price was high, and the winter was cold. The newspapers featured tips on how to conserve coal, and producers placed ads explaining the high costs of mining.

Then, Albany's Montgomery Coal Company filed bankruptcy, so that its affairs were laid open to public scrutiny. The well respected Judge William Woollard was appointed trustee. It was soon revealed that 79 carloads of coal, billed to the city, had never existed. The taxpayers were left holding the bag to the tune of $18,000. Other jolting revelations followed. While people were husbanding their pennies to buy coal, high city officials had received it free and delivered.

When Boss Barnes looked Albany in the eye in 1921, he saw hot coals glaring at him.

The new young leadership of Albany's Democratic party had done well in the previous election. Despite a national Republican landslide, Governor Al Smith had carried Albany, and Peter G. Ten Eyck was elected to Congress. The *Times-Union* was now reconciled to the new Democratic leaders, who were attracting back into the fold some of those whom Barnes had seduced or who were repelled by Packy McCabe. Republican enrollment was dropping, and local issues were undermining the G.O.P. even before the coal scandals. As 1921 opened, the city was gripped by a transit strike; riders apparently supported the strikers, since patronage of the lines dwindled almost to nil. But the city fathers, inspired no doubt by the anti-labor attitude of Boss Barnes, refused to give in, and the strike remained unsettled by election time. An epic battle was shaping up for Albany's mayoralty.

In the Republican party, Barnes' opponents launched a primary fight, running Dr. James N. Vander Veer for mayor. Barnes was ready to dump Mayor James Watt, and while this would be standard at the end of two terms, the malodor of scandal infected the air. Thus, Watt's enthusiasts were disturbed that his retirement would reflect badly upon him, and demanded his vindication through renomination.

Despite this, Barnes put up a new slate, headed by William Van Rensselaer Erving, who had been Albany's public safety commissioner. But ignoring pleas from his cronies, Barnes refused to run the campaign himself. Instead he stayed at a pleasant mountain retreat until just before the primary, leaving matters in the hands of County Chairman Frank Wiswall and trusted henchman Ellis J. Staley.

As the vote approached, so did the readiness of the Watson Report. This was to be a report to the Common Council on a school construction scandal as well as the distribution of free coal to high political officials. Since these scandals could no longer be concealed, the tactic devised was to "hang all the Barnes dirty linen" on Mayor Watt. Even before this development, Watt felt humiliated by those who had put him in office, and was growing restive in his affiliation with them. The Mayor, however, did not in the end break with the machine—nor was he smeared by it. That one was traded for the other is altogether plausible. In any event, at the last minute, the Watson report was suppressed. "It's an ill bird that fouls its own nest" was the wisdom purveyed against the scapegoat plan.

The high point of the primary battle was reached when the rivals debated at Chancellor's Hall. Erving came off badly, minimizing the importance of the scandals. It is true that the public sometimes wants reassurance that all is well and that its officials are not thieving rascals. But once the voters become convinced that the officials *are* thieves, they want to hear what will be done about it. They are beyond patronizing, and Erving was courting disaster.

In the voting, the insurgents did remarkably well against the machine. Erving won the nomination for mayor, 11,138 to 8,670, but the small majority was scant comfort to the boss. While he had won the battle, it seemed the war was lost.

By this time, it was clear that the name William Barnes was a hated one, and his henchmen took to claiming that Barnes was no longer the boss at all. Barnes, who had come to town for the primary, returned to his mountain retreat. But despite this camouflage of his "retirement," Barnes' followers did not attempt to make peace within the party. Alwin Quentel and Edward Dempsey, who had backed Dr. Vander Veer, were purged from their ward leaderships. The regular organization met and re-elected its old slate of officers. The insurgent Roosevelt Republican Club decided to incorporate, so that the situation congealed into a permanent party schism.

The Barnes Republicans loudly and proudly unfurled the endorsements of numerous Doctors Vander Veer. But they never did get one from the particular Dr. Vander Veer who had run in the primary. Evidently the machine hoped that at least some voters could not tell one Dr. Vander Veer from another.

Meanwhile the Democratic ticket was put together without dissension. Twelve hundred people packed an August meeting at Union Hall, over which Edwin Corning presided. Nominated for mayor was William S. Hackett, a prominent banker and native Albanian. Hackett was a self-made man, and sold newspapers as a boy, of which the Democrats made much in their campaign. A graduate of Albany High School in 1884, he was admitted to the bar in 1889. At the time of his nomination, Hackett was head of the City Safe Deposit Company and also president of the newly organized New York Mortgage and Home Building Company, geared to aiding people of small means in building their own homes. Until this time, the O'Connells had not been acquainted with Hackett, and it was Edwin Corning who arranged for him to make the race.*

Hackett and the Democrats launched their campaign for a

---

* Interview with Erastus Corning, September 1971.

Left: Mayor John Boyd Thacher, 2d (*Author's Collection*)

Right: Mayor William S. Hackett (*Courtesy of Capital Newspapers*)

"business administration," calling for economy and making much of the charge that Albany's cost of government was extravagant. This year's campaign was unusual for its lavish use of newspaper advertising. The Democrats had new sources of funds, with a leading banker on the ticket, and through Edwin Corning's business connections. Corning himself contributed heavily. The Republicans responded in kind to the Democrats' newspaper blitz, matching their opponents full page for full page.

The Democrats attributed the high cost of Barnesism to the ever mounting need for patronage jobs to keep the machine in power. Coming in for special attention was the County Penitentiary, supposedly larded with political goldbricks. A cartoon in the October 3 *Times-Union* asked, "Who would not be a prisoner in the Albany Penitentiary under the Barnes administration, 29 prison attendants for 36 prisoners—how soft! Every prisoner has his own valet or personal attendant." The drawing showed prisoners asking their "attendants" for matches, to run baths, etc. By October 15, prison services were extended to include a lecture program, manicures and flower deliveries.

The alleged reason why this and other scandals were possible was the lack of ready access by the public to the facts. "WE MUST OPEN THE BOOKS!" demanded a Democratic advertisement. "WE MUST HAVE FULL KNOWLEDGE OF WHAT THE CITY LEDGERS SHOW, AND THEY REFUSE TO TELL US ANYTHING OF OUR OWN BUSINESS AFFAIRS! WE WANT THOSE BOOKS OPENED AND WE WANT THEM IN THE HANDS OF MEN WHO ARE NOT IN THE CONTROL OF THE BARNES MACHINE!"

Hackett also hammered away upon law and order as an issue, promising to appoint a public safety commissioner "who with an iron hand and with fearless and nonpolitical efforts will see . . . the city rid of gangsters, dope peddlers, thieves, house breakers and murderers." Erving too campaigned on such themes, but the Democrats pointed out the contradiction between this stance and Erving's castigations against those whom he saw as running Albany down for political gain. And they labelled his cleanup pledge as itself an indictment of Erving and his party, since he had recently been commissioner of public safety in charge of the police. Thus Erving was personally responsible for the conditions he now promised to remedy, while simultaneously denying their existence.

But the real issues that decided the campaign were the scandals, chief among them the coal affair. Dan O'Connell long afterward indicated that the newspapers had carried the ball on this, and that his candidates had simply gone along with a good thing. He felt that the newspapers had blown the scandal far out of proportion, unfairly to the Republicans. Furthermore, as to the free deliveries to city officials, one close to Republican affairs of this era believes that the officials acted behind Barnes' back; and this was more a case of the company trying to feather its nest than of a shakedown by the officials.

The Republicans tried to blame the missing coal on a negligent lower echelon employee who had failed to check the falsified bills given him by an unscrupulous contractor. But the opposition countered that the city fathers had known of this months before its public disclosure, and had conspired to cover it up, causing the city to forfeit its bond against such losses.

As for candidate Erving, he took the position that since he had not personally been implicated, he had no cause for concern. This met with savage ridicule. Erving was mock-quoted as saying, "Hi didn't steal the coal. Mr. Barnes didn't steal the coal. 'Ow do hi know who stole the coal?"

The subject of the coal fraud was cartooned mercilessly. A repeated favorite was captioned ERVING WHITEWASHING THE COAL STEAL, and showed a stoic Republican candidate painting an endless train of coal cars. Another cartoon showed Erving in bed, aghast, besieged by a horde of little coal cars. He is still protesting that he did not steal the coal—but the expression on his face, and the coal in his bed, strongly imply that he did. According to yet another cartoon, "Mother Albany finds Willie a very evasive youngster when she interrogates him on the condition of her household." "Everything is black with coal dust, Erving," she says, and the candidate, depicted in knickers, answers, "But I'm a clean little boy, ma"—again insinuating that he really is not, beneath a veneer of making the point that it doesn't matter whether he is or not.

The coal scandal was not the only one receiving attention in the campaign. There was also Public School 14, whose construction was called gravely deficient and unsafe. There was the Park Avenue paving scandal, with the city having supposedly done a slipshod job and diverting attention by dropping its effort to assess the abutting property owners. A similar case was that of the Beaver Creek Sewer.

Few of the revelations might shock the consciences of civilized men. Yet throughout the campaign, the Watson probe report, despite having been on the verge of release, remained buried. Having already blundered by making its readiness known, the Republicans could only have suffered from the implications inherent in their refusal to release it, firing voters' imaginations as to what scandalous material it might contain. The Democrats repeatedly demanded that the report be made public, to no avail.

Such blundering was characteristic of the G.O.P. campaign. After Erving's disastrous experience debating in Chancellor's Hall, he squirmed mightily to avoid a repeat. When the City Club, a women's organization, invited him to speak, his reply was a surly refusal, which could not have endeared Erving to the female electorate. Then, when he tried to rectify the situation, he got himself into even worse trouble with another group of voters.

In what the *Evening Journal* headlined as a tribute to womanhood, Erving told Albany's ladies, "you will save this city from the disgrace which would come to it if its government were turned over to the O'Connells and their followers," and commended them for keeping Albany "out of the clutches of the O'Connells, men brought up in an environment and atmosphere not conducive to good government, not conducive to the well-being and honor of our city."

He was pounced upon at once, asked just what was the matter with the O'Connells. They, it was pointed out, had never robbed the city of $18,000 worth of coal (nor, it might also have been pointed out, ever had the opportunity). The *Times-Union* headlined, SOUTH END IS ABLAZE FROM ERVING ABUSE, and speculated that the Republican had "handed himself a considerable hoist toward political oblivion" by trying to read an important section of the town out of the realm of decency. Now glowing praise was heaped on the South End as solidly representative of America. Hackett pointed with pride to his own early life there, and Reynolds Townsend said he felt perfectly at home in that neighborhood. The O'Connells were hailed as sterling citizens, with Dan's war record prominently mentioned.

The tenor of the campaign was to degenerate further yet. It was on October 26, 1921 that the mysterious potato hurtled into Albany politics.

Young Senator Frank Wiswall was holding forth at a street corner rally, attacking among others Edwin Corning. When Wiswall began talking about the conditions in the 1890's under Democratic rule, a heckler shouted, "What happened in 1492?"

Wiswall replied on the bombastic uptake that "in 1492, the country was discovered of which you today should be proud to be a citizen."

At that point, the recently assailed Corning happened by. Having heard himself maligned, he shouted out, "Here I am, what have you got to say about me?"

Just then, an overripe potato hit Wiswall in the face. Others were claimed to have hit his truck. The Republicans instantly made this the main issue of the campaign, decrying the "Rowdyism of the Corning Democrats." The accusation that the patrician Corning had deliberately instigated the throwing of the potato was not even veiled.

The Democrats treated the incident all in fun, purveying a "rumor" that Wiswall would thenceforward campaign from a potato-proof tank. But apparently the Republicans thought they had hit upon an effective issue—or at least one that might keep voters' minds off the scandals. Other vegetable throwing incidents would gain strident attention in the *Evening Journal*.

The opposition was not going to be put on the defensive. They kept up their lambasting of the administration. One additional issue they pounded was labor. William Barnes had delivered a speech in which he had maintained that the labor of a human being is a "commodity," the laws and courts of the United States to the contrary notwithstanding. This rent asunder once and for all the Barnes alliance with organized labor. Another facet of the issue was the labor strife plaguing Albany, especially the transit strike. The machine's leadership being in cahoots with the company owners repelled the public as well as organized labor.

Money was naturally held to be the last resort of the G.O.P. The emergency was said to warrant a price as high as $25 per vote —although it was hoped that most of the purchaseable supply could be garnered nearer to $10. Other charges of intimidation were levelled at the machine, and Corning signed a newspaper ad guaranteeing voters a secret ballot. Meanwhile, the Republicans made their usual charges of Democratic fraud and strongarm tactics. For all this, the election took place peacefully.

William S. Hackett was elected mayor of Albany by a solid margin, piling up 29,425 votes to Erving's 22,203.

Every other candidate on the Democratic city and county

tickets also won, and the party captured a majority of the alder-men, making it a clean sweep.

The *Times-Union,* originally opposed to them, editorialized that "the direction of affairs of the Democratic party by Edwin Corning and Edward J. O'Connell demonstrates rare wisdom and judgment." In their second year, the new leaders had managed a triumph beyond anything McCabe in his twenty years had dreamed.

The O'Connells had come to power.

Part Two:

IN POWER

» »

CHAPTER 5

Happily Ever After (I)

ONCE the O'Connells had come to power, they naturally set about perpetuating their rule. The two methods chosen to solidify the support of Albany's voters were popular government actions, and the building of a political machine.

Water supply had always been a vexing problem and a political issue in Albany. During the late nineteenth century, much of the city's water came from the Hudson River, bringing with it pollution and a high death rate. At the end of the century a filtration plant was installed which greatly reduced the incidence of typhoid fever. In 1913, however, this system was flooded, resulting in a typhoid epidemic. Republican administrations attempted projects to deal with the water supply problem, but without notable success. This remained a political headache for the party, and was an incidental cause of the Republican defeat in 1921.

Mayor Hackett inaugurated a program to eliminate the Hudson entirely as a source of Albany's water, and his successor, Mayor Thacher, would carry the plan through to conclusion. This was the sort of progressive action that made the Hackett regime popular.

A similar albeit less urgent issue was that of parks, which had become a political football through the insensitivity of Republican mayors to popular demands for expanded park facilities. While plans for parks were made, years and decades slipped by without their implementation. It remained for the Democrats to finish the job, and since the 1920's, this has ceased to be an area of political concern.

The flurry of civic improvement was largely confined to the administration of Mayor Hackett and the early part of Mayor Thacher's. During these years, the Democrats gave Albany good and progressive government, building up a reserve of popularity that lingers to the present day. The Depression intervened to halt this progress, and the O'Connells' political machine became so entrenched that it slipped into the torpor that so often overtakes regimes without challengers.

Since the 1920's, the Democrats of Albany have rested upon their laurels, however yellowed and withered with age those laurels might be. In 1971, Mayor Corning said that the most significant development in his city in a decade was the South Mall project—a state office building complex planned and executed by Governor Rockefeller.°

In 1921, William S. Hackett was elected mayor, defeating Republican W. V. R. Erving, who in turn had beaten James Vander Veer in a party primary. Had Vander Veer been nominated that year, as an upright and untarnished Republican in a Republican-dominated town, he would probably have won, and the history of Albany would be quite different. But it was in 1923 that Republicans finally did nominate him, with former boss William Barnes in retirement in Westchester. Vander Veer's opponent was now an already popular incumbent, who easily won re-election.

Hackett's fledgling administration was hailed for its general businesslike efficiency, which included a reorganization of many of the city's departments. There were the already noted efforts being made to solve the long-standing water supply problem and to meet long neglected park needs. The city was free of the ugly and disruptive labor disputes that had plagued the last years of Barnes' reign. A citywide system was instituted for the collection and disposal of ashes and garbage. A new listing system was inaugurated for property assessment, after a realty expert from New York City

---

° Interview, September 1971.

had been brought in. Four new schools were under construction, and every school was renovated.

The Democratic party leaders capitalized upon their sudden popularity by whipping into shape one of the most efficient political organizations in the country. Their success at the polls had stifled intra-party dissension against the Corning-O'Connell leadership, and their success at city administration, combined with revulsion against the delinquencies of the Barnes crowd, made it easy for them to attract followers. The comparison between the new regime and the old was so stark that a complete turnabout occurred in Albany's party loyalty. By 1923, the Democrats evened up the two-to-one Republican advantage of two scant years before (itself down from three-to-one in 1920). By 1927, the city was two-to-one Democratic in voter enrollments.

The usual pattern in municipal politics is for reform administrations to be elected periodically, at moments of great voter dissatisfaction over machine excesses. Such reform regimes usually encounter serious roadblocks in the form of recalcitrant bureaucracies and political hostility in government arms like the city council, which may remain in the hands of the opposition. While most voters endorse abstract virtue, it has proven difficult in practice for reform administrations to gain popularity. Those reforms actually capable of being accomplished generally do not affect voters sufficiently to engender their interest. Meanwhile, the ousted political machine does not go away; its grassroots organization based on years of personal contact continues to operate throughout the reform administration's term, sowing goodwill. At the next election, the reformers are thrown out and the rascals return to power.

In Albany, an apparent departure from this pattern occurred, with the reform administration elected in 1921 managing to entrench itself permanently, even to sway the majority of voters to its party column. The surface reason for this was the genuine popularity of the Hackett administration. A less obvious reason lies in the machine that was replaced. Albany, a heavily Catholic, heavily Irish city, had had a long history of Democratic party allegiance, of which the Barnes years were but a temporary interruption.

Thus, when they came to power, the O'Connells had a great advantage over most newborn reform administrations. Voters who had enrolled Republican during the Barnes years for convenience

now returned to the Democratic fold. Many of Barnes' hench-
men, it will be recalled, were actually former Democrats whom
Barnes had seduced into Republicans of expediency. Now with the
Democrats back in power, expediency meant being a Democrat
once more. These wayward politicians were eager converts to
O'Connellism.

As we have seen, the leadership of the machine during its early
years was collective among the Corning brothers and the
O'Connells—the patricians and the plebeians. Edwin Corning held
the chairmanship, giving a respectable face to the party and ar-
ranging much of its financing. Parker Corning played a subordinate role, going to Washington as congressman in 1923.

Edward J. O'Connell had by now successfully opened a law
firm of his own, a partnership with law school classmate Samuel
Aronowitz.* O'Connell's legal practice was a general one, encom-
passing corporate, real estate and probate matters. He represented
several Albany banks. No criminal, bankruptcy or matrimonial
cases were handled by him. Other financial activities included su-
pervision of the family's Hedrick Brewery, and broadcasting—he
was an organizer of WTRY Radio and WAST Television.

Edward J. O'Connell assumed public office only once, when
the Board of Supervisors named him county attorney. In this capacity, he represented the county government in all non-criminal
legal matters. Ed held his office for just one year, in 1922, but in
that year he educated himself thoroughly on all facets of local administration. This expertise strengthened his political power
throughout the rest of his career, because few of the other politicians in the machine had any such knowledge. Ed was called upon
to make most of the decisions in the governmental sphere—
decisions which often had important political ramifications.

Ed, despite being the youngest of the O'Connell brothers, had
the dominant voice among them. But he did not have the last
word; it was preferred that decisions be reached by consensus. Ed
acted as the brains of the organization, the intellectual, conversant
with county and local affairs and government financing, wise in
the ways of the law. Yet the division of authority between Ed and
Dan O'Connell was vague even to their closest associates, and it

---

* The office remains operating today at 100 State Street under the name
O'Connell and Aronowitz. Aronowitz is still practicing law. A Republican, he
was never politically close to Dan O'Connell, and if anything has been antagonistic toward him.

was said that neither made any decision without consulting the other.

Edward O'Connell was a six-footer of commanding personal appearance. But like his brothers, he almost pathologically shunned publicity, preferring to work in the shadows. Ed had no hobbies, indulged in no particular recreations, and refused to take extended vacations. Instead he concentrated almost exclusively on his law practice and politics. His only other pleasure seemed to be his home and extensive gardens, superintended by Mrs. O'Connell, the former Kathryn Brandow, whom he married in 1921.

Daniel P. O'Connell, elected city assessor in 1919, held the job until the board of assessors was reduced in size. That was in 1923, and Dan decided not to run for re-election. Meanwhile, he served for a time during the 1920's as Democratic city chairman and as state committeeman.

His chief role was essentially that of "public relations man" for the party. This did not mean that he sent out press releases. Dan kept contact with the rank-and-file of party workers and also with as many voters as he could, making thousands of friends. Edward O'Connell, the leader, was hard to reach, but Dan was very easy to see; in fact, he spread himself all around town so that he could be available. He would discuss a matter with a supplicant and then take it up with Ed if required. It was often unnecessary, in fact, to seek Dan out. If you told the right person (such as a Democratic committeeman) of your problem, word would reach Dan, and he would come to you.

He would do almost anything to get you out of a jam, and this included giving you money. A typical story is told of a tailor during the Depression who was going under. Dan loaned him $500 and told him he didn't have to pay his local taxes until he was back on his feet financially. Dan would respond like this, with only one proviso—you had to directly ask him for help, in person. It had to be made very evident that you were getting a favor, and that you were indebted to Dan. That debt was never forgotten by either party; if you ever afterward strayed in your loyalty, you would be reminded of it. Almost always, though, the gratitude engendered was genuine and long living. The above tailor story was told by the beneficiary's son, a well-to-do businessman and a supporter of O'Connell today for no other reason.

One of Albany's legends is that Dan would walk down from his home to city hall during the hard years, by a different route each day, and with hundreds of dollars or more in his pockets. By

the time he reached his destination, he would have hardly enough
left to buy his breakfast.

Patrick O'Connell was also politically influential, but never at-
tained the notoriety of Ed or Dan. This was partly because
"Packy" avoided the spotlight even more assiduously than his
brothers. Ed and Dan, though, were greenhorns in their early thir-
ties during those first years in power, and they inevitably looked to
their more seasoned older brother for sage counsel. Thus, Packy
was called the "dean of the Democratic dictators of Albany," and
"the foremost counsellor" of the party leadership.

It has been common for big-city political machines to dominate, or constantly strive to dominate, their states. The Illinois
Democratic party was for years the creature of Mayor Daley's Chicago machine, as the New York State Democracy was once in the
Tammany tiger's paw. But the O'Connells have never been much
taken with the vision of statewide power, being quite content to
lord over Albany and perhaps a few neighboring counties. Part of
this was mere pragmatics, since not even electing a governor
would give little Albany clout over the rest of the state's Democrats. On the other hand, it was inevitable that so strong a local organization would play a significant role in state affairs.

The O'Connells came to power in 1921. The following year's
Democratic state convention at Syracuse was one of the most dramatic in the party's history. It was a tale of two titans: former Governor Alfred E. Smith, seeking a comeback after having gone down
in the 1920 Republican landslide, and William Randolph Hearst,
imperious publishing magnate, nourishing presidential dreams.
Hearst had tried for the governorship before, but this time, the
party favored Smith so strongly that Hearst was after the senate
nomination instead. The problem was that Smith swore that he
would refuse to run on the same ticket with Hearst.

Albany was supporting its own Congressman Peter G. Ten
Eyck for governor, but the county's delegation ultimately withdrew
him and plumped for Smith. The Albany leaders still hoped to win
a place on the ticket, that of comptroller, for either Ten Eyck or
City Comptroller Thomas Fitzgerald. This aspiration, too, had to
be abandoned by County Leader Edwin Corning. The Albanians
felt that sufficient honors had come their way: Mayor Hackett was
elected permanent chairman of the convention, and William T.
Byrne was chosen to make the nominating speech for Smith, which
he would do again in 1924.

Al Smith implacably stood against Hearst, and in the face of this, Hearst finally withdrew. Smith was then harmoniously nominated for governor, with Dr. Royal S. Copeland named for the Senate, and both were elected.

Albany jumped into an even more powerful political role in January, 1926, when Democratic State Chairman Herbert C. Pell resigned. Governor Smith's personal choice to fill this vacancy was Edwin Corning, who had impressed the party's leaders by his role in turning a staunch Republican bastion into a Democratic one. Corning was unanimously elected state chairman. He was naturally succeeded as Albany County leader by Edward O'Connell.

When the new Chairman Corning introduced Governor Smith to the assembled state committee, he hailed Smith as "the next President of the United States."

Smith unhesitatingly responded, "I accept the nomination!"

Meanwhile, the presidential hopeful announced that he would not run for another term as the Empire State's chief executive, and Democrats had to start thinking about a new candidate. The selection of Corning as chairman was seen as significant in the jockeying for the gubernatorial nomination, and the name being prominently mentioned for governor was Albany's Mayor William S. Hackett. The Mayor was a proven vote-getter; in 1923, he had been re-elected by 33,673 to 18,353, an overwhelming margin, and had repeated the feat two years later. Smith himself was said to look with favor upon Hackett being nominated.

However, Smith in the end bowed to pleas that he run for a fifth time; and meanwhile, on March 4, Mayor Hackett died of complications after an automobile accident in Cuba. His successor under the terms of the city charter was the president of the Common Council, John Boyd Thacher, 2d.

At the state Democratic convention of 1926, Albany once again had the honor of placing Smith's name in nomination, this time with Mayor Thacher waxing eloquent. Further recognition was given to Albany with, at last, a place on the ticket: Edwin Corning was nominated for lieutenant governor. As Corning's son, the present mayor, explains the choice, Smith was already preparing to run for the presidency, and wanted to leave the state in strong, competent hands while campaigning. He picked Corning specifically for that reason, it is said, with Smith also having promised Corning support for governor in 1928.

However, in August, 1928, Edwin Corning resigned as party chairman, and revealed that he was retiring completely from politics, for health reasons. He was then only 45 years old, and some have speculated that he left public life for fear he would be implicated in the unfolding baseball pool gambling scandal (detailed in Chapter 6). The pool trials would indeed feature some dramatic testimony naming Corning, which he contradicted. On the other hand, it was true that the lieutenant governor's health was poor for a man of his age, and he did not long survive, dying in 1934.

In 1928, Governor Alfred E. Smith received the presidential nomination. With Edwin Corning out of the picture, the most prominent names being mentioned for the governor's chair were Senator Robert F. Wagner and former Assistant Secretary of the Navy Franklin D. Roosevelt. Meanwhile, the most active campaign for the job was being waged by Albany's favorite son, Peter G. Ten Eyck. Mayor Thacher was readying a nominating speech for Ten Eyck in hopes that the party would want an upstater and would look to Albany. But Governor Smith instead backed Roosevelt.

John Boyd Thacher was forty-three years old when he became mayor of Albany in March, 1926. A descendant of two previous mayors, he was born in Leadville, Colorado, and came to Albany as a youth. Thacher was a graduate of Albany Academy, Princeton University and Albany Law School. His career in public service began as deputy attorney general under Governor John A. Dix (1911–12) and during World War I he participated as a YMCA athletic director in charge of a field behind the lines. After that field was bombed, he became an ambulance driver. In 1919, Thacher was nominated for District Attorney, but refused to run. Two years later, he joined the Hackett slate as candidate for city treasurer, winning the office. He later moved up to the council presidency.

Despite his short record as an incumbent, Thacher proved even more popular at the polls than his predecessor. He won a special election for the mayoralty in November, 1926, by a vote of 39,309 to 18,181. Following in Hackett's footsteps in civic development programs, Thacher's administration would also be marked by a pay-as-you-go fiscal policy, and the Mayor's interest in augmenting Albany's recreational opportunities. The city constructed municipal playgrounds, swimming pools and a golf course.

Yet, beneath this glossy exterior of accomplishment, the opposition was beginning to find some festering areas. With the mayoralty term now increased to four years, the Republicans in 1929 waged a combative campaign to recapture it. They finally had some real ammunition to hurl at the Democrats in the form of corruption issues. The baseball pool scandals had broken, implicating the Albany political leaders in a gambling operation not only illegal but dishonest as well. Lawmen were chasing Dan O'Connell. It was becoming evident that far from reforming property tax assessment, the Democrats had borrowed the political tricks previously played by the Barnes machine. The Republicans hammered away on these issues, and charged too that the county's debt had suspiciously increased from three million to four million dollars in the preceding year. An instance of what may be termed classical "honest graft" * was cited, the purchase of a site for a new almshouse, at $160,000 after a costly condemnation proceeding. It was contended that the property could have been acquired for as little as $60,000—but that a Utica real estate dealer, who had been a classmate of Ed O'Connell, had bilked the city for the difference.

By the time of this 1929 campaign, the *Times-Union* had soured on the O'Connell regime, and was now printing unfavorable articles about it. The Albany *Evening News* expressed dismay at both camps, and declined to endorse either candidate for mayor. The paper did note, however, that the political system of tax assessments was the major issue. That could only have suggested a vote against the Democrats.

Despite all this, the Republican candidate polled only 18,657 votes. Mayor Thacher piled up 41,180, the machine's most impressive triumph yet. It may be observed that while the Republican vote—and the city's population—had held fairly stable during the past four elections, the Democratic vote had increased steadily. In 1933, it reached 47,830, and in 1937, Thacher polled an astonishing 61,257. The machine's efficiency was in high gear, and the enormous Democratic vote totals prompted general recognition that not all votes cast were legitimate. (Fraudulent voting in Albany is covered in Chapter 15.)

The machine was rolling up these triumphs despite further scandals. In 1930–31, a series of revelations rocked the City Treasurer's office. State auditors uncovered shortages approaching $40,-000, connected with fixing of tax payments and an interest sharing

---

* The distinction between honest and dishonest graft has been drawn by that legendary Tammany politician, George Washington Plunkitt, in William Riordan's *Plunkitt of Tammany Hall*. An example of honest graft would be utilizing inside information as to where the government intends to erect a building, to purchase the land cheaply and then sell it to the government at a big profit. Dishonest graft might be stealing the roof off the building and selling it for scrap. This, in Plunkitt's opinion, is going too far.

and tax receipt forgery conspiracy. District Attorney John Delaney obtained a dozen indictments, and one city employee was sentenced to a year in jail. Prompted by this scandal, a joint state legislative committee on the assessment of real property was established, with George Z. Medalie engaged to investigate the Albany tax system. The final report was a scathing indictment of Albany's practices, pointing up the political manipulation of tax assessments and slipshod procedures in the Treasurer's office. The O'Connell machine was accused of taking advantage of an antiquated system to enhance its power, and of "corruption . . . leading directly to the highest political powers in the city." Of using tax assessments to intimidate voters, it was said in the report that "a more serious threat to free government than such methods of political proselytizing can scarcely be imagined."

The report was virtually ignored by city officials. Some of the corrupt practices charged continue to the present day.

Meanwhile, a number of reform-minded clergymen began attacking District Attorney Delaney and Sheriff Keegan for condoning vice and gambling in the city. The police were accused of protecting known gangsters. All of these derelictions caused a coalition of Republicans and disenchanted Democrats to back a fusion campaign in 1933, with erstwhile Democrat Reynolds King Townsend as the candidate for mayor. The fusion device was being employed successfully in New York City that year by Fiorello La Guardia. But the Albany machine's victory margin only increased in the face of this challenge.

» »

CHAPTER 6

Dan O'Connell Goes to Jail

It was called the "greatest lottery in history," and the "$35 million swindle." Dan O'Connell was imprisoned over the affair, yet managed to avoid the stigma of direct complicity. His explanation nowadays is that he went to prison only because he knew the real culprits, and was unwilling to turn them in; and forty years have blurred the memory of many Albanians.

The baseball pool was humbly born in 1905 in the J. B. Lyon Company printing plant. Each printer chipped in a dollar and was assigned at random a group of baseball teams. At the end of the week, whichever player's teams scored the most runs won the pot. The pool, initially a friendly game in just one of the shops, spread to the entire plant.

James Wright was given the job of collecting the money and operating the pool, once it became a complicated plantwide enterprise. After that, word of mouth spread the pool even beyond the plant and it mushroomed rapidly. The management of the Lyon Company became concerned, and decreed a halt; but by this time, Wright was finding it more lucrative to operate the pool and rake off a percentage than to labor as a printer. He quit his job in order to run the pool full-time.

It was illegal gambling, of course. Wright was soon arrested on the complaint of a disgruntled player. He served a thirty day jail sentence—after deciding that was preferable to having the case fixed and becoming a permanent shakedown victim.

The pool grew too big for one man to handle. Others wormed their way into Wright's moneymaking operation, including some Albany political figures, one William "Cooch" Buchanan among them. Businesslike methods were applied to the pool operations, spread throughout New England. By the 1920's, millions of dollars were involved.

Responding to complaints in 1925, Governor Smith directed the local sheriffs to act against the pool. To escape, it simply moved its headquarters, though in the course of the crisis, James Otto, a Republican who had come in during the Barnes days, and Wright himself were kicked out of the pool ring. While the involvement of the O'Connells was never fully revealed in court, by now they controlled Albany, and had insinuated themselves into the pool.

In that year, 1925, about four million dollars was netted throughout the northeast. To make it a year-round operation, a stock market pool was inaugurated for the winter months. Then James Otto resurfaced with a new, rival pool, and competition between the two pushed prizes up to the $20,000 level. In 1927, the original ("Hudson") pool was prosecuted in Boston, where Dan O'Connell pleaded guilty to a minor charge of conspiring to evade the federal anti-lottery laws, and was fined $750. His brother, John "Solly" O'Connell, with wide gambling interests, was also among those implicated in Boston. These prosecutions left Otto's new "Administration" pool alone in the field. But it seems the O'Connells had gotten a finger into that one, too.

At about this time, the pool's operators began cheating to make it even more profitable. They used dummy players to win some of the prizes themselves. Then they stopped releasing the names of the winners. Ultimately the swindle was perfected, with the management carefully picking its own teams, leaving everyone else to chance. This reduced almost to zero the possibility that any ticket-buying sucker would win. A further gimmick was splitting the prizes between the real winners and imaginary "tie" winners. Dan O'Connell—a baseball expert himself—was identified as the man who directed the dummy player operation.

After the successful prosecution in Boston of the original "Hudson" pool, U.S. District Attorney Charles H. Tuttle of Manhat-

tan went after James Otto's "Administration" pool still operating in
Albany. Some convictions including Otto's were obtained, but Tuttle didn't believe the real leaders had been brought to justice. One
of those whom he was anxious to nail was Dan O'Connell.

O'Connell was being sought as a material witness for the new
perjury trial of James Otto (already serving a term in the Atlanta
Penitentiary). For months, O'Connell had managed to evade the
deputy U.S. marshals trying to serve him with a subpoena. Now finally, in July, 1929, the marshals lay in wait for their quarry outside
the Albany Democratic headquarters at 75 State Street.

O'Connell emerged from the building and was able to slip
past them into an automobile. A long chase ensued, and
O'Connell's car was overtaken just as it reached his summer cottage in the Helderberg Mountains. Dan then tried to lose his pur-
suers on foot in the woods, only to be stopped when a marshal
drew his gun and threatened to shoot. The Albany Democratic
leader was arrested.

O'Connell was taken to the federal grand jury in New York
City, held on $10,000 bail as a material witness. But he refused to
answer the grand jury's questions, and was then brought before
Judge Julian Mack, who rejected his excuse that to answer would
"incriminate and degrade" him. Sent back to the grand jury, Dan
was asked whether he knew certain persons, to which he replied
that he knew several persons by those names and "might know
them to nod to." Questioned on his own business affairs, he said
that he had had no business for several years, and no income. He
claimed to have lived by betting and borrowing, and gave equally
indefinite answers to the remaining questions.

Judge Mack thereupon slapped O'Connell with a ninety day
sentence for contempt of court, citing his "wilfully, deliberately
and contumaciously obstructing the process of justice." The judge
observed that "if there was ever a flagrant case of contempt, this is
it." District Attorney Tuttle told the press, "The moral of this episode is that no one, no matter how influential, is more powerful
than the United States government."

Daniel O'Connell served two days of his sentence and was
then released by order of Judge Martin Manton on $1,000 bail,
pending appeal of the contempt sentence.*

While the O'Connell appeal was underway, the Otto perjury

---

* Manton is remembered for having been convicted for soliciting and receiving bribes, later in his judicial career.

case continued with some revealing testimony. "Cooch" Buchanan
swore that large sums had been paid to Albany politicians for protection. These payments were split five ways, according to the
witness—among himself, Otto, Dan O'Connell, Ed O'Connell and
Edwin Corning, the former lieutenant governor. One $16,000 pay-
ment, he recalled, was divided up in an Albany cafe run by the
O'Connells. The five-way split, he said, had been arranged by Dan,
who demanded 2½% of the pool's receipts on threat of jailing its
operators. Buchanan also explained that James Wright, being a Republican, "had no right to run a pool in Albany"—so the political
machine, in addition to milking Wright for protection money, set
up its own pool. Its proceeds were also divided five ways. Buchanan told how an Albany police captain had assigned patrolmen
to guard the pool operators whenever they were carrying large
amounts of cash.°

On December 23, 1929, because of his earlier answers to the
grand jury, Dan O'Connell was indicted on 27 counts of perjury.
Among the counts were his denial under oath that he had received
a $40,000 payoff from Buchanan.

Four days later, when called to plead to this new indictment,
O'Connell failed to appear. He was then at liberty on $10,000 bail
in the Otto case and $1,000 bail in his own contempt case. His law-
yers told the court that bad roads on the drive from Albany were
holding him up and that he was not a fugitive from justice. Hours
went by, and the courtroom waited in vain for his appearance.
Finally, exasperated, Federal Judge Alfred Coxe issued a bench
warrant for O'Connell's arrest. But no one knew where the politician was.

When he did not show up by year-end, the $11,000 bail was
declared forfeited. O'Connell's attorneys pleaded for more time to
produce him, but District Attorney Tuttle was dubious. "Word has
come to me," he said, "that O'Connell has departed in an automobile for parts unknown . . . if O'Connell is not a fugitive from justice, I do not know what a fugitive from justice is." Rumors soon
floated placing the missing politician in Canada or in Cuba.

Finally on January 7, O'Connell gave himself up in Albany to
the U.S. Commissioner, and was freed once more—this time on
bail of $30,000. When newsmen inquired where he'd been, he told
them, "You'll have to ask my lawyers about that." °° O'Connell

---

° *New York Times*, November 27, 1929. Corning publicly denied that he
was involved.

°° His lawyers in this case included James I. Cuff of Brooklyn and Joseph
L. Delaney, Joseph Murphy and Neile Towner of Albany.

also told the press that he would fight proceedings for his removal to New York City—although the court had warned that it would refuse to decide his contempt appeal until he was in custody.

Proceedings were soon started to bring O'Connell back to New York, and Federal Judge Frank Cooper ruled that he must go. But O'Connell stayed in Albany while the ruling was appealed. Meanwhile, in May, the United States Supreme Court consented to hear the appeal of the ninety day contempt conviction that had resulted from O'Connell's refusal to answer grand jury questions the previous December.

At that point, however, O'Connell made a deal with District Attorney Tuttle. He agreed to withdraw his Supreme Court appeal and serve the ninety days; in return, the perjury indictment was dropped. Thus, after serving a short term in jail, O'Connell's troubles with the law would be over. Tuttle may have sensed a moral victory in putting O'Connell in jail at all; perhaps too, the District Attorney was unsure that his evidence was strong enough to convict Dan of perjury. It would have been a case of Buchanan's word against O'Connell's.

At noon on the thirteenth of June, 1930, Daniel P. O'Connell surrendered himself to serve three months for contempt of court, in the Federal House of Detention in Manhattan. He went to jail for refusing to answer questions, and was not convicted of any involvement in the baseball pool itself. This is the basis for O'Connell's explanation in later years that he had never been personally involved, but had "taken the rap" for some of his associates. However, in the earlier Boston case, he did plead guilty to direct involvement, and there remains the Buchanan testimony in the Otto case which clearly pointed up his role.

While serving his sentence, Dan O'Connell did not break rocks. In fact, he enjoyed a fairly pleasant stay in the penitentiary, and was even escorted out to night clubs and shows by the warden and his friends.

As for the notorious baseball pool itself, it pretty well collapsed under the prosecutions, and especially the publicity given to its cheating methods. However, pools of that sort continued to be a problem; in 1930, Governor Roosevelt was forced to threaten renewed prosecutions.

The proceeds of the pool were enormous, and the O'Connell machine, reigning at the pool's headquarters city, received a fat cut, as would almost any political machine in a similar position. The O'Connells not only got a cut for protection, but were involved in conducting the pool itself. While some of the money went into the pockets of the O'Connells, much of it also went out again to finance the machine's welfare operations for the needy. There was a little bit of Robin Hood in this—they swindled money from the not-so-poor, and handed out coal and food to those in want. And if they did well for themselves in the process—perhaps they subscribed to the view of Louisiana Governor Richard Leche, that his oath of office did not include a vow of poverty.

CHAPTER 7
Kidnapped

IT WAS July, 1933. At one o'clock one morning, John J. O'Connell, Jr., twenty-three years old, drove up to his Putnam Street home. Four men emerged from the shadows. They put a gun to young John's head and hustled him into their car; he was blindfolded, bound, gagged and thrown to the floor of the car, which took off on a long ride.

Thus was effected one of the most famous kidnappings in American history—that of "Solly" O'Connell's son, the nephew of the political bosses of Albany. To this day, many Albanians believe that the youth was abducted in order to force his father, involved in big-time gambling, to pay a gambling debt on which he had reneged. Others point out that "Solly" had the reputation of paying all his debts.

A confidential source close to the kidnappers tells this story: that gangster "Legs" Diamond had been trying to muscle in on the O'Connell bootlegging business. He was murdered in a Dove Street rooming house. To those who had done the job, the O'Connells had promised a share in their own Hedrick brewery, but then refused to pay up. The kidnapping was supposedly to enforce this debt.

Finally, it is even believed by a few in Albany that O'Connell was never kidnapped at all, but that the family wanted, for reasons unknown, to keep him out of sight for a while, and that the "kidnappers" were framed. This notion seems rather fanciful.

The night of the abduction, an anonymous telephone call was received at the law office of John's uncle, Edward O'Connell, demanding a ransom of $250,000 and promising a letter with further details. The letter soon arrived, instructing the family to place a classified ad in one of Albany's dailies, naming in code a list of suggested intermediaries to negotiate with the kidnappers.

Announcement of the dramatic crime was withheld for a time,* while three suspects were immediately singled out by the police on the basis of their absence from their usual hangouts. These were Manning "Manny" Strewl, a one-time Albany beer runner, released from prison; his beer running partner, John Oley, also an ex-convict; and Percy "Angel-Face" Geary, an Albany hoodlum who had served time for robbery.

It was apparently decided to let the culprits know that they had been identified. The first coded advertisement contained a list of men prominent in Albany sporting circles—with John Oley's name in the middle. However, this brought no response, as did the second list. The third list included the name of Strewl. By this time, the O'Connells were trying to list names who might really be acceptable to the kidnappers as intermediaries. In so doing, the politicians demonstrated their acquaintanceship with many members of Albany's criminal underworld.

The kidnappers bit. A letter was mailed by them from New York City, naming Strewl as an acceptable intermediary. A week after the abduction, a meeting was held between Strewl and Dan O'Connell in Albany's Washington Park, at which ransom terms were discussed. After three or four further conferences, the family finally handed Strewl $42,500 in cash. But he reported back that the kidnappers feared the serial numbers of the bills had been taken down, and they insisted on fresh money. Strewl's call was made from a phone booth in New York's Pennsylvania Station. Dan arranged for the money to be exchanged at a New York City bank.

---

* The authorities gave out publicly that they were not receiving cooperation from the O'Connells. This was intended to put the kidnappers at ease. It was eventually revealed that in fact, the O'Connells had worked closely with the authorities throughout.

Early on the morning of July 30, 1933, an automobile arrived at Dan O'Connell's Helderberg retreat. Three men got out— Strewl, an Albany attorney named Louis Snyder, and the kidnap victim. John Jr. now told of being held blindfolded and manacled to a bed during most of his 23-day confinement. He was sent to a hospital, while Strewl was allowed to leave.

Strewl was arrested the following evening while walking on North Pearl Street, taken to police headquarters and questioned at length. He was eventually charged with the kidnapping.

The two-week trial in Albany County Court in March, 1934, was a dramatic one. Handwriting experts testified that Strewl had written the negotiation letters. A more startling witness was Sam Gross, a Toronto knit goods salesman, who testified that early in 1933, he had been in a woman's suite in a New York City hotel while the kidnap plans were first being discussed. While two mobsters indulged in opium, Gross described two others as having a businesslike demeanor. These were Manny Strewl and John Oley. Gross said that he had informed the F.B.I. of this some time after the abduction had taken place.

Strewl, convicted, was sentenced to fifty years by County Judge Earl Gallup and incarcerated at Dannemora prison. The authorities now said that they were seeking Oley and Geary. While the search for those two dragged on, late in 1936, Strewl was granted a new trial by the courts; it began in January, 1937.

The bombshell during Strewl's second trial was the arrest of Frank Fisher, a beefy six-footer and ex-South African diamond miner, who had stayed in the room guarding John Jr. during the kidnapping. Word of Fisher's arrest leaked out, frustrating District Attorney John Delaney's idea of slipping him unnoticed into the court room, and then having the victim dramatically identify both Fisher and Strewl. John Jr. had already identified Fisher outside of court, since at one point during his captivity the blindfold had slipped and he had gotten a glimpse of the man.

This time, Strewl pleaded guilty to a reduced charge of blackmail and was sentenced to fifteen years. Now after Fisher's arrest, the full story began to unfold. The hideout at which the victim had been held was in Hoboken, New Jersey, verified by John Jr.'s identifying types of sounds he had heard coming through the window. The kidnap mob included some major criminals already in prison elsewhere on other charges. Those still at large were soon rounded up. Francis Oley, John Oley's brother, was seized in Denver after a family there recognized his picture while perusing a detective

John J. O'Connell, Jr. (left) entering courtroom with his uncle, Daniel O'Connell. (*Courtesy of Capital Newspapers*)

1935 Reward poster issued by the O'Connells. Pictured are, first row: John Oley, Percy Geary; second row: Mrs. John Oley, Francis Oley, Mrs. Francis Oley and Mrs. Percy Geary.

(*Knickerbocker Press*)

the activities
service. You may assist in this service
by telephoning the addresses of new
residents to 8-1458.

SEDGEWICK
10-9-13-13-9-5—7-9-12-12-15-21-7-8-12-25
16-1-20—3-1-19-5-25
10-15-8-14—15-12-5-25
6-18-5-4—3-1-18-18-15-12-12
20-15-13—12-25-14-3-8
2-1-18-14-5-25—18-9-12-5-25 .
10-9-13—15-8-1-7-5-14
20-15-13—4-25-11-5
13-21-19-8—20-18-1-3-20-14-5-18
2-9-14-4-25—18-9-12-5-25
* 1-13-5-19—15-2-18-5-9-14

Wanted   5

Kidnapper Manny Strewl
(*Gerber Collection*)

Coded advertisement nam-
ing contact men to deal
with kidnappers. Key: A
for 1, B for 2, etc. (*Courtesy of Capital Newspa-
pers*)

Bottom: Percy Geary apprehended, being carried because of a
leg injury due to an escape attempt from a second floor apartment. (*Gerber Collection*)

Dan O'Connell on the witness stand in the Strewl trial, before Judge Earl H. Gallup.

(Courtesy of Capital Newspapers)

magazine. They received a $15,000 reward from the O'Connells. Two days later, John Oley himself was seized in New York City, and the same night saw "Angel-Face" Geary trapped in a Brooklyn rooming house.

The complete gang consisted of Strewl, Geary, the Oleys, Harold "Red" Crowley, Charles Harrigan, John "Sonny" McGlone, George Gargillio and Thomas Dugan. In August, 1937, the federal government put all except Francis Oley on trial under the Lindbergh law.° Francis Oley had escaped prosecution by hanging himself in his cell.

The entire gang was convicted. Oley and Geary were sentenced to 77 years each; Strewl drew a 58 year term and a $10,000 fine. Fisher had turned state's evidence and got a minor sentence, eventually returning to the South African diamond mines. As a sidelight to the kidnapping case, it was revealed that Geary and the Oleys, while at liberty in 1933, had allegedly taken part in another "crime of the century," the $475,000 hold-up of an armored truck in Brooklyn.

In November 1937, Oley, Geary and Crowley were in Onondaga County Penitentiary near Syracuse. Geary yelled down the cell block to a guard, "Hey, Oley's hanging himself!" The guard came running—into a gun that Oley had managed to smuggle in. The trio escaped, only to be caught two days later in a Syracuse rooming house. They were eventually taken to Alcatraz.

After more than a score of years in prison, "Angel-Face" Geary could not face the prospect of living outside. He begged to remain in prison, and three days before his scheduled release, jumped under a moving truck and was killed.

John J. O'Connell, Jr., was installed as Democratic County Chairman by his Uncle Dan in 1939 and kicked out in 1945. He went to work in the Hedrick Brewery and died in 1954, at the age of 45.

In 1957 and 1958, Crowley, Oley and Strewl were each released from prison. Manning Strewl resides today in New Jersey.

The ransom money was never recovered. Legend has the abductors going into Albany's Washington Park with it, and coming out without it—the money remaining buried somewhere in the park to this day.

° Since among other blunders, the kidnappers had crossed state lines, thereby committing federal as well as state offenses. The U.S. and the State could each separately try and punish the culprits.

CHAPTER 8

Happily Ever After (II)

DAN O'CONNELL's prison term and unfolding tales of corruption in Albany in the early 1930's did not dampen the machine's interest in high level political maneuvers. It was not long before the O'Connells plunged themselves into the battle for the presidency of the United States.

In 1932, Governor Franklin D. Roosevelt and his political mastermind, Democratic State Chairman James A. Farley, set out to capture the presidential nomination. Former Governor Al Smith was the leading challenger.

At the national convention in Chicago, New York's delegation was dominated by a pro-Smith group made up of John F. Curry's Tammany, the Brooklyn organization led by John H. McCooey, and some upstate allies. Prominent among the latter were the O'Connells of Albany. They opposed the Roosevelt-inspired move to dispense with the two-thirds requirement for nomination, and stood steadfastly behind their Tammany allies and Smith, until Roosevelt was finally nominated on the sixth ballot.

Dan O'Connell would in later years support Roosevelt, but never took a shine to him. "He was all right," Dan has said of F.D.R., "but he was a bigot. He didn't like Tammany. He just didn't like poor people. He was a patronizing son-of-a-bitch, he was." *

Shortly after the 1932 convention, Albany leader Edward O'Connell unveiled the gubernatorial candidacy of Mayor John Boyd Thacher, to succeed Roosevelt. At this point, Lieutenant Governor Lehman was thought to be the leading contender for the nomination. But the Albany machine, it was said, "has built itself up in the past few years to a point where it will have to be reckoned with in any major movement such as the selection of a candidate for Governor." **

The Thacher candidacy quickly attracted significant upstate support, but was elsewhere seen as merely a demonstration of strength by the forces which had backed Smith at the national convention. The purpose was to drive home to Roosevelt, before he became president, that these men had to be dealt with. Tammany Hall also opposed the Lehman candidacy for this reason. While the O'Connells were in close touch with chieftains Curry and McCooey, the Roosevelt-Farley forces belittled them, considering Thacher at most a likely prospect for lieutenant governor on a Lehman ticket.

Ed O'Connell, to squelch any notion that Thacher was only interested in the second spot, wrote a public letter to Farley denying it and asking state committee neutrality in the contest. But when Lehman announced his own candidacy, Roosevelt chimed in with an endorsement, and there was no doubt where Chairman Farley stood.

The political picture was clouded even further with a new development at the beginning of September. In the wake of the Seabury investigations into Tammany corruption, and Governor Roosevelt's own inquiry into his conduct, Mayor Jimmy Walker of New York resigned. Until then, he had been under threat of removal from office by Roosevelt.*** This heightened the resentment harbored by Tammany against Roosevelt, and whetted the Hall's appetite for revenge through blocking Lehman.

The anti-Lehman combine scored a victory in an early round when the state committee designated Albany as the convention site. However, strangely enough, Tammany was soon found lending a hand in the Roosevelt presidential campaign, and this was

---

* *Knickerbocker News,* May 15, 1973.
** *New York Times,* July 14, 1932.
*** In New York State, the Governor has the power to remove any local official, including the mayor of New York, for cause.

Standing (left to right): John H. McCooey of Brooklyn, Edward J. O'Connell and Tammany Leader John F. Curry. *Seated:* Rensselaer County Democratic Leader Joseph Murphy, former Governor Alfred E. Smith and Mayor Cornelius Burns of Troy. (*Courtesy of Capital Newspapers*)

interpreted as a sign of reconciliation toward him and possibly toward Lehman. While Tammany had the power to thwart Lehman, its shrewder leaders knew that this would be an unpopular move that could seriously endanger the entire ticket.

Lehman was further bolstered when Al Smith agreed to place his name in nomination. Tammany was now believed to be holding out only for a pledge by Roosevelt that he would deal with them, through McCooey, the state's national committeeman. As a further trump, Tammany threatened to nominate the besmirched Jimmy Walker for the special mayoral election occasioned by Walker's own resignation. Such a nomination would have been a direct slap at Roosevelt.

Roosevelt took time out from his presidential campaign to fight for Lehman, arriving in Albany on October 2. Al Smith was now urging the O'Connells to relent and accept Lehman. At one point, in a conference among them, an O'Connell underling proposed that Smith himself be the candidate, but the ex-governor demurred.

As far as the mayoralty problem was concerned, he countered Curry's threat to name Walker with a threat of his own: that Smith would himself run for mayor.

"On what ticket?" sneered Curry.

"On a Chinese laundry ticket, I could beat you and your crowd," retorted Smith.

As the convention opened, Tammany's lines crumbled. Eighteen of the 24 Brooklyn leaders announced that they would back Lehman—and McCooey did not try to stop them. The Ahearn faction of Tammany broke from Curry to endorse Lehman. Thacher's support now seemed limited to the O'Connells, M. William Bray of Utica and Joseph Murphy of Troy. Tammany made a final proposal that Senator Robert Wagner run for governor, and Lehman for the Senate. When this was rejected, the Hall capitulated.

Herbert H. Lehman was nominated for governor by acclamation. John Boyd Thacher, true to his word, rejected offers of lieutenant governor or comptroller. Instead, as a sop to the beaten forces, M. William Bray was given the second spot on the successful ticket.

Early in 1933, Patrick O'Connell, eldest of the brothers, was elected clerk of the newly Democrat-controlled State Senate. After Boss Curry and the other leaders had received their share of legislative patronage, Curry, apparently as a peace gesture, gave Farley about thirty Senate jobs to dole out. No sooner did Farley submit a list of names for those jobs than Ed O'Connell and his upstate cohorts charged him with using them as a weapon of retaliation against the former Thacher men. With Clerk Packy O'Connell holding the appointive power over these jobs, the upstaters were able to tie up the entire legislature in what became a month-long patronage wrangle. The upstate members of the O'Connell-McCooey-Curry bloc served notice that those jobs would not be filled until they got a fair share of them. The men endorsed by Farley cooled their heels in the capitol.

The response was not long in coming: the Senate voted to strip the clerk of the appointive power. Before this could become law, Packy O'Connell defied the Senate by quickly filling the vacancies. But his appointees were fired, and Farley's list was installed as soon as the bill became effective. Farley won the round decisively—bolstered by the fact that he now controlled federal patronage for President-elect Roosevelt. (The O'Connells and their allies apparently felt they could well risk exclusion from federal patronage on account of their power play, since they were likely to be excluded in any event.)

Patrick H. O'Connell died in June of 1933, stricken with apoplexy in his car. He had just shot the best golf score of his fifty-four years. The state senate clerkship was inherited by his widow, Marguerite.

In the aftermath of the 1932–33 battle for control of the state, Curry was voted out by his colleagues, the first Tammany leader ever to suffer such a fate, and the city-upstate combine had lost power to the Roosevelt-Farley forces. However, despite the fact that Roosevelt was pre-eminent in Washington, and Lehman in the state, the O'Connells remained recalcitrant and in alliance with Tammany. Not until about 1937 did the Albany bosses give in to pragmatism and align themselves with Roosevelt, Farley and Lehman. Eventually, Roosevelt's victory became complete, and he was even able to install his own choice, Michael J. Kennedy, as leader of Tammany Hall.

At the 1934 state convention, in spite of the unhealed party rift, Albany was honored by the selection of John Boyd Thacher as permanent chairman. Al Smith said that if anyone had told him not so long before that he would address a convention presided over by a three-term Democratic mayor of Albany, he'd have had the man examined by the committee on lunacy. Governor Lehman and Senator Copeland were renominated by this convention without opposition.

The following conclave was noted primarily for something that did not happen. Al Smith by now had fallen out again with Roosevelt, becoming one of the New Deal's bitterest critics. The "Happy Warrior" had not seen the President in some time; when they did meet at the Syracuse convention, Smith, according to legend, greeted his old adversary with "How are you, you old potato?" Jim Farley was there, and relates that Smith never uttered the colorful line; a reporter concocted it and sent it over the wires. When Farley told him of its falsity, the reporter begged that the story not be killed publicly. "Don't worry, I won't kill it," said Farley, "it's too good a line to kill." *

Governor Lehman entered the 1938 convention refusing to run a fourth time for governor. Senator Royal Copeland had died, and Lehman had announced his candidacy for that vacancy. Meanwhile, the Republican nominee for governor, Thomas E. Dewey, loomed as the toughest challenger the Democrats had faced in many years. Ed and Dan O'Connell, having now made peace with Farley, were part of a meeting of state leaders who decided that Lehman must be drafted for governor again. At Lehman's Rochester convention hotel room, Farley, Dan O'Connell and the Tammany chiefs gathered to persuade Lehman to accept the nomination. The Governor relented and agreed to run.**

At this convention, John Boyd Thacher served as permanent chairman for the third time. Thacher was also supposedly offered the senatorial nomination, which he declined. It went instead to Congressman James M. Mead, who was elected, along with Lehman.

The fact that the O'Connells had aligned themselves with Roosevelt and Farley in 1937 became beside the point in 1940, when Farley broke with the President over the third-term issue, and allowed his own name to be placed in nomination at the national convention. While Dan O'Connell had little use for F.D.R. and his

---

* Letter to the author from James A. Farley, 1972.

** During the campaign, Dewey milked the picture of "twice convicted Dan O'Connell" sitting on the Governor's bed and pleading with him to run. Farley disputed the accuracy of Dewey's charge. Dan, he said, did not sit on the bed at all, but like a gentleman sat in a chair. Dewey accepted the correction.

policies, Farley's posture smacked to O'Connell of party disloyalty, an unforgivable sin. Once more, Farley became *persona non grata* in Albany. "Why, Farley would still be selling sporting goods if it hadn't been for Roosevelt," O'Connell has said. Farley's attitude toward O'Connell's longtime antagonism is one of bemusement, regarding it as stemming from his refusal to take O'Connell all that seriously and disregarding O'Connell's carping letters.°

The final showdown between the President of the United States and his erstwhile political partner over control of New York came in 1942, with Governor Lehman retiring after a decade in office. Roosevelt, Lehman, Senator Wagner, O'Connell, and Tammany leader Michael Kennedy all united behind the gubernatorial candidacy of Senator James M. Mead. Against this impressive array of power stood James A. Farley, backing State Attorney General John J. Bennett.

The fight was a bitter one. Recriminations were rife over Brooklyn leader Frank V. Kelly's support of Bennett, with grumblings that his delegation was not as unified as Kelly gave out, and demands for the minority Mead faction there to be unmuzzled from the unit rule. At the convention, Albany Congressman William T. Byrne, Mead's floor manager, was taunted by surly delegates when he gave a seconding speech. Farley had to intercede for quiet; both he and Lehman shook Byrne's hand as he left the podium.

Despite the lineup against him, Farley won, 623 to 393. The split in the party, and the nomination of a candidate against the open wishes of the President, contributed to the election of Thomas Dewey in November, the first Republican governor in twenty years. Only once since then have the Democrats managed to win a gubernatorial election.

Victory for Farley at the convention having turned into defeat at the polls, he relinquished the state chairmanship in July, 1944, nearly ending his role in New York politics. This left Edward J. Flynn of the Bronx as the most powerful Democrat in the state. At a conference presided over by Flynn, Paul E. Fitzpatrick of Buffalo—advocate of a fourth term for F.D.R.—was agreed upon by the leaders as Farley's successor.

In the meantime, the leadership of the Albany machine had also changed hands.

° Letter, *op. cit.*

Ed O'Connell was in his office on June 6, 1939. But that evening, at his home at 107 South Manning Boulevard, he suffered a fatal heart attack. The unexpected and untimely death at fifty-one brought in its wake rumors of suicide that persist to the present day. Some believe that Ed took his life rather than face some imminent personal or political scandal. While Dan had weathered a scandal that sent him to prison, Ed might have felt humiliated by the prospect. Yet no unseemly revelations followed his death, and political scandals by nature involve more than one culprit.

Edward O'Connell was honored with one of the most Lucullan funerals ever seen in Albany. One local resident remembers a crowd so thick that you couldn't get near the O'Connell house, and a dozen or more open cadillacs following the hearse, each filled with flowers. It reminded him of a Chicago gangster lord's funeral.

Albany had for many years seen an unusual form of political bossdom, embodied in a team of brothers. That was history, and in its place came a much more common form: one man rule.

Dan, however, did not take the chairmanship at this juncture. He didn't have to—after decades of political work and cementing loyalties, as well as by being the last survivor—Dan was the boss even without holding any formal position. So he passed the chairmanship to John J. O'Connell, Jr., his nephew, little more than thirty years old. Since Dan had no children of his own, it was his hope to continue the family dynasty through young John.

But the young man had no political know-how, and the real power remained in his uncle's hands. Dan made the decisions while his nephew was chairman. In 1945, he finally put the young man aside in favor of his dying old crony, John Murphy. After Murphy's death later that year, Dan himself finally took over the chairmanship.

By 1940, John Boyd Thacher, 2d, had served fourteen years as Albany's mayor, the longest term since colonial times. That year he left the office, being elected judge of the Albany County Children's Court. Thacher sat on the bench until 1947, when he finally retired, and he died in 1957 at the age of 74.

The man next in line for the mayoralty was the president of the Common Council, Major Frank S. Harris. He had served in that position 1922–25, having been a member of the first Hackett ticket, and was returned to office as Thacher's running mate in 1937. A distinguished veteran of World War I, he was now 72 years old, and in addition to his city office was serving as the state's deputy commissioner of taxation and finance, equivalent to

state treasurer. Becoming mayor would have required Harris to re-
linquish his state post. Disinclined to do that, he stepped aside by
resigning the council presidency at the close of 1940.

From its members the Council then elected a new president,
who immediately took another step up, to the mayoralty. This was
Herman F. Hoogkamp, who sat for sixteen years on the Council,
becoming majority leader. At the time he skyrocketed to the may-
or's chair, Hoogkamp was still employed as a machinist in the
Knickerbocker News composing room. He served as mayor
throughout the year 1941, but the organization did not tap him to
run for a full term. Hoogkamp later became chairman of the Albany War Price and Rationing Board.

The next mayor—and the only one since—was Erastus Corning, 2d. The son of Edwin Corning, Erastus was born October 7,
1909, and attended Albany Academy and Groton School. Following his father's path, he graduated Yale University in 1932. That
same year he married the former Elizabeth Platt of Philadelphia.

While in college, Erastus Corning showed a particular flair for
history, government and mathematics. Regarding the latter, he is
held to be that rare public official who revels in the seemingly dry
figures and statistics with which he must deal. He has been described as beaming while going over budget figures with newsmen.
Corning at college also played golf, was on the boxing squad and
won a Phi Beta Kappa key for his academic prowess. His current
recreations include hunting and fishing, and he is a collector of
memorabilia concerning Albany. When the author interviewed
Corning in connection with this book, the Mayor pulled out of a
drawer in his city hall desk a selection of obsolete paper currency
of the nineteenth century issued by local banks. Many items bore
the signatures of his grandfather and great-grandfather, both also
named Erastus Corning.

After college, Corning went into insurance as a profession. Although his family had been prominent and successful in business
for several generations, by the time young Erastus reached man-
hood, there was not a great fortune left. He did become wealthy in
his own right through the insurance company, no doubt aided by
his political influence. Corning today is still president of Albany
Associates, Inc., a firm which receives over $100,000 a year in
premiums for insuring the property of Albany County alone; he
has denied any conflict of interest by pointing out that he is not a
county official. His firm also participates in insuring the State's
South Mall project, on which Corning's total profits have been
estimated at $250,000.

During his father's term as lieutenant governor in 1927 and 1928, Erastus Corning recalls spending as much time as he could at the State Senate, over which the lieutenant governor presides. He had also been initiated into the world of politics by accompanying his father on the campaign trail. In August of 1934, Edwin Corning died. He had previously been named a delegate to the Democratic State Convention, and now, 24 year old Erastus was substituted for his father. This was his first public role, and it was soon followed by a much more significant one. In 1935, Erastus Corning was elected as assemblyman.

His uncle, Parker Corning, was at that time Albany's representative in the United States Congress. As a member of the House Interstate and Foreign Commerce Committee, he had fostered legislation which created the Port of Albany, and was in addition responsible for the Parker-Dunn Memorial and Troy-Menands Bridges over the Hudson River. Congressman Parker Corning, in tune with the local Democratic party, was a conservative, and opposed Franklin Roosevelt's New Deal. By 1936, Parker Corning was thoroughly disgusted and disheartened by the trend of the national administration, and decided to retire to his farm, where he died in 1943.

This opened the way for Erastus Corning's quick advancement. Following the O'Connell organization's practice of orderly promotions, the congressional seat was taken by State Senator William T. Byrne, fiery orator and veteran of the machine's earliest days. Naturally, young Corning moved up from the Assembly to take Byrne's place in the Senate.

In 1941, with Herman Hoogkamp serving as temporary mayor, Dan O'Connell was casting about for a man to take the job permanently. He didn't have to look far. He had known Erastus Corning since the latter was six, when Dan, then a young committeeman in the ranks, attended political meetings at Edwin Corning's house. Corning describes his own selection for the mayoralty this way: "They knew me and I knew them. It was what they wanted, and it was what I wanted to do." He candidly points out, too, that despite Albany's preponderant Catholicism, a need was felt to balance the strong Catholic flavor of the O'Connell group with a Protestant mayor. Corning is an Episcopalian, and he notes that although he himself is not a Mason, both Mayors Hackett and Thacher before him had been Masons.[*]

Corning, thirty-two years old, had no difficulty winning the

_____

[*] Interview, September 1971.

election in November, 1941. He defeated his Republican opponent, Benjamin R. Hoff, by a vote of 57,868 to 11,807.

Before the new mayor took office, World War II began for the United States. Eventually, Corning was drafted at his own request. The New York legislature had passed the "La Guardia Law" to deal with military absences of municipal officials, in anticipation of New York City's mayor being commissioned a general. That never came to pass, but the law was on the books, giving a mayor the right to enter the service without resigning, and to appoint someone to act in his place during his absence. Corning took advantage of this law and remained as mayor while in the service, appointing Major Frank S. Harris as his stand-in. Harris, well up in his seventies, had foregone the job once before. Now he took it, and served as acting mayor from Corning's departure on April 15, 1944 until his discharge September 18, 1945.

Corning left Albany with a contingent of other local draftees, and turned down the chance to become an officer. He served instead as a private with the 314th Army Infantry Division. After basic training at Camp Blanding, he saw duty in France, Belgium, Germany and Czechoslovakia. His unprivileged army career earned him the nickname "G.I. Mayor."

He returned to Albany just in time to campaign for re-election in 1945. Four years later, his vote reached its numerical peak of 60,497, and in 1957, he won with an unequalled 80% of the total. Corning has been elected mayor eight times, and his three decades in office more than doubled the previous record. Among present American mayors, only one has held office longer than Corning.

Corning as mayor prides himself on his attention to detail; no matter is too trivial to engage his concern. In a sense, he is campaigning the year-round. For example, the Mayor once learned that a man quite unknown to him was interested in getting a hand-gun license. Corning telephoned the man and offered to personally take care of it. By doing thousands of such tiny favors through the years, the Mayor has developed a large reservoir of popularity. His door is always open to people seeking help with all sorts of problems.

Corning has also held himself out as something of a one-man government, always on top of every facet of municipal affairs.* He spent one recent Saturday morning at his desk, painstakingly put-

---

* The need to maintain this image yielded, apparently, to more pressing considerations when Corning was publicly questioned by the State Investigation Commission in 1972 on city purchasing practices. In his answers, the Mayor professed ignorance of the operations of major city agencies.

ting his signature on a large stack of city bonds. His political importance has also resulted in Corning's taking a major, albeit unofficial, role in the county government.

While some have regarded Corning as the mere puppet of Dan O'Connell, this has never been really true. Dan was not as deeply interested in government as Ed O'Connell had been, so that while Corning has always dutifully kept Dan abreast of city affairs, he has not been dictated to.

Erastus Corning is acknowledged to be a man of considerable ability. For a long time, a bright future in state and even national politics was foreseen for him. Now he is in his sixties, and has been mayor so long that speculations of higher office have petered out. Some view him as a tragic figure for never having been able to exercise his talents in a more significant way. Corning is a very big fish in a small pond. But he might have been a big fish in a big pond.

» »

CHAPTER 9

The Great War

IT WAS wartime. The battle for democracy raged in the Far East, in Africa, in Europe—and in Albany County, as some would have it.

In 1938, Manhattan's young racket-busting district attorney, Thomas E. Dewey, ran for governor. One of his campaign pledges was to launch an investigation into corruption in the state's capital city that would curl the hair of its voters and politically destroy its boss, Dan O'Connell. "The Tammany machine braves are pikers compared to this machine," said the candidate. But he was unable to carry out his pledge, being narrowly defeated by Governor Herbert Lehman.

Four years later Lehman retired; Dewey once again campaigned with pledges to clean up Albany, assailing its "political dictatorship" and saying that he didn't "know the difference between a Democratic crook and a Republican crook."

This time, Dewey was elected. Of course, his promise of a cleanup had been intended to get him votes. Now, further, besmirching O'Connell's machine could hurt the Democrats across the state; and if the efficient Albany organization could be broken, the Democratic vote margins rolled up there would surely suffer.

Also, Dewey had presidential ambitions, and hoped to net some favorable publicity. Finally, the Governor was the sort who could not look upon evil without wanting to be the one to stamp it out.

It began in August, 1943, with his instructing the State Tax Commission to sift Albany's tax records. A number of city officials were subpoenaed to a hearing at which testimony revealed slipshod practices with respect to tax assessment of property—aside from any political chicanery in that area.

Then twenty examiners checked the City's books and found a shortage of over $1,600,000, the City having illegally channeled bond issue money into its budget. This prompted the Governor to order a wide-ranging probe into all city accounts and fiscal affairs. Mayor Corning, City Comptroller Lawrence Ehrhardt and Corporation Counsel McGuiness were called to testify, but all three refused to waive immunity. Waiver would have left them open to prosecution on the basis of their testimony; thus they were silent. But Corning publicly reacted to the charges by claiming that Albany's fiscal policies were prudent and economical, and arguing that the so-called "shortage" had in fact saved the City interest costs. He attacked Dewey for a "highly unjust and dishonest effort to destroy Albany's credit and smear its officials" for political advantage.

The campaign season was then underway, and New York State was holding a special election for lieutenant governor. This was important to Dewey because of his presidential ambitions, which would be advanced if he could leave the state in Republican hands.

State Comptroller Moore's next move was to prohibit the City from refunding some of its bonds because of "unwise and illegal fiscal practices." The City went ahead with a bond sale anyway, defying Moore. This battle ended in a stalemate, and nothing ever came of the Comptroller's charges.

Another battle had meanwhile been joined, when the Election Frauds Bureau of the State Attorney General's office seized Albany County's records pertaining to the 1942 election. A report to the Governor followed, recommending a searching examination of election practices in the county, and suggesting that its people had been denied fundamental political liberty. Dewey immediately dispatched a letter to the City noting "wholesale and shocking violations of the election laws" and warning that District Attorney Delaney and Sheriff Decker would be held responsible for the enforcement of the law during the upcoming elections.

Mayor Corning and State Comptroller Frank C. Moore (right)
looking over the records. (*Gerber Collection*)

Right: Governor Thomas E. Dewey (*Gerber Collection*)

Below: Former District Attorney John T. Delaney (left) with Assemblyman Frank P. Cox, in 1964. (*Courtesy of Capital Newspapers*)

In a predictable response, the Albany County Democratic Committee branded the charge as "cheap political trickery." While the Democrats admitted that the irregularities cited were "technically correct," such practices, they said, were commonplace throughout the state.

As voter registration got underway, state troopers patrolled the polling places. Despite this, and allegations that the voter rolls were grossly padded, registration in 1943 was only four percent lower than in the previous year. This fact was hailed by the machine as refuting any notion that Albany's electoral process was corrupt. On the other hand, the Chief of the Frauds Bureau later observed that the presence of the troopers had curbed many of the previously prevalent abuses, and that some 2,000 more than usual had foregone voting after having registered—implying that their registrations had been illegal.

The next move was a strategic counter-attack by the Democrats, and they retaliated with more than just words. District Attorney Delaney went before the Albany Board of Supervisors for support in launching an investigation of his own, this one to probe the Republican-run towns in Albany County and the Republican-dominated state legislature. The objective was to cause these Republicans to cringe with fear lest their own dirty linen be exposed—and to appeal to the Governor to save them by dropping his own probe of O'Connell. The ploy was easily arranged since the machine controlled the local grand jury. Delaney went so far as to subpoena State Tax Commissioner Brown and Comptroller Moore, but these subpoenas were quashed by the State Supreme Court.

The G.O.P. was not intimidated by Delaney's investigation. After the 1943 election (in which Dewey's man won the lieutenant governorship) the attack upon the Albany machine broadened. The Governor now appointed an extraordinary special and trial term of the State Supreme Court to investigate and prosecute election frauds in Albany County. A special grand jury would be selected, circumventing the regular one, controlled by the machine. By the time this special session convened, Dewey had broadened its powers to investigating and prosecuting "any and all violations relating to the administration of justice, failure to prosecute crime, pressure by political leaders upon public officials and transactions of business by individuals or corporations with the County or any of its political subdivisions." George P. Monaghan was appointed Special Prosecutor.

The practical effect of this was to supersede District Attorney Delaney in his usual functions, since the new body could look into any crime in the county. This attempt to disarm the machine was completed when Dewey created yet another new grand jury in Albany County—to investigate the state legislature, pre-empting the Democrats' own brainchild! They were now powerless to retaliate against the Republicans, at least in an official way. There was still ordinary blackmail, and it was rumored that O'Connell had plenty of dirt on important Republicans.

Special Prosecutor Monaghan immediately ran into controversy in selecting his jurors. He would hand each prospective juror a list of names—evidently of Democratic leaders and wardheelers —and if the juror knew anyone on that list, he would be rejected. So pervasive was the machine influence throughout the area that after a month of trying to impanel a jury, ten people had been selected out of two hundred called. At that point, the Democrats brought a court challenge to Monaghan's selection methods, but the move failed. Meanwhile, the imminent exhaustion of the panel to be drawn upon prompted the legislature to pass a bill which amounted to setting up a special grand jury system for Albany County. The Governor signed it into law, but it would shortly be voided by the Court of Appeals.

Monaghan eventually did manage to impanel a full complement of 24 grand jurors. Subpoenas were issued and indictments handed down. A welter of witnesses were heard—including City Comptroller Ehrhardt, Fire Chief Michael Fleming (later renowned for holding that office until well up in his nineties), and young Donald Lynch, then deputy county treasurer, who was castigated by a Monaghan aide for "contemptuous and insolent behavior." The grand jury also summoned fifteen Democratic ward leaders including County Chairman John J. O'Connell, Jr. All of the latter refused to sign waivers of immunity and gave no testimony.

Monaghan could pick the grand jurors who would hand down the indictments, but he had no such hand in the trials themselves, which had to take place in the Albany County court system. At the end of the investigation, some lesser guilty pleas, but not a single conviction, had been obtained.

John J. Murphy, treasurer of the Albany County Democratic Committee, was indicted on 29 counts of stealing $85,000 of the *machine's own money*. Far from throwing Murphy to the wolves,

Dan O'Connell made a public demonstration of his confidence in the man by installing him as Democratic county chairman in April, 1945. The case of Murphy was held in abeyance when he fell ill. He died of cancer on October 15, 1945.

Although Murphy's death prevented any resolution of the case, Monaghan, in moving for a change of venue, complained that Supreme Court Justices Schenck, Schirick, Murray and Bergan were all beholden to, if not under the thumb of, the O'Connell machine. If it accomplished nothing else, the investigation did point up the bias of the local judges and their willingness to come to the machine's aid. One judge, Gilbert Schenck, was almost removed from office because of a recorded telephone conversation with Dan O'Connell. This aspect of the Dewey investigation is covered along with the judiciary in general in Chapter 14.

O'Connell was aware of the fact that his phones were liable to be tapped during this fight. He even mentioned to Schenck in one of the taped conversations that they had to be careful over the phone. Eventually, the machine resorted to a "write, don't call" policy.

But Dan took advantage of the situation to have some fun with his presumed Republican eavesdroppers. "Did you hear the latest?" he said to one caller, "Dewey was in bed with Oswald Heck last night." Heck was the rather rotund Assembly speaker.

Another controversial incident enlivening the investigation was the Sonny Jones case. Jones, a black former capitol janitor, had been called to Monaghan's offices in the Smith State Office Building to be questioned about his role in buying votes, in February, 1944. Through his attorney, Morris Zuckman, Jones subsequently filed an affidavit charging that he had been beaten by state policemen as well as questioned, and had been dangled by his heels from the 29th floor window for fifteen minutes. Jones and Zuckman went to the State Assembly to press their pleas for an inquiry. But Judge Finch, asked by the Attorney General to make a private investigation, reported that Jones' charges were groundless, and that people who had seen him shortly after the alleged 3½ hour beating did not recall his having appeared maltreated.

Monaghan contended that the whole incident was concocted by the Democrats to create a diversion and make him look bad. Despite this, and Judge Finch's conclusion, the Albany Police Inspector issued "John Doe" warrants for the arrest of the six state troopers. The warrants were eventually quashed by the Appellate Division, ending the case.

To this day, the Jones incident is commonly referred to, even taught in the schools, as fact, in Albany. Almost any longtime resident will graphically describe the poor fellow being dangled out the window by the cruel Republicans, even though no one ever saw it take place. This is consistent with the Albany mentality that however rascally the O'Connell gang might be, Heaven save the city from the alternative.

It was not long after the Jones affair that Dewey finally succeeded in ending the nettlesome stewardship of District Attorney John Delaney. (The Governor had been unwilling to exercise his removal power.) The special grand jury, ordered to investigate all of the D.A.'s acts, indicted several Albany junk dealers and a railroad policeman for theft of $650,000 worth of iron and brass, citing Delaney for having failed to act. Delaney resigned, saying that "developments clearly indicate a design to make me a political football . . . I do not propose to be kicked around any longer." *

Early in 1946, after nearly three years of conflict, the war ended. Special Prosecutor Monaghan gave up, reporting to the Governor that although some indictments remained outstanding on which the evidence was clear and overwhelming, "until some remedial action is taken to correct the present abuses of the Albany jury system, it would harm the administration of justice and bring it into disrepute, were we to engage in trials of the existing indictments or to seek new indictments, the trials of which under the present law would necessarily be held in Albany County." Monaghan pointed out that while only 12 out of 24 grand jurors were necessary to hand down an indictment, conviction by a petit jury required a unanimous vote, so that one juror loyal to the machine could block conviction. And with the Albany County jury lists controlled by the machine, conviction in the local courts seemed an impossibility. So, out of a total of 52 indictments, the probe realized 38 guilty pleas, mostly to election law violations, and there were no jury convictions. A few minor party functionaries went to jail for short terms.

As for the concurrent investigation of legislative spending, launched by the Republicans only to deflect the Democrats' attempted counter-blow, Hiram C. Todd was appointed special prosecutor. His investigation was immediately suspect in some quarters

---

* Governor Dewey appointed the temporary successor to Delaney. In November, 1944, O'Connellcrat Julian B. Erway was elected district attorney, later to become state senator. Delaney for many years remained as secretary of the Democratic County Committee.

merely by being a Republican probe of Republicans. However, it was elsewhere noted that Todd was "forceful and independent, and there will be difficulty in keeping the investigation within [politically] safe bounds." *

The Todd probe's first report, in December, 1944, found practices that, while not criminal, were reprehensible. The cost of running the legislature seemed exorbitant. The payrolls were padded with political appointees having no visible duties. Several recommendations were made for reform. A second report some months later cited a few specific cases of kickbacks and padding. Almost nothing concrete resulted from the Todd investigation.

Belief persists that the Albany investigation was abandoned by Governor Dewey under threat by Dan O'Connell to expose Republican corruption. While the warfare dragged on for nearly three years before it was called off, it may be argued that O'Connell was holding this threat in reserve. If so, he never had to use it, for the investigation was already hopeless by the time it ended. It seems reasonable to suppose that Governor Dewey gave up because there was no chance of accomplishing anything, and the matter was hence becoming an embarrassment.

Warren Moscow observed before the investigation's end that to call it "a failure is only to report the opinion of both Republicans and Democrats in and around the State Capitol. It has even some of the aspects of a boomerang. The constant use of the State Police and wiretapping, and the constant pressure to produce evidence of criminality that would stand up in court, has produced a sympathy and an objection to what is called further persecution." **

The failure of the investigation was largely due to Monaghan's plaint of packed jury lists and politically biased judges. Also, as I. F. Stone observed, "Albanians have the civic patriotism of a Greek City-State," so that Governor Dewey, in whatever garb of virtue he might clothe himself, was regarded as a foreign invader.*** And of course, as well as being a downstater, Dewey was a Republican. Despite the misdeeds of the local Democrats, Albany was still happily Democratic. Besides excusing O'Connell-crat corruption by speculating that anyone else would be worse, Albanians felt that O'Connell was giving the city the kind of cheap government they wanted, and they gave no aid or comfort to the

---

* I. F. Stone, "Thomas E. Dewey," *The Nation*, May 20, 1944, p. 587.
** *New York Times*, October 20, 1945.
*** Stone, *op. cit.*, p. 588.

"outsiders" trying to change things. Moscow described thusly what the voters liked about the Albany status quo: "pretty good municipal services, public officials accessible to the citizenry, and in general, the live and let live attitude of the practical political machine." He also pointed out that Albany was one of the few places in the country where the local machine got more votes for itself than Franklin D. Roosevelt got for himself.[*]

As Stone put it, "We Americans are for clean government in theory and political favors in practice. This makes the Dewey type popular—at a distance." [**]

At home, they still liked Dan O'Connell.

---

[*] *New York Times*, October 24, 1946.
[**] Stone, *loc. cit.*

» »

CHAPTER 10

"You're Not Finished
Until You're Dead"

NOT ONLY did Governor Dewey's lengthy war against the machine fail to dislodge it as the power running Albany, but it had no adverse impact upon O'Connell's role in state and national politics.

Senator James Mead had received O'Connell's support for governor in 1942, but was beaten by Farley's candidate. Four years later, however, Farley was no longer important, and there was scant opposition to Mead as the nominee for governor. Also at the 1946 convention, despite protestations that he wasn't interested, Albany's "G.I. Mayor" Erastus Corning was drafted to run for lieutenant governor. Dan O'Connell had ostensibly opposed Corning's joining the ticket; and when he yielded to the widespread sentiment that Corning would strengthen the slate, Dan was in a position to virtually dictate the nomination of his choice, Henry Epstein, to the Court of Appeals. Completing the ticket was Herbert Lehman for the Senate. Defeating the ticket was the postwar "had enough" Republican tide.*

---

* Lehman ran for the Senate again in 1949, after the death of the elder Robert Wagner, and won. He served through 1956.

In 1948, President Truman, who had succeeded to his office on the death of Franklin Roosevelt, was a candidate for a full term. The Republicans had swept the congressional elections two years earlier, and most observers gave Truman no hope of beating Dewey. There was considerable unhappiness in the Democratic party over Truman's nomination. Dan O'Connell called those who wanted to dump Truman "a bunch of rats deserting a sinking ship." Dan put himself squarely in Truman's corner. "We'll be for Truman right down the line," he said, and called his candidate "the greatest President since Jefferson." O'Connell avowed that Truman was the only Democrat who could win, "by taking advantage of the mistakes of the Eightieth Congress in which the Republicans demonstrated anew that they are for big business first," thereby foreshadowing the very campaign Truman would wage.

During that campaign, Truman paid a visit to Albany, where more than five thousand turned out at eight o'clock in the morning to parade down State Street in welcome. It was said that no other organization in the state could have done as well proportionately.

After the election, a group of New Yorkers called upon Truman to discuss patronage distribution. "I don't care," said the President, "but whatever that guy up in Albany wants, he can have."

Dan O'Connell first began feuding with Democratic State Chairman Paul Fitzpatrick in the spring of 1950. Governor Dewey was backing a residential rent control bill, which Fitzpatrick called a "landlords' bill," intending to make it an issue in the upcoming gubernatorial campaign. Dewey needed one Democratic vote in the State Senate to put the bill through—and got it from Albany's Peter Dalessandro, who at the last minute revealed that he had been "directed" to support the bill.

However, O'Connell and Fitzpatrick soon held a public get-together to douse the stories of a feud between them. O'Connell told the State Chairman that he would support any candidate for governor acceptable to the leadership. Until that time, Albany had been regarded as favoring Oscar R. Ewing of the Bronx, Federal Security Administrator. At the convention in 1950, O'Connell did wind up behind Ewing but the nomination went to another Bronx man, Congressman Walter Lynch (who was easily beaten by Dewey). Jim Farley tells the story that O'Connell offered to support him for governor at this convention. "You wouldn't back me if you thought I had a chance," Farley told Dan, "you only want to oppose the slate."

Dissatisfaction over the election defeat moved O'Connell to instigate a petition for Fitzpatrick's ouster. Dan's candidate for chairman was Thomas Cullen of Orange County. The chairman was required under the rules to call a state committee meeting if petitioned by 25% of its members. While Fitzpatrick granted O'Connell the support of not more than fifty of the three hundred committeemen, he called a meeting to bring matters to a head.

Fitzpatrick's supporters believed that O'Connell's animus was really resentment over a patronage matter, the Fitzpatrick endorsement of **Port Edmund** of Syracuse for U.S. District Attorney. "I wasn't after Paul," the Albany leader explained afterwards, however, "I was after Flynn. He is an amazing fellow, but you never get anywhere with him."

Edward J. Flynn was indeed "an amazing fellow." A meteoric rise had put him in control of the Bronx Democratic party in 1922, when he was thirty. He became Democratic national committeeman, a legendary political boss and a close associate of Franklin Roosevelt. Flynn served for a time as national chairman, and was now the most powerful New York Democrat. It was this control which O'Connell sought to break, for the claimed reason that it could eventually lead to the Liberal party controlling the Democratic.

Meanwhile, Vincent R. Impellitteri, protégé of underworld czar Thomas Luchese, had in 1950 succeeded William O'Dwyer as mayor of New York City. The same year, running independently on his own Experience Party ticket, "Impy" won a special election for the mayoralty. But he still regarded himself, and was regarded, a Democrat.

As O'Connell told it, several months after the Impellitteri victory, the Mayor's close associates gave him assurances that both Kings and Queens Counties, in New York City, would support a move to change the state leadership. O'Connell then undertook to pull together upstate votes. The effort also gained a scattering of miscellaneous backing; Robert Blaikie, an insurgent Tammany leader, would argue that poor leadership was to blame for recent Democratic defeats, and allegations flew of patronage discriminations by the state chairman against blacks.

The anti-Flynn putsch, however, foundered. A week before the state committee meeting, Mayor Impellitteri took a hands-off stance. Evidently on the basis of the prior assurances he had received, O'Connell had never directly contacted the leaders of Kings and Queens Counties, whose support was crucial. Now they were lost to him and his upstate confreres.

O'Connell retreated and released those pledged to support his move. Fitzpatrick was given an overwhelming vote of confidence.*

Party dissension between upstaters and city men continued even after the collapse of O'Connell's bid to oust Fitzpatrick. Early the next year, Democratic leaders of 31 upstate counties banded together into a formal organization to battle New York City leaders for a voice in party affairs. At the Democratic national convention, while Fitzpatrick supported Averell Harriman for president, O'Connell steadfastly backed Oscar Ewing, his choice for governor two years earlier.

1952 was another bad year for the Democrats. Dwight Eisenhower beat Adlai Stevenson for president by a large margin; in New York, Senator Irving Ives won re-election over Democrat John Cashmore. O'Connell had supported Cashmore's nomination, but the continuing defeats heightened dissatisfaction with the leadership. Shortly after the election, Paul Fitzpatrick finally resigned the state chairmanship.

The ensuing contest over the position brought James A. Farley back into the fray, actively supporting the candidacy of William Morgan. Mayor Impellitteri backed Morgan, and Farley as leader of the more conservative elements in the party placed Morgan's name in nomination. But the winner was Richard H. Balch of Utica, the candidate of Ed Flynn, who was firmly in control. (O'Connell's Albany committeemen and those from neighboring Rensselaer County boycotted the meeting, knowing how it would end.)

Flynn's years as leader of the party came to an abrupt end with his untimely death in 1953. The power vacuum thus created was soon filled by Carmine DeSapio, the first Tammany boss since Murphy to dominate the state. Bolstered by the success of installing Robert Wagner as New York's mayor, DeSapio moved to elect a Governor in 1954. His choice was Averell Harriman.

Dan O'Connell had other ideas. He openly supported the nomination bid of Franklin D. Roosevelt, Jr., who had been elected to Congress as an independent on the Liberal Party ticket.

---

* A bitter O'Connell afterwards announced a belief that Mayor Impellitteri was serving his first and last term, and that Council President Rudolph Halley was likely to succeed him. Halley had been elected as a Liberal Party candidate; he carried that same banner in the mayoral election of 1953, but without success. As for Impellitteri, he did not even get that far, fulfilling one aspect of O'Connell's prediction. Some of New York City's Democratic chieftains, spurred by a nascent Carmine DeSapio of Manhattan, united behind Robert F. Wagner, Jr., who defeated Impellitteri in the Democratic primary and was elected mayor.

O'Connell would eventually vilify Roosevelt for that very independence, but in 1954, young FDR became the vehicle for upstate resistance to Tammany.

At the state convention, Assemblyman James J. McGuiness of Albany placed Roosevelt's name in nomination. When the delegates voted, Harriman was the winner. He was victorious again in November when he nosed out Republican candidate Ives by the narrowest margin in modern times.

DeSapio's star, having risen so swiftly, began its fall four years later, when the political boss got into a tiff with Governor Harriman over the senatorial nomination. Harriman wanted Thomas Murray to be the candidate, but DeSapio, seeing little party enthusiasm for Murray, backed Manhattan District Attorney Frank S. Hogan. Albany went along with Harriman and Murray, but Hogan was nominated. This spectacle of the Governor being beaten in his own party by DeSapio raised the campaign charge that the Democrats were boss-ridden. The issue contributed to the election victory of Nelson Rockefeller for governor and Kenneth Keating for senator, and sowed the seeds of serious party dissatisfaction with DeSapio's leadership.

Dan O'Connell was a warm and early supporter of fellow Irishman John F. Kennedy for the presidency, having been a long-time acquaintance of the candidate's father. The Albany boss was, by his own account, the first man whom Joseph P. Kennedy contacted in New York State, even before the 1960 presidential effort had openly begun. O'Connell told the elder Kennedy, "you needn't bother to come up here again—we're for your boy."

The Democratic state chairman at this time was Michael H. Prendergast, completely within the thrall of Carmine DeSapio. Prendergast undermined his popularity with fellow Democrats, especially O'Connell, by refusing to join the Kennedy bandwagon until the last minute, and by opposing forceful promotion of the national ticket in New York State. Prendergast soon gave O'Connell a pretext for urging his removal.

By this time DeSapio had become anathema to the voters on account of his "boss" label. Mayor Wagner doubted his ability to win re-election in 1961 while tied to DeSapio, and finally broke with him. The Democratic county leaders then put State Comptroller Arthur Levitt into the mayoral primary—and Wagner, running against "bossism," won overwhelmingly. Unrepentant, State Chairman Prendergast endorsed the maverick candidacy of Lawrence

Gerosa in the November election, putting himself outside the party.

That was the last straw. Dan O'Connell called for the ouster of Prendergast, and this time, he had a powerful ally—Wagner. The Albany leader told the New York Mayor that he was not pushing anyone in particular for chairman and was willing to back the Mayor's choice. Opposed by these two powerhouses, Prendergast was doomed. It was said at this time that O'Connell's "thinking permeates, if not controls outright the thinking of the leaders of the 7 counties making up the 3rd Judicial District," and that his influence also affected the Niagara frontier area centering around Buffalo and the eight counties of the 8th Judicial District.*

Chairman Prendergast was replaced by Wagner's choice, William McKeon. Meanwhile, Wagner's primary triumph had weeded DeSapio's allies out of the Manhattan party hierarchy, and he too was ousted. (He had, in fact, lost his own district leadership.) Since the demise of DeSapio, New York State Democrats have been without a dominant leader.

1962 was a gubernatorial year, and Schenectady Congressman Samuel S. Stratton, an Albany neighbor, was running. But he was regarded as something of a troublemaker for entrenched party leaders. A former aide explains that for a long time, "Albany County was frozen" toward Stratton. Finally a conference was arranged between Stratton and Dan O'Connell at the latter's Helderberg retreat. While the meeting was cordial, no support was forthcoming.**

O'Connell was thinking of someone else to run for governor that year: Judge Bernard Botein, who was being touted by some as a draft possibility. The hope was to regain some of the Jewish vote that had been lost to Rockefeller four years earlier. O'Connell pledged all of Albany's state convention votes to Botein, the first solid support the draft movement gained. "He'll make a grand candidate—excellent," effused the boss in his usual hyperbole for a man he is backing. As to what weight his endorsement might carry in neighboring counties, O'Connell was more restrained: "Possibly some of them might be influenced by what I have to say."

---

* *New York Herald Tribune*, November 1, 1961.
** The Albany machine would warm rapidly toward Stratton when he was forced by redistricting to run within its bailiwick—a warming that was quite mutual.

Botein, however, refused to run, and the Democrats turned to another Jewish candidate, United States Attorney Robert Morgenthau. Governor Rockefeller repeated his 1958 feat, outdistancing the colorless challenger by half a million votes.

The election two years later brought a new face to the New York Democratic party. Robert F. Kennedy moved into the state at the last minute to run for the Senate, winning the nomination over Congressman Stratton. In the Democratic landslide of 1964, Kennedy was elected, immediately becoming the major figure— although not the boss—of the party, since Wagner remained a powerful force. Also, for the first time since the 1930's, the Democrats won control of both houses of the state legislature.

When the state legislative caucuses met, Wagner's choices for the leadership positions were defeated. For speaker of the Assembly, Brooklyn party leader Stanley Steingut was picked over Anthony Travia, who had been minority leader. In place of their former Senate leader, Joseph Zaretzki, the Senators chose Dan O'Connell's own Julian B. Erway. O'Connell was said to have agreed only reluctantly to Erway's running for the post, at the request of Robert Kennedy. The choice of Erway, a conservative member of an old political machine, met with widespread criticism.

When the legislative session opened, Wagner's followers broke party discipline and refused to vote for the caucus selections. With the Republicans voting for their own men, neither an Assembly speaker nor a Senate majority leader could be elected. The legislature was completely stymied, unable to begin work. Senator Kennedy stood aloof from this political crisis.

Dan O'Connell supported Erway in the Senate, while backing Wagner's man, Travia, in the Assembly. However, when Erway's candidacy floundered, and Wagner shifted his support from Zaretzki to Thomas Mackell, O'Connell endorsed the latter. In explaining the choice of Mackell, O'Connell quipped, "Well, they tried everybody else, didn't they?" Mackell was put forth as a compromise, but Dan didn't think Erway was quite through. "You're not finished," he said, "until you're dead."

O'Connell's role was pivotal, since he controlled at least two senators and a number of assemblymen. Those few votes counted heavily in the close battle. And O'Connell's ability to influence the course of affairs was paradoxically enhanced by the fact that he had little to gain or lose upon the outcome. Many of the lesser patronage jobs in the legislature would be his no matter who the leaders were, since the jobs were so low-paying that they had to be filled locally. O'Connell was therefore free to support anyone.

The battle became even more bitter when Wagner charged State Chairman William McKeon with offering bribes to legislators.° Dan O'Connell had never been a McKeon man, having in fact earlier referred to him as "little leader." But Dan and many other party chiefs were infuriated by Wagner's public charges, which could only harm the Democratic party. Forty-two county leaders met at Albany and gave McKeon an overwhelming vote of confidence; and O'Connell switched his support in the Senate battle to Jack Bronston, now the anti-Wagner candidate.

O'Connell would have liked a compromise, with the leadership of one legislative house going to Wagner, the other to his enemies. But amid this acrimony, compromise was impossible. The struggle dragged on for a month, until the Republicans finally intervened, throwing their own votes to Wagner's men, electing Travia speaker and Zaretzki as Senate majority leader.

Despite this apparent victory, the Mayor announced in June that he would not seek another term at New York's Gracie Mansion.°°

In the ensuing 1965 mayoral contest the city's Democratic bosses backed Comptroller Abraham Beame. Queens' popular District Attorney Frank D. O'Connor, with gubernatorial ambitions, was also in the race; but before long, he dropped out and resurfaced as Beame's running-mate for council president. It was strongly surmised that O'Connor did this in return for Bronx boss Charles Buckley's promise of support for the governor's race. Beame lost in November to John Lindsay; O'Connor won, though, giving him a boost in his quest for the governorship.

O'Connell had long worked closely with Bronx leader Buckley, and in 1966, the Albany boss endorsed O'Connor for governor. This was after having first leaned toward Franklin D. Roosevelt, Jr. What undid Roosevelt in O'Connell's eyes was his act of pub-

---

° The State Investigation Commission held hearings on this and other Wagner charges. No crimes were found to have been committed.

°° Some have speculated that Wagner was hoping to become available for the governorship the following year, but such a candidacy never emerged from the shadows. The man Wagner backed as his successor was meanwhile defeated in the Democratic primary, and William McKeon resigned as state chairman, to be replaced by John Burns of Binghamton. Robert F. Wagner would make a comeback bid for the mayoralty in 1969, and lose the primary. Four years later, he refused to run as Rockefeller's endorsee.

licly airing the 1965 O'Connor-Buckley deal, an indiscretion which infuriated many old-line Democrats. When Mayor Erastus Corning announced that Albany's delegates would back O'Connor, Roosevelt responded that "the action today by boss Dan O'Connell . . . confirms my warning to the party that the principals to this unprincipled arrangement are determined to brazen it out and steamroller an O'Connor candidacy through the Buffalo convention. . . ."

Once again, Senator Robert Kennedy proved unable or unwilling to exert influence. Although O'Connor was patently not a Kennedy favorite, he was nominated, and the "bossism" issue was revived against the Democrats. In a four-way race including a Conservative and Franklin Roosevelt, Jr. on the Liberal ticket, Governor Rockefeller prevailed once more.

Rockefeller carried Albany County, and lost the city by only 15,000 votes, despite a generally lackluster run for a Republican in other upstate areas. One observer close to Democratic affairs at this time gives the following explanation:

Rockefeller's South Mall project was stalled by a political dispute over the lucrative insurance premiums. A conference was held among the Governor, Mayor Corning, and some others.

"Where do you think those premiums will go," posed Rockefeller, "if Frank O'Connor is elected?"

"I'm beginning to get the message," said Corning, who has an insurance firm of his own.

So supposedly, the deal was that Corning and the Albany Democrats would get the insurance contracts on the Mall. In return, the machine would not work against the Governor's re-election.*

Senator Kennedy's half-hearted support for the O'Connor ticket led some to expect a move to take control of the party after its defeat. But nonesuch occurred. He did not even enjoy predominant support in the state party for his presidential bid. When that campaign was cut short by an assassin's bullet, New York was left without so much as a major Democratic office-holder, much less a leader.

---

* This source also believes that as part of the deal, Republican Daniel Button was not to be vigorously opposed for congressman. Interestingly, Button ran ahead of Rockefeller outside the city, but behind the Governor in the city. This would support a hypothesis that the machine aided Rockefeller deliberately in the city, while letting its congressional candidate languish from a poor campaign (see Chapter 23 on that campaign).

Still, the Democrats went into the 1970 campaign with high hopes of defeating Governor Rockefeller. Their ideal candidate seemed to be former Supreme Court Justice Arthur J. Goldberg. Dan O'Connell thought so, and supported Goldberg, along with former Kennedy aide Theodore C. Sorensen for the Senate (who came to Albany to meet with its leader). Under a new primary law, the state convention designated Goldberg and Sorensen.

Albany County played a curious role at this convention in respect to the other nominations. Under the new law, a candidate needed 25% of the convention vote for the right to contest the designee in a primary. Mayor Corning delivered the largest block of votes received by Jerome Ambro, an obscure Long Island politician seeking to challenge State Senator Basil Paterson for lieutenant governor. Ambro tallied just barely enough votes to get on the ballot. Corning and Albany also backed the insurgency bid of Robert Meehan against the nomination of Adam Walinsky for attorney general.

Both Walinsky and Paterson easily disposed of their opponents in the primary, while Goldberg had a surprisingly hard time defeating Howard Samuels for governor. The senatorial nomination was won by Congressman Richard Ottinger, after a television commercial blitz; the convention choice, O'Connell-backed Ted Sorensen, placed a dismal third.

Goldberg proved to be a far from ideal candidate. His campaign was as ineffectual as any waged by the Democrats in modern times, and he gave Rockefeller his greatest margin of victory. Running on the Conservative party ticket, James L. Buckley accomplished the upset of the year by winning election to the United States Senate.

There had been considerable resentment in the party over the makeup of the ticket, laden as it was with downstate Jews. After the defeat, Dan O'Connell remarked to State Chairman John Burns in explanation, "Basil Paterson was the only white man on the ticket." Paterson, a black, is a Catholic. O'Connell later said of the slate that it wasn't even a Democratic one, and that he hated to vote for it.

Albany Democrats kept their options open for a long time before supporting any candidate for president in 1972, and elected a slate of uncommitted delegates to the national convention (Albany was the only place in the state where a McGovern slate was defeated). Not until the convention itself did the Albanians declare for Hubert Humphrey, who promptly withdrew from the race.

Mayor Corning then switched the delegation to Senator Henry Jackson. Although after McGovern's nomination, Corning quickly jumped on the bandwagon, and in fact was named to head McGovern's campaign in upstate New York, Dan O'Connell never reconciled himself to the McGovern candidacy, and publicly expressed disagreement over Corning's joining the campaign.

The Albany machine's tradition of bickering with Democratic state chairmen was continued after the 1972 election, with Corning calling for the removal of Chairman Joseph Crangle. The Mayor's complaint was frankly that Crangle had turned down a proposed bipartisan deal on the three Court of Appeals judgeships up for election, and had instead attempted to elect three Democrats. Three Republicans won. As for Crangle's replacement, Corning intimated that he himself would be interested in the job. The challenge attracted little support outside of Albany, and was soon dropped.

» »

CHAPTER 11

Uncle Dan

"UNCLE DAN," as he is called by friends and en-
emies alike, is the redoubtable leader of the longest functioning
personal political organization in the entire history of the United
States. Dan O'Connell is the most famous of his clan—mainly by
grace of having outlived all the others by so many years. If he was
not the dominant force in 1920 (and the newspapers then seemed
to think he was) he has been since 1939, and has rounded out one-
third of a century of leadership.

For all this, Dan O'Connell has not basked in the limelight.
On the contrary, he has been one of the most self-effacing of political chieftains imaginable, the epitome of the behind-the-scenes operator. Despite the thousands who pride themselves on calling him
a friend, he is paradoxically very much the man nobody knows. Interviews and photographs of him are rare, important occasions.
Not until his eighty-fifth birthday did he ever consent to be interviewed on television. He is not a man to be encountered anywhere
but in his own home, limiting his public appearances to only one a
year, the annual meeting of his organization. Between meetings he
runs it by telephone.

O'Connell seems indifferent to his own fame. "I'd rather paint the town red than be Michelangelo," he has explained. But mainly, his shunning of the spotlight is a very canny political ploy, part and parcel of his mystique. Despite this general aversion to the public eye, he does not mind being called a political boss, and likes people to know at least that much about him. Once, Congressman Leo O'Brien complained of Dan's being constantly labelled as "the boss."

"But Obie," said Dan O'Connell, "I *am* the boss."

Otherwise, he is a very private person who spends the warm months at his mountain camp retreat in the Helderbergs. Except for trips to Florida, he lives during the winter in a yellow clapboard house at 142 Whitehall Road. The house is sometimes referred to as "The Castle" because he lives there, but is not an imposing structure, and is located in an ordinary, quiet middle class neighborhood. No name or ornamental initial, nor even the house number can be found on it, and the front door does not even open on Whitehall Road.

O'Connell holds court in a large living room entered through glass-paneled doors. He receives visitors sitting in a chair under a light, his legs covered by a blanket; the guests sit in darkness. The living room has a quality of unostentatious affluence. (In contrast, the furnishings of a waiting room appear almost ramshackle.) Near at hand to Dan is a telephone; he answers it himself when it rings. The number is said to be unlisted, but this is not strictly true—it is listed under the name of nephew-in-law Donald Lynch.

At his Helderberg cottage, O'Connell allowed some photographs to be taken only once, in 1963. The lensman was prize-winning Bernard J. Kolenberg of the *Times-Union*. In 1969, the old man was visited in the Helderbergs on his birthday, the last day he spends there, by *Knickerbocker News* reporter Edward Swietnicki.

As Swietnicki described the scene, O'Connell was just packing to move to his winter home. The old man sat in his living room in a favorite chair on a small round rubber air-filled cushion. With him in the chair was an already dog-eared copy of the morning paper.

He had read that paper with care. When conversation turned to the political scene, and who might run for governor, attention was called to an item in the paper about a dinner honoring State Comptroller Arthur Levitt, a potential candidate.

"And did you notice," said O'Connell, "who is sponsoring the dinner? A Rockefeller," referring to David Rockefeller, the Governor's brother.

Right beside the leader's chair was a table piled with books and topped by a telephone. The volumes were a current Albany voters directory, a telephone directory, a history of the United States from 1806 to 1837 by Henry Adams, a book about Tammany Hall, a biography of O. Henry, the American short story writer, and a book of Robert Burns' poems. When he saw the reporter eyeing the last named volume, O'Connell commented on the variety of moods in Burns' writings.

His chief interests, however, are baseball, of which his knowledge is said to be encyclopedic, and the Civil War. The latter subject is believed to receive more of his attention than politics; when he visits battlefield sites, he knows more about them than the professional guides.

The living room sports a large stuffed Democratic donkey on a chair; there is another donkey on the front lawn. A small campaign poster sixty years old hangs on a wall, along with a tattered yellow newspaper clipping showing ten football players, the Delphian League of 1910–11.

"Howard Myers and I are the only ones alive today from that group," said O'Connell of what was known as one of Albany's best semi-professional teams.

The room also featured several photographs of O'Connell's nieces and nephews and several religious pictures. There was a holy water container, an old fashioned chest-high radio, and a television set.

And, to round out the scene, on a chair in a small anteroom, its proper place, lay the battered, wide-brimmed fedora hat that is Dan O'Connell's trademark.

He receives regular visits from the neighborhood's canine population, whom he feeds from a stock of food kept for them. There is also a stream of human visitors, on both political and friendship bases.

He had just turned eighty-four at the time of this particular visit, and was asked how he felt about that.

Dan grumbled amiably and smiled. "You know all you're going to at 35 or 40. After that, you get old. I hope and pray I don't live too long."

Dan O'Connell married Leta H. Burnside when he was in his forties. A native of Oneonta, she resided in Albany and was a retiring woman who did not participate in public activities but devoted herself to her home and close circle of friends until her death in 1963. The couple had no children.

Although Dan O'Connell had little formal education, he is today an avid reader of many types of literature; a favorite novelist is Charles Dickens. His sports interests, too, have always been many and varied. Besides baseball and football, Dan has been a devotee of cockfighting, outlawed for its cruelty. He is said to have owned and raised some of the best fighting cocks in the country, and to be willing to travel almost anywhere to put them in matches. Large amounts have been wagered on these cockfights. Dan has been quoted as frequently saying, "One person you can trust is a chicken fighter."

O'Connell has been fascinated by fights between humans as well as between cocks, and he has travelled quite a bit around the country just to attend prize fight bouts. Mayor Corning mentions Dan's having gone all the way to Reno to see a match. He was once a good amateur boxer himself and knew such old-time boxing greats as Jim Jeffries and Jess Willard. This interest of his prompted a move to get him appointed to the State Boxing Commission at its inception in 1920, but Dan never got the job.

As we have already seen, Dan O'Connell's political role in the 1920's and 30's called for him to give away large sums of money to needy people both inside and outside the machine. Dan was always known as a soft touch. Once, while he was standing on the steps of the Elks Club, a panhandler came up and asked for a hand-out. Dan pulled out his roll and peeled off a twenty dollar bill. "Gee, thanks a lot," the bum exclaimed, "this is my lucky day!"

"You always get lucky before you die," said Dan.

Other stories of Dan's generosity are legion in Albany, and many may be apocryphal. There is the tale of the man who needed false teeth; Dan got him some, but they didn't fit. The man carried them around in his pocket, and every time he saw his benefactor, slipped them into his mouth. There is the story of the priest given $1,000 each Christmas and Easter, who turned out to be a Republican. "Now you're going to have to bury me for nothing," quipped Dan when he found out. He is even said to have loaned $10,000 to his predecessor as boss, William Barnes.

Little of this changed over half a century. The favors were still doled out by Dan O'Connell personally, even into his eighties. He would no longer trek out to visit the person in difficulty, but his door would be open to anyone who walked up and rang the bell, with or without an appointment. He frequently has seen up to fifty people a day in his home.

Dan O'Connell gives every outward evidence of being a religious man. He is a patron and friend of churches and churchmen and attends mass. Some who know him describe him as a faultlessly clean living man whose morals are above reproach, while others believe him to be a disreputable old sinner whose involvements have included big time gambling and prostitution. No one has ever been able to link him with the skin trade. But gambling is another matter.

In 1922, after the O'Connell takeover in Albany, Solly O'Connell was put in charge of all the gambling and every proprietor of a gaming casino was ordered to report to him and Dan. They all complained of having a new partner foisted upon them. Eventually, Dan and Solly centralized gambling at 560 Broadway, with a few branch offices, and operated one of the largest Monte Carlos in the east. Every known form of gambling was offered, and as many as 250 players were seen in a single room at one time. The O'Connells also had a finger in the policy or numbers racket (in which players bet small amounts on numbers which they pick. The winning number is taken from some random event such as a racetrack payoff rate). The machine has even employed policy workers on election day as thugs and vote repeaters. Finally, there was the lucrative, illegal and dishonest baseball pool, Dan's deep involvement in which caused his prison term in 1930.

Thus, at least in years past, Albany has been a wide open town for gambling, with slot machines, policy rackets and horse rooms (the most flourishing of which in 1971, accordng to Mayor Corning, was located in the State Capitol Building itself). It has been claimed, though, that Dan O'Connell never had a large share in the take—that instead, he shrewdly allowed this to be the province of his ward leaders, many of whom made fortunes at it. The story went the rounds that one of the ward leaders used to gather up all the slugs played on his slot machines, to play them on slot machines elsewhere in the state—run by his brother-in-law.

Another gambling activity of O'Connell's was election betting. A classic story is told of the 1942 race for governor. The Democratic nominee was John J. Bennett, who as attorney general had conducted an investigation of Albany, which made him distinctly unpopular there. A group of big gamblers from New York figured to make a killing, and offered to wager that Bennett would not carry Albany by 20,000 votes. Dan turned them away, saying, "those guys are anxious and will be back." A few days later they did return, this time offering to bet on a margin less than 15,000. Dan took all the bets he could on that figure, and the amount involved may have approached $100,000.

Bennett lost the election to Thomas Dewey, but carried Albany. By 19,000 votes.

O'Connell had some losses on occasion, too. He once made a large bet on a margin of 20,000 votes in Albany, only to fall short by a hairsbreadth 300.

Aside from gambling, another of his favorite pastimes is to go for simple automobile drives. A political crony, often Jimmy Ryan, takes the wheel and as Dan has explained, "we have a route for most any occasion. If we have an hour, we go this way, and if we have three hours, we go that way."

Dan is not much of a drinker. He likes beer and prefers people around him to drink it rather than hard liquor. When he frequented the Elks Club, highballs would be hurriedly swept off the bar upon his entrance. Until recently, he smoked Camel cigarettes incessantly, and once said, "I feel sorry for anyone who doesn't smoke . . . They always look nervous and upset." Smoking was probably the major contributor to O'Connell's raspy voice, which was so difficult to understand that subtitles had to be used in one television interview. At the age of 86, Dan noted this problem publicly, and revealed that he had quit smoking. While he feared he may have done so too late, there followed a distinct improvement in his voice.

As political leaders of his type go, Dan O'Connell has not been greedy and has not amassed a very great fortune. He seems to revel in his political activity and to enjoy a modest life style, never showing any interest in big houses, cars or boats. His personal wealth has been estimated at less than a million dollars, certainly a small fraction of all the money that has passed through his hands.

While the O'Connells have participated in a number of business ventures including some warehouses, much of Dan's money probably derives from the Hedrick Brewery, which was sold a few years ago. The family had originally gained control of the brewery in the course of normal political operations, loaning the owners money in order to keep them going. The owners finally decided to opt out, and told the O'Connells that for an additional payment, they could have the whole brewery.

Hedrick's was naturally Albany's leading beer. If the owner of a saloon used Hedrick's beer exclusively, he had full privileges— staying open 24 hours a day, the right to have prostitutes maintain headquarters there, no license worries and the profits from O'Connell slot machines. If the owner used two kinds of beer, one of them Hedrick's, he may have been even better off, since the courts would not be receptive to a suit by the competing firm to collect an unpaid bill. Albany is full of stories of strongarm tactics *a la* Chicago gangsterism being used to promote the sale of Hedrick beer—of heads being knocked in and of rival beers spilling out onto pavement. Most of this is probably fanciful, the product of naive assumptions that violence was necessary to push the beer. The fact was that any saloonkeeper would know Hedrick was O'Connell's beer, and most would act accordingly without being pressured. Any who failed to get the message on their own would be closed down at the midnight curfew while their competitors stayed open, or a few sanitary code violations could be slapped on them. Hedrick beer sold well enough.

A similar case is that of the Desormeaux Vending Corporation in the capital district, run by a man named DeSormo and James Ryan. One barkeeper told of his venture in selling some items over the counter and being advised that he would be better off selling them through vending machines. In short order he received four summonses for violations of the health and building codes, and gave up selling over the counter.

O'Connell's commercial interests are not the only ones that have prospered by the grace of the machine's power. One local entrepreneur found his business unexpectedly zooming. The cause was a false rumor that O'Connell was a part owner.

It has, predictably enough, been said of Dan O'Connell that his gruff exterior conceals a kind nature. A close associate, Leo O'Brien, has said that "Even when he turns a fellow down, the guy somehow goes away with the feeling that maybe Dan knows best."

O'Brien also maintains that "Even when he makes a mistake —Dan's a good judge of people, but he's human—and we find we've put a clinker in office, he manages to work it out gently. I remember once we put a real clinker into the State Senate and I said to him: 'we've got to get rid of that fellow. He's an embarrassment.' Dan said 'No, Obie, we owe him something.' So the next thing I know, the clinker was out of the Senate and into a job more suited to his ability. Everybody was happy and no harm done." °

The ability to avoid making enemies is one of Dan O'Connell's greatest talents. For a political boss of his sort, he has amazingly few antagonists, even among Republicans, and he has kept the Democratic party virtually free of dissension. One of the few dissident Democrats calls Dan "a master untrained psychologist,"

° *Times-Union*, February 23, 1970.

whose adroit carrot-and-stick approach has held him in everyone's good graces for half a century.

The characteristic of Dan O'Connell perhaps best known to the public is that he does not want to be known to the public. He has explained: "politically you should not be seen nor heard. I've always thought that if you talked too much, you got into trouble . . . I've seen it finish a lot of them." Yet in 1972—possibly due to an improved voice—he suddenly became talkative. Over the radio, he called a Roman Catholic priest "that Dago son of a bitch." In a television interview, he said that there had indeed been politics behind the controversial cancellation of a sale of bonds. When asked if he could hint at the political background, O'Connell offered to tell the reporter if it would be kept quiet. Although he refused to apologize to the priest, he did indicate that he was sorry for having gotten into hot water over the incident. In any event, it was political expediency, and a wise one, rather than modesty that kept him out of the limelight for so many years.

O'Connell's views on politics and life in general are conservative. He opposed Franklin Roosevelt's New Deal, and in New York State, he opposed the "little New Deal" of Governor Lehman. Before World War II, he was in the isolationist camp. This deep-seated conservatism has had some strange impacts on Albany. Some time ago, for example, it was proposed to extend a runway at Albany Airport, but the project was stalled year after year. The reason: "Dan O'Connell does not believe in airplanes." Renovation of Public School 17 was also deferred for many years, because that was where Dan O'Connell had gone. "We don't want to renovate it," explained an official, "because if it was good enough for Dan, he must think it's good enough now."

O'Connell has said that the militance of many young people today and the divisions in the country don't bother him. "They'll get over it . . . I think those teachers are the cause of most of the trouble. Children shouldn't have anything to say about a college . . . I think the teachers are somewhat soft . . . The teachers were always that way, I think."

He believes that modern America is basically in sound condition. "There's only one thing that concerns me [and it's] over-publicized. The growing drug thing. They get on them, they're never off. They're public charges. There's only one cure for them—to take care of them." As for himself, he avowed never to have taken so much as an aspirin in his life.

Today in his late eighties, Dan O'Connell is in faltering

health. He is plagued by emphysema and throat polyps, which sent him to the hospital several times in 1971. The same year he fell in his home and suffered a broken hip. Up to about that point, he remained in full control of the Democratic party, and no one in Albany doubted it for a minute. However, his interest resided strictly in the organization's political affairs, leaving the running of the government and questions of public policy to Mayor Corning, with whom he is in daily contact. O'Connell's word has been law on matters of personnel—appointments to public jobs and political candidacies. As to the latter, he has said, "I never nominated a candidate in my life. They're always nominated by a consensus of opinion around headquarters. It didn't make any difference to me who they run. If they wanted him, it was his." That may have been a bit disingenuous, to say the least. No one ran on the Democratic ticket in Albany whom O'Connell didn't want.

In 1972, although not retiring, Dan began shifting the rest of his power to Mayor Erastus Corning, calling Corning the chairman of the party in fact if not in name. Corning for his own part insisted that Dan O'Connell was still the leader.

On his own terms, Daniel P. O'Connell no doubt believes that he has done good in this world. While he believes that he has given Albany good administration, he perceives that good in individual terms—all of the thousands of people whose lives he has helped. It is mostly *his* people whom he has helped, both through the government and his personal largesse. Some in Albany feel that Dan O'Connell is not the leader of all the people, and that the government of the city and county is not the government of all the people.

Whether the good he has done outweighs what has suffered for his having been in power is a question that has often been answered and will continue to be answered by the voters of Albany. But it is also a question for Dan O'Connell and his conscience.

For all the world can tell, his conscience is clear.

Part Three:

THE WAYS OF POWER

» »

CHAPTER 12

The Machine People

THERE IS a building in the City of Albany known as the Polish Hall. Once a year, it is the scene of the meeting of the County Committee of the Albany Democratic party. Once a year, the local papers headline, FOR ALBANY DEMOCRATS, IT'S ALWAYS 'THE SAME'.

The headline would refer to the results of the meeting, but the people attending it are always the same as well. The rows of chairs, packed close together, would chiefly be occupied by the women, shoulder to shoulder. The men would stand at the sides or the rear of the hall, slapping each other on the back and renewing acquaintances. They would be packed so thickly that one must shove one's way through to the seats.

A few of them would not be middle aged or old. A few of them would not be of Irish or German ancestry. A few of them would not be blue collar or municipal employees, and most of those few would be lawyers. A very few of them would not be white. And none of them would be contentious here this night. This is a political meeting, but they have not come for the business. The business is brief and a foregone conclusion. They have come instead for the camaraderie. They have come to consume hot

Left: Donald L. Lynch (*Author's Collection*)

Right: Lynch's business partner, State Senator Julian B. Erway. (*Author's Collection*)

At the Polish Hall: Leo C. Quinn, Mayor Corning, Mary Marcy and Congressman Leo W. O'Brien (*Gerber Collection*)

dogs and beer over hurried conversations with their old buddies. They have come to be seen here. They have come to hobnob with people of power, to be treated as friends by them, and to reassure themselves that when they go home, they will be people of consequence in their neighborhoods.

"That was a nice party," said octogenarian machine functionary Mary Marcy at the end of one meeting.

Her teutonic figure has been a familiar one at these gatherings for half a century. Through the thick haze of cigar and cigarette smoke hanging in the air, one catches glimpses of all the other familiar faces—Donald Lynch in sartorial splendor, John Clyne with the frames of his glasses hugging the sides of his head, the ubiquitous Ryan brothers, the towering, aloof Mayor Corning, and all the nameless faces seen year after year, nameless to an outsider but not among themselves.

Up at the podium, the proceedings are conducted mechanically by script. One at a time the chair calls upon the pre-arranged nominators, who hand up their nominations in writing. The papers are read in a rapid, droning voice, full of the knowledge that no one is listening. Only a sharp ear can tell who is being nominated for what. But the committeemen approve all of the nominations with a casual chorus of ayes. No one takes issue with anything. This is how they make such selections as their county chairman and their candidate for mayor. The leaders are named in seconds, and each year, the speed record is improved. The entire business is generally concluded within ten minutes.

At the back of the hall, there is a center of attraction. It is a modestly dressed old man wearing a floppy wide-brimmed grey fedora hat. He is being pressed from all sides by photographers, and a steady stream of people is passing by to shake his hand and exchange a word or two. The reporters are milling around and asking the leader of the party how the election will turn out this year. They already know what the answer will be.

"Same as usual," says the old man. He doesn't stop to talk to reporters, but keeps on shaking hands and saying hello to his people. He knows how important they are.

The word "machine" connotes an impersonal quality, with the human element reduced to a minimum. But a political machine is a very human thing. Its cogs and gears are people, and the power that makes it work is the power of personal relationships.

That is something reformers and machine opponents often forget. While they may crusade against the corrupt mayor, the people are voting for their friend, the neighborhood committeeman. While the reformers may campaign on the issues, a citizen may be influenced more by who asks for his vote than by any question of policy.

The O'Connells, experienced in neighborhood politics, knew this well when they began to build their machine in the early 1920's. Knowing it, they placed the main emphasis on their network of committeemen, and selected them carefully. Not anyone could be allowed the position. That key individual would, more than anything else, refract an image for the party into his neighborhood. He would be chosen for his reputation, friendliness, decency and community acceptability as well as his loyalty to the O'Connells and his adeptness at performing the many duties of a diligent committeeman.

And diligent they were, wherein lies the key to the O'Connell machine's success. The committeeman was on the job not only at election time but year-round. He knew personally every single human being in his district; when someone new moved in, the committeeman would soon visit. He was neighborly toward his people, stopping by often, did his homework to find out what their problems were, and found solutions. Through pull at city hall, the committeeman had the power to do many favors, and was happy to do them, since it bound the voters more closely to the Democratic party.

During the campaigns themselves, there was no substitute for work. The committeeman had to make sure everyone registered, and saw to it that whoever needed an absentee ballot got one, and that it was turned in to the Election Board. Every voter was canvassed to make sure he hadn't strayed. For election day, the committeeman organized his inspectors and runners, and oversaw the polling place. He kept track of who was voting, and late in the day, would send runners to roust out those Democrats who hadn't voted yet. One Albany resident recalls that his father, a Democratic politician during the machine's early days, would be absent from the family almost the entire three months preceding an election. The committeemen, as a result of all this spade-work, knew their districts like the backs of their hands. They knew what the vote tally would be within two or three, and if there was a deviation, they knew where to look for it.

The committeemen, along with other party runners and workers who have not yet reached committeeman status, are the bulwark of any political machine. They are also the base of the organizational structure. Each district (or precinct) has two committeemen elected, in theory, by the district's enrolled Democrats at a primary every two years. Although the position is coveted, carrying with it power, prestige and often a patronage job, there is almost never a contested election. In practice, a ward leader selects his committeemen.

Five to nine districts make up a ward, and there have been nineteen wards in the city (sixteen starting in 1973). The ward leader is supposed to be chosen by the committeemen in his ward, but in fact, he is selected by Dan O'Connell and his circle of party leaders. They may select a committeeman from the ranks for promotion, or may give the job to some city official or a member of a trusted old family. As examples, the Third Ward Leader is Joseph Yavonditte, formerly a City Court judge; and John P. Martin, leader of the 13th, is the son of a man who was on the ticket with Dan O'Connell in 1919.

The committeemen accept the leadership's selection of their ward leader, and there is never an open fight for the position. Most committeemen may be unaware of their technical right to choose a leader; in any event, the ward leader is too important to allow committeemen to select him on their own. Furthermore, the O'Connell machine does not believe in contests of any sort within the party, and instead cultivates solidarity. Of course, it is necessary that committeemen be kept happy, so the leadership will not impose unpopular ward leaders on them. And if there is dissatisfaction over the choice of a ward leader, it will be talked out; no one would think of an open fight.*

The ward leader is responsible for organizing and coordinating all the committeemen in his ward. It is indispensable for a committeeman to have a good working relationship with his ward leader, since it is through the leader, and not on his own, that favors for a committeeman's constituents can be accomplished. This is another reason why a committeeman is not wise to oppose the ward leader selected by the party bosses.

Ward leaders are the focal points of the organization. They keep in touch with the people of their wards through their committeemen, and the top leadership keeps in touch with the committee-

---

* The Albany Republican Party has not been able to impose such control; in 1972 the silk stocking Fifth Ward's committeemen unanimously elected a new leader over a candidate openly endorsed by the city leadership. Of course, threats of reprisals carried little weight with the Republican committeemen, who earn scant reward if any for their service.

men through the ward leaders. It is thus the ward leaders who keep the bosses attuned to the mood of the voters, an important element in any group's staying in power.

While in most places, citizens nowadays seek help with problems through local elected officials like city councilmen and state legislators, Albany retains the old-fashioned Tammany-like reliance upon the party ward leaders for this function. The problems put before the committeemen are resolved through the ward leaders, and requests for favors are channelled through them. If an Albanian goes to his alderman with a problem, the alderman will either refer him to the ward leader, or contact the ward leader himself. At least, nothing is ever done without a ward leader's knowledge and approval.

In many cases, however, the ward leader cannot take action completely on his own. He in turn goes to the party headquarters, and deals directly with O'Connell's close confidants, like Donald Lynch, Robert Bender or Jimmy Ryan. These are the men who, merely by their say-so, can influence a city contract award, have a street cleaned or put people on the payroll. For example, if a ward leader has someone who needs a job, he goes to headquarters to get a "white slip" with the approving signature of Jimmy Ryan or another of the top leaders. The job hunter need only present this slip at the place of employment, and he will go onto the payroll without further ado. Other favors, like fixing traffic tickets or getting taxicab licenses, the ward leader can arrange directly with the city officials involved. City officials know who all the ward leaders are, and treat their requests accordingly.

Thus, the ward leader's job is by no means limited to organizing the Democratic party in his ward. He is a combination ombudsman and Santa Claus, looked on by his people as the man to see, no matter what the problem. John Martin of the old 13th Ward tells the story of an elderly woman who called him at work one afternoon to complain about children playing on her roof.

"Yes, ma'am," said Martin, "what would you like me to do about it?"

"Get them to stop it."

Martin answered that he could call the police if she liked, but otherwise, frankly, he could not chase the children off her roof.

"Listen, you've *got* to help me," the woman pleaded, "you're the ward leader!"

In this instance, the woman instinctively turned to the ward leader, even though a moment's reflection would have shown her that he could do nothing more than she herself could. On the other hand, the idea of ward leaders having mystical powers is not without foundation. There are things that ward leaders can do that no one else is able to.

For instance, in order to get a taxi license in Albany, one must go through a complicated procedure including a lengthy waiting period, pending a security clearance. Temporary licenses, however, may be issued so that a driver can work during this period. The official channels for getting a temporary license are none too clear, but one thing is certain: a taxi driver cannot get one. A ward leader, and only a ward leader, must be the one who asks for it.

Situations in which people are in effect forced to turn to the ward leaders for help, however, may sometimes ironically create resentment rather than gratitude. One Albany woman told a Republican worker that she'd heard her husband would have to go to the Democratic ward leader for a taxi license. The Republican inquired at his headquarters, found that the woman was correct, and advised her to see the Democratic ward leader after all. The woman thanked the Republican for his honesty, and reluctantly did as he suggested. In this instance, the Democrats gained an opponent, not an adherent, for their "favor."

Unfortunately, however, most voters do not realize that they are being exploited by the Democrats in such matters, and that many things are given out as "favors" which should be theirs by right.

What are the ward leaders like? They are mostly Irish Catholics, fifty or older, lifetime Albany residents, with blue-collar backgrounds. Typical of them is Ray Joyce of the old 12th Ward, a former railroad foreman. Now 75 years of age, Joyce has been a lifelong friend of Dan O'Connell. He has been a Democratic committeeman for forty years, and a ward leader for five. Naturally, not being in business like some other leaders, Joyce is on the public payroll, as clerk of the Albany County Legislature. He got the job simply by asking headquarters for it, when his advancing years made railroad work too strenuous.

Joyce keeps in close touch with those both above and below him in the party hierarchy. He visits the State Street Democratic headquarters at least once every day, usually confers with his alderman once a week, and meets with his committeemen once or twice a month. He is always on call to do favors for his constituents. "Party work is a full time job," he says, "it's not a pastime. If a fella doesn't want to work hard—to get out and even ring doorbells—well, then he doesn't belong in politics."

Ray Joyce's $12,000 a year job with the County Legislature is a dignified and not very demanding one. Other ward leaders occupy similarly congenial offices. Bill Devane has been water commissioner, Pat Prendergast fire commissioner, and Jack Dwyer, Jr., like his father, has been superintendent of the Ann Lee Old Age Home. George Hettie of the old First Ward has been on the city payroll to the tune of $5,000 a year, with the nebulous title of "consultant" to Mayor Corning. Ed McHugh of the 11th Ward was foreman of the Albany County Airport until the party gave him an easier post as Port Authority public relations director.

While no Democratic ward leader starves in Albany, the ones who profit most from the position are not those on the payroll, but those who contract for City work. John Martin is a plumbing contractor who is frequently employed on projects by the City. During one thirty day period he performed ten different jobs for the City and garnered $5,000. The king of the politician-contractors is William Carey of the old Ninth Ward, whose North End Contracting has received about a million dollars in each of the last three years on one job alone, the city's sanitary landfill. The contract was given to his firm without competitive bidding, and on a cost-plus basis which guaranteed a fat profit. Carey's dealings with the City have been the subject of state investigation, which is covered in Chapter 16.

To complete the picture of the organizational structure, its base is composed of the committeemen who report to the ward leaders, and the ward leaders report to the county chairman, at the top of the pyramid. Also reporting to him are the leaders of the other cities, towns and villages in Albany County. Again, in theory, the county chairman is elected every two years by all of the committeemen in the county. The present incumbent is Daniel P. O'Connell.

The O'Connell organization's structure of ward leaders and committeemen has changed little since it was put together in the 1920's. Almost unique among city political machines in this century, it has experienced only minor deterioration. But even this paragon of machines has developed some crotchets of old age.

The best party worker is one who has been at it for long years, building up personal relationships with the people of the neighborhood. Many of the machine's present committeemen and ward leaders have worked for thirty or forty years and more. But this carries with it an inevitable problem: these party stalwarts are now very old, and thus hobbled in making their rounds. Even if there is a younger man ready and able to step into the oldster's shoes, personal factors, including a large debt to the old man for his faithful service, may prohibit his being replaced.

Committeemen and leaders who move their homes do not forfeit their positions, so that today, a substantial proportion do not live in the districts assigned them, an inevitable handicap to their effectiveness.°

The geographical boundaries of the constituencies have changed, and the people in them are changing too, perhaps subtly, but inexorably. Life is not as simple as it used to be, and the relationships between the wardheelers and their people are different. This relationship, one observer has written, "has become more of a business deal and less of a social institution. Business deals are far more transitory than institutions, and the party . . . is rapidly losing its traditional hold on its residents."°°

The extent to which Democratic committeemen are falling down on the job was perhaps revealed when in 1973, some of the nominating petitions were examined. In the seventh ward, some committeemen had made the job of collecting signatures easier for themselves through forgery. At least one "signature" of a man long dead was found. The petitions for that ward were challenged by insurgent aldermanic candidate Jane Ramos, leaving open the question of how slack signature-gathering might have been in other wards.°°°

And while it is becoming increasingly difficult for aging ward workers to perform as of old, a greater problem, perhaps in its potential more than in current force, is that of replacing the workers themselves. The old time party loyalists with their great diligence, patience and attention to detail simply aren't being made any more. The world that spawned them no longer exists; young people getting interested in politics have broader horizons than their

---

° This proportion has been estimated as high as half; but it is pointed out that in most cases the district still contains people bearing the same last name as the no longer resident committeeman.

°° Ira Wolfman, "Old Ward Leaders Face a Changing City," *Washington Park Spirit*, July 25, 1972.

°°° Seventh Ward Alderwoman Ballien indicated that the negligent committeemen were made sorry for what they had done. The outcome of this primary race produced another surprise for some smug committeemen who thought they knew their districts (See chapter 24).

parents, and are moved by national, not local, issues and problems. They might work with dedication on an occasional campaign, but have scant interest in taking on year-round chores of attending to petty neighborhood troubles. Few of them can be enticed by the city jobs which for years held committeemen in harness. Few of them can be attracted by the neighborhood prestige which used to go hand-in-hand with being a committeeman. Indeed, a recent public opinion survey revealed that only garage mechanics and used car salesmen are held in lower esteem than politicians.

Albany, with its quaint but effective political machine, has been out of the mainstream of twentieth century American development. But the mainstream is more powerful than the fragile links with the past that hold the machine together. Albany will one day be swept along.

We have discussed the grass-roots of the machine, the people who make it up and who do its work. These people, committeemen and ward leaders, are powerful in the sense that they can get things done that the average citizen cannot. But their influence stops here. They do not make the decisions of the organization. They are not power brokers between the organization and the financial interests, they do not pick candidates for important offices, they do not decide upon city government policies.

These decisions are made by the boss or bosses of the organization. True one-man rule is a real rarity among political institutions. Any man in power tends to have around him a flock of subordinate characters in various roles. They may be mere sycophants, or henchmen who carry out the leader's dictates. On the other hand, they may be trusted advisers, or even men of power in their own right.

Definitely in the latter category is Mayor Erastus Corning. While he played a subordinate role when he first took office, through the years, Corning has increased his sphere of authority. Recently, he has overshadowed the aging Dan O'Connell as the real decision-maker and boss of the machine.

Corning is a leading public figure in Albany. Another man of great influence, but of whom the community is scarcely aware, has been Judge Francis Bergan of the New York Court of Appeals, the State's highest. This alone makes him one of the most important citizens of Albany. Bergan has been described as perhaps the second closest, after Corning, to Dan O'Connell as an adviser on major matters. A graduate of Albany Law School and a protégé of the machine, he was elected to the State Supreme Court at the age of 32, and retired in 1972. Throughout his career he has been a valuable judicial ally of O'Connell. Because of his judgeship, Bergan was compelled to remain deep in the background of political affairs, but has devoted considerable energy to community involvement. Another judicial confidant of O'Connell's is State Supreme Court Justice Russell G. Hunt, also at the twilight of his career on the bench—a career marked by a willingness to make outrageous decisions favoring the machine (see Chapter 14).

Ubiquitous in the councils of the Democratic party are the Ryan brothers. The legend goes that when Dan O'Connell was imprisoned in 1930 in New York City in connection with the baseball pool scandals, he met the Ryans' father, a friend of the warden, who secured liberal treatment for Dan. While O'Connell himself has said that he did meet Mr. Ryan during his prison term, Jimmy Ryan disclaims the whole story, terming it a fabrication of unknown provenance. In any event, it was Dan O'Connell who beckoned the brothers to Albany, taking them under his wing.

Jimmy Ryan was county purchasing agent until the State Investigation Commission found that the County had been cheated out of hundreds of thousands of dollars by sellers who had delivered less than what the County was billed for. The 1963 S.I.C. report criticized a whole range of purchasing practices: collusive bidding, awarding contracts without bidding, extravagant prices paid for merchandise, favored vendors, and delivery of inferior meat described as "sticky and slimy" to the County Ann Lee home. Ryan refused to appear at public hearings, was questioned privately, and held to be an uncooperative witness. The Board of Supervisors reappointed him purchasing agent two weeks after the S.I.C. hearings ended, which action the S.I.C. report called "an affront to the people of Albany County and a contempt for honest and responsible government." He eventually resigned the position.

Jimmy Ryan is a friendly confidant of Dan O'Connell, and will act as his chauffeur several times a week. In 1972, Ryan was installed as manager of the party's headquarters, traditionally a seat of power in the machine. However, his taking that job is seen as a diminution of its influence, since he is not expected to be as effectual as his predecessor, Donald Lynch.

Charles Ryan, Albany County Elections Commissioner and party treasurer, is more of a wheeler-dealer in business affairs and not as close to O'Connell as Jimmy is. His influence in smaller matters is nevertheless termed substantial. In 1973, Charles Ryan was

Right: Charles W. Ryan, 1959 (*Courtesy of Capital Newspapers*)

Left: James A. Ryan, 1966 (*Courtesy of Knickerbocker News*)

Left: Ward Leader William E. Carey (*Courtesy of Times-Union*)

Below Left: Common Council President Richard J. Conners, 1966. (*Courtesy of R. J. Conners*)

Below Right: John T. Garry, while Assistant District Attorney in 1956 (*Gerber Collection*)

indicted for extortion in offering protection to a gambling operation. A third Ryan brother, John, is a federal bankruptcy referee, and while less political than the others, he has been a regular Saturday visitor to O'Connell.

Other leading lights of the organization today include Mrs. Mary Marcy, its vice chairman and hence leader of the women. She has held that position since 1931, and is the same age as Dan O'Connell. The Albany County attorney until the end of 1972 was John J. Clyne. Appointed by the County Legislature, he acted as liaison between O'Connell, to whom he is intensely loyal, and the subservient legislators. Albany has no county executive, but Clyne has been the nearest thing to such an official. He has also served on the regional planning commission. Clyne was nominated for the State Supreme Court in 1971 but was defeated by a Republican in the multi-county district. The following year, however, he won a closely contested race for Albany County Court Judge.

Other attorneys high in party councils are John T. Garry, former district attorney and at present leader of the Democrats in Colonie township, and Andrew Pinckney, son of Elizabeth Pinckney, the longtime commissioner of jurors. He held the position of County public defender until his troubles with the law in 1973.*

The number two man in the city government is Richard J. Conners, who has served a dozen years as president of the Common Council. He had previously been a member of the Council since 1941, and by profession has been a sportswriter and insurance executive. Conners is regarded as an unusually amiable politician in Albany, as opposed to some others who play the game more roughly. Nominated for Congress in 1966, he was defeated, but is now considered in the running as a potential successor to Mayor Corning.

For forty-three years ending in 1965, the city's comptroller was Lawrence J. Ehrhardt. An infantry machine gunner in World War I, Ehrhardt worked with the Albany Trust Company until given a job in the comptroller's office at the advent of the Hackett administration. He had the good fortune of being Dan O'Connell's neighbor, and was soon appointed comptroller. Ehrhardt died in 1970 at the age of 79.

---

* Pinckney was indicted in connection with an alleged stock fraud. Wide-ranging charges of professional misconduct were also lodged against him, and he resigned his license to practice law. After that, Pinckney was allowed to plead guilty to a lesser charge, avoiding a jail sentence; but County Judge Clyne forbade Pinckney to engage in any investment business for three years.

His counterpart at the county level is Treasurer Eugene Devine, held to be a man of wealth as a result of a stock market play some years ago. He is an attorney and once served as president of the County Bar Association. While he is not thought to be very close to Dan O'Connell—and is definitely on the outs with Mayor Corning—Devine has wielded considerable influence on country affairs. After a hairsbreadth re-election in 1971, Mr. Devine has hinted at a retirement from the political scene.

One of the machine's most beloved personages has been Leo W. O'Brien. Born at the turn of the century, he came to Albany from Boston in the early 1920's, with a vague idea of going to law school. He couldn't afford that, however, and so took a job as a copy boy on the *Knickerbocker Press.* To support himself, he also worked nights at a market selling vegetables. By 1926, O'Brien had become a capitol hill reporter for the *Times-Union,* and developed a wide and admiring readership. He never ran for office until 1950, when the organization installed him as successor to Congressman William T. Byrne.

The high point of O'Brien's congressional career came in 1959, with the admission of Alaska and Hawaii into the Union. He is credited with having been a major force in bringing this about. O'Brien retired from Congress in 1966, rejoining the fourth estate as a newspaper columnist. His political role in Albany continues, however.

For many years one of Dan O'Connell's closest legal advisers and friends was "Sir Robert" Whalen. Whalen played a major role during the machine's epic battle with Governor Dewey in the 1940's, handling among other things its case brought against Special Prosecutor Monaghan's methods of impaneling his jury. In this, Whalen lost, but he was a more successful advocate in other types of cases. One specialty was handling tax assessment matters. For example, the New York Central Railroad was annually forced to appeal a million dollar hike in its property tax assessment. The railroad played ball each year by retaining Whalen to represent it, and thereby succeeded in having the assessments reduced. On another occasion, Whalen was hired by the City as a special counsel in a case in which the very practice of such annual assessment increases (detailed in chapter 13) was under attack. Whalen beat off this effort to make an assessment, once given, permanent—allowing the machine to continue milking the corporations annually, much to the benefit of his own law practice.

For nearly two decades, Dan O'Connell's second-in-command and right hand man was Leo C. Quinn. He was executive secretary and treasurer of the Albany Democratic party, and overseer of the county headquarters. He was also the spokesman for the organization and for O'Connell personally, representing the latter in various conferences, and always present at meetings in which O'Connell himself took part. When Leo Quinn spoke for Dan O'Connell, though, there could be no doubt that he bore the leader's exact sentiments. In addition to the above roles, Quinn also acted as the machine's patronage dispenser.

Leo C. Quinn was born in Jessup, Pennsylvania. His family was a religious one; a brother became a monsignor and Quinn himself was known for private charities. He worked his way through school with coal mine jobs, attending Catholic University and its law school, earning his law degree in 1923. Arriving in Albany about 1929, he obtained a clerkship in a law office and also worked as chief elevator starter at the state office building.

Quinn became active in the local Democratic organization and close to Dan O'Connell. At the death of John Murphy in 1945, he took over the key post of executive secretary. Through the Quinn era, it was said that watches could be set by the punctuality of his daily one o'clock conferences with the County Chairman, Uncle Dan.

During his political career, he also held the position of Superintendent of the County Tax Delinquent Bureau. The settlement of delinquent tax accounts and levying upon the properties involved is a fertile area for political favoritism and boodling, discussed in chapter 13.

Leo C. Quinn was a stereotype of the politician in his appearance, always sporting a cigar and a fedora. He would go to the Saratoga track during the racing season in a sharply pressed white summer suit and panama hat worn at a jaunty angle; his private box would become a mecca for politicians, stopping by to pay their respects.

Quinn was not, however, the back-slapping type. Emulating his leader, he was ostensibly a gruff man of few words, often seeming almost curt. He was not given to small talk, and it was said that he knew how to keep a secret.

Leo Quinn died suddenly of a heart attack on January 21, 1964.

His successor as executive secretary and headquarters manager was Donald L. Lynch. Lynch, who married a niece of Dan

O'Connell, was born in 1916 and graduated Albany Law School. While in his twenties he held the post of deputy county treasurer. From 1946 to 1962, when he left office under fire, Lynch was Albany County clerk.

George Washington Plunkitt explained his wealth accumulated during a political career with the epigram, "I seen my opportunities and I took 'em." Lynch was an apt student of Plunkitt while county clerk. In partnership with State Senator Julian B. Erway in a real estate venture known as Erly Development, Inc., Lynch gained control of many large and valuable properties. He was also president of the Colwash Corporation, formed in 1956 and dissolved in 1971, which held considerable parcels of land in the Pine Bush. Donald Lynch is now considered the wealthiest man in the machine, certainly a millionaire.

In his role as Dan O'Connell's close political sidekick, Lynch is sometimes known as "The Arranger." While he may have tried to build an independent following of his own, many in the party resented his ostentatious life style, regarding it as bad for their image. There must also have been some envy of his power. Thus there was no lamenting his departure from the headquarters in 1972. This was reported as occurring after an acrimonious telephone conversation, Lynch being miffed because his choice for city court judge was passed over, even though Lynch thought he had a commitment on the matter. He may also have been disgusted with his confreres' politically imprudent handling of a contract dispute with Albany's firemen. He remains as the party's second vice chairman, and close to Dan O'Connell.

» »

CHAPTER 13
Games and Taxes

NOBODY likes to pay taxes, and the aversion to taxation in Albany is especially strong. The political viewpoint prevailing here is conservative and inward-looking. Incomes and life
styles in the city are generally modest; Albanians are savers rather
than spenders—and they want their government run along the
same lines.

Dan O'Connell and those who have run the city with him
have always been aware of this keen sensitivity in Albany toward
taxes. For years, and integral to their holding power, they played
the whole matter of taxes like a fine violin. Through taxes, allegiance to the machine has been encouraged, and opposition to it
demoralized. Friends have been rewarded and enemies punished.
Through tax manipulation, the facade of a balanced budget was
maintained, while Albany plunged deeply into debt. Through their
handling of tax delinquent properties, machine leaders made fortunes.

When Dan O'Connell ran for tax assessor in 1919, his campaign theme was that Republicans were manipulating the property
assessments for political advantage. He was elected and his party

came to power—but assessment practices didn't change. The only difference was that Democrats were now doing what Republicans had done before, and doing it with greater finesse. It is known as the "assessment racket."

The machine plays it subtly nowadays, but that was not always so. As in the case of other machine abuses, there was a time when it was much more brazen. During the 1930's, the Albany *Evening News* (then a Gannett paper) ran side by side photographs of Democrat and Republican-owned houses. One would be an imposing mansion with sprawling lawns, its assessment tagged at $2,500. The other property would be a humble abode in every respect, assessed at $8,500. Governor Dewey in his campaigns assailed the machine for what he called the "Albany Poll Tax," telling the story of Dan Dugan, a retired plumber. Dan lived in a modest home which had cost $6,000, but when he registered Republican, that assessment zoomed to $10,500. It cost Dan Dugan $192 in extra yearly taxes for the privilege of being a Republican.

Times have changed. Here's the way it works today:

In July of every year, assessments on property in Albany are set. When a property has changed hands during the preceding year, the assessment is raised drastically. The owner of the property receives no notice of the new assessment, and unless he goes down to city hall to look at the assessment rolls, he could remain unaware of the change until he gets his tax bill. By then, it is too late to do anything about it.

There is, however, another way by which an Albanian is informed of his assessment. As soon as it is raised, the Democratic committeeman will pay a call. "I've seen the new assessment on your house, and I'm shocked at how high it is," he will say, and indeed, the new owner had been counting on lower taxes than now seem likely.

The committeeman will then tell the good news: he can get the assessment lowered. All he needs is the homeowner's signature on a protest form; the committeeman fills out the rest of the form, and files it at city hall. Sure enough, the assessment is cut back to what the previous owner carried.°

An alternative plan occasionally practiced is for the committeeman to recommend a lawyer who is good at getting assessments

---

° Even though the filing by the committeeman is technically illegal, since the law requires such protests to be filed in person by the owner of the property. The forms are often sloppily filled out by the committeemen, making them even more defective.

lowered. The lawyer charges a fee for his services, so that the transaction amounts to patronage channelled his way by the organization. These lawyers are always machine boys. One lawyer antagonistic to the machine indicated that lowering a residential assessment is so simple that he never charges for it. (The role of lawyers is much more significant in commercial assessment cases, discussed later herein.)

The assessment system provides the Democratic committeeman with a useful entree through the front door of anyone moving into his bailiwick. He meets the newcomer and shows what the party can do for him: saving hundreds of dollars in taxes. This ingratiates the committeeman, and the party, with the new homeowner, and also plants in his mind the threat that should he ever give evidence of Republican sympathies, his assessment will go back up. All of his neighbors tell him that this is the way things work in Albany; the city is famous for it. Real estate dealers, cooperating with the machine, tell their clients the same thing.

Depending upon the technique of the particular committeeman, the political angle may be more than just implicit. In recent years, one new arrival in town was visited by a committeeman who said, "You haven't registered to vote yet. You better go do it quick, and then I'll come back and talk about your assessment." Another was told that the assessment would be lowered in return for a promise to vote for Keegan for district attorney.

Even if some people realize how little effort the committeeman expends in getting the assessment lowered, what most do not know is that anyone can get it lowered himself. After setting of the assessments, there is a grievance period. It takes no political pull to obtain a protest form, fill it out, and bring it to the Assessor's office at city hall. All protests, whether or not they are supported by a committeeman, are routinely processed, and the assessments are cut back to prior levels. The story is even told of one Republican who angrily chased the committeeman out of his house, went to city hall, and got the assessment lowered by himself.

It remains a tenet of faith in Albany that Republicans get higher assessments than Democrats. But students in recent years, bent on proving such discrimination, examined the assessments on similar properties owned by Democrats and Republicans, and were no longer able to find any significant variations. A comprehensive review of assessments by the anti-machine Albany Taxpayers' Association in 1972 came up with similar results. While the machine's best friends may get some break in their assessments, it no longer uses assessments for the financial harassment of Republicans. In fact, the ultimate assessment level on a house is to an extent a product of happenstance, because while most localities assess at a uniform percentage of the sale price, Albany simply cuts all assessments back to those carried by the previous owners. The assessments on some houses are thereby keyed to their 1930's levels—so that if a Republican is lucky enough to stumble upon a house once owned by a loyal machine Democrat, his assessment might actually come out a little lower than those of his Democratic neighbors.

The O'Connell machine is too shrewd nowadays to get caught discriminating against Republicans in assessments, when such discrimination is unnecessary. It is enough that people believe there is discrimination. Many property owners are afraid to enroll Republican for fear of tax retaliation. This is a devastating dampener and demoralizer of the Albany Republican party. In the words of one observer, "the implied intimidation works—you don't have to hit people over the head, they do it to themselves."

And there is no harm to the machine if an occasional upstart goes to city hall and gets his own assessment changed—as long as few know how easily this can be done. What the machine preys on in working the assessment racket is people's ignorance of their rights, and their natural readiness to believe that in a machine-controlled city, it takes political pull to get an assessment changed. Ironically, that is naive.

Keeping the O'Connell machine in power is not the only effect its assessment practices have had upon the city. This may be one reason for the lack of high-rise apartment developments in Albany. Since apartment dwellers do not pay property taxes, the assessment game could not be played on them. Also, apartment buildings are notoriously difficult for party committeemen who like to keep close contact with, and tabs on, their constituents. Apartment housing has long been tight in Albany, especially during the legislative sessions.

Republicans and others have also charged that the machine's policies are detrimental to business and civic growth, because of the inequity of treatment between residential and business property. In 1960 the Temporary State Commission on Economic Expansion found that Albany in effect penalizes business and industry. The following year, the State Board of Equalization and

Assessment found that "in Albany, there is the biggest spread between high and low percentages of assessment that can be found anywhere in the state. Houses are assessed at 41.86 per cent of true value while the commercial [properties are assessed] at 93.62 per cent."

Since that time, the overall level of assessments in the city has dropped from 60% of true value to 40%. The residential ratio has dropped to 28.3% market value, the commercial ratio to 64.4%. This was probably due to a general increase in property values without a corresponding increase in assessments. At the same time, however, the bottom has dropped out of the real estate market in the downtown area, so that there, the assessments are even higher than the real values. (The State Board found the assessments on commercial property to vary from 16% to 193% of real value. A similar range, it may be noted, was observed for residential assessments.) The upshot is a crushingly high tax rate on downtown businesses, contributing to their lack of viability and the deterioration of the area.*

The high level of commercial assessments reflects the machine's understanding that houses supply voters, while businesses do not. The pragmatic tendency is to put coddling voters ahead of coddling business. The voters keep the machine in power; their loyalty is indispensable. The businesses have never really squawked at this, because even for them, the overall taxation rate was still low until recently. The machine's power can be used to keep businesses in line, once again using the stick and the carrot. For big business there is the lure of dealing with the City and County, and the small fry know they can be put out of business by flyspecking sanitary and building inspections, pressure on local banks, etc. They don't have to be treated to low assessments. The machine would rather soak them to keep tax rates for the mass of voters low. The city has had, at least until the big 1972 jump, one of the lowest real estate tax rates in the state (with city services at an equally abysmal level).

City Assessor Bruce McDonald has given this excuse for the discrimination between residential and commercial assessments: "If a man is making money from a property, deriving a living from it, he should be assessed at a higher rate than a homeowner." This

---

* Another factor here is that downtown land prices may be artificially high, following a $2 million price paid by the federally funded Urban Development Corporation for the site of the Hotel Ten Eyck.

view is not shared by assessors in other cities, and in fact, contravenes Section 306 of the Real Property Tax Law. McDonald admitted being unaware of that law.

Section 306 is the basis for court actions underway in Syracuse at this writing, challenging an assessment discrimination between residential and commercial properties that is much less drastic than Albany's. If the challenge is sustained, the discrimination in Albany may be ended too—sharply increasing residential taxes.

Like residential assessments, commercial assessments in Albany are generally set at high initial levels, only to be cut back later. This is usually accomplished through legal processes. There used to be continuing rounds of court litigation over assessments. They would be published in July, lowered by court order by January, and raised again the following July. Since the court orders were good for only one year, the City was not deterred from pegging assessments at previously disallowed levels. In recent years, this has been illegal; the new trend has been for the City to settle such cases out of court, so that it can raise the assessment again the following year, only to lower it once more.

These out-of-court settlements are possible because businessmen do not seem intent upon permanent judicial determinations of proper assessments. They apparently understand that the annual litigation is a game, and so does the City. And the City does have a rationale for the seemingly pointless routine. Under state law, the City's tax and debt limitations are based upon a five year average of the full values of assessed properties. However, the "full values" are not actual figures, but are derived by dividing the assessed values by the equalization rate (computed by the State Board of Equalization and Assessment by comparing actual values against assessments). In making this determination, the official assessment roll is used, and this does not reflect subsequent lowering of assessments. As an example, if a property really worth $12,000 (for which a $5,000 assessment is proper) is assessed initially at $10,000, application of the 40% equalization rate to the latter figure would put the imaginary "full value" at $20,000. Thus, the city can increase its tax and debt limits by setting initial assessments at inflated levels, that is, above 40% of real value. Subsequent lowering of the assessments does not affect the tax and debt limits.

This allows the City to put out a seemingly balanced budget. Each year's budget shows that a certain amount of money must be raised through real estate taxes. If the assessments in effect at budget time are inflated, the amount of tax revenues coming in will be overestimated. By the same token, the city will appear to need a lower tax rate than it actually does need. Of course, when the assessments upon which the taxes are actually paid get cut back, there results a deficit. The city must borrow money to make up this deficit—hence its need for a high debt limit. This budgetary practice has put Albany deeply into the red. A few years ago, the state legislature had to bail the city out by authorizing a special $14 million bond issue. Today, interest and service on Albany's debt is close to 30% of the entire budget, a level grossly out of line with what prevails in other cities.*

Turning back to commercial assessments, a subsidiary function of setting them high at the outset lies in the fact that the lawyers who handle the court challenges to them are often good machine followers. Robert Whalen, a confidant of Dan O'Connell, used to handle some of the biggest assessment cases. Today, perhaps the most active law firm in these cases is Garry, Cahill & Edmunds, headed by former Albany District Attorney John T. Garry. Another leading firm of the assessment bar is Cooper, Erving & Savage, one of whose partners is County Treasurer Eugene Devine. Other frequent assessment lawyers include Traffic Judge John Holt-Harris, his successor as School Board President, Simon Rosenstock, and former City Court Judge Evariste LaVigne, or their law firms. Assessment work is a very lucrative field, since fees generally range between a third and half of the tax savings.

Finally, unlike residential assessments where political favoritism would be easy to spot, big commercial assessment breaks can be given to friends of the machine with no one able to prove wrongdoing. There is little doubt that the machine takes advantage of this opportunity, and there is probably not a political outfit in the country that doesn't. As an example, in 1938, the assessment on the O'Connell family's own Hedrick brewery was cut by fully half, while that of a rival Albany brewery was adjusted upward.

At the end of 1971, Mayor Erastus Corning announced that there would be a whopping increase of 84% in real estate taxes. The city's overall tax rate leaped from $33.38 per thousand dollars

---

* Another trick which Mayor Corning has used to balance his budget is the underbudgeting of certain items. Street cleaning, budgeted at $489,000 in 1972, cost $848,000; street maintenance, budgeted at $478,000, cost $739,000; and the landfill, with $650,000 allotted, cost $909,000. These are standard items in every year's budget, consistently underbudgeted, so that the divergences cannot be explained away as mere mis-guesses.

of assessed valuation to $59.32. This made Albany's tax rate the third highest among the state's sixty largest cities, and highest among its "big six." The Mayor openly admitted that this increase was necessitated, at long last, by the budgetary tricks practiced through the years, which had resulted in large deficits.[*]

The recent tax increases may be only a foretaste of what is in store for Albany. Despite the machine's general lack of concern over high business assessments, the deterioration of the downtown area is becoming an acute embarrassment in a city never noted for its economic vibrancy. If the downtown trend is to be reversed, the tax burden on businesses there may have to be eased by cutting assessments sharply. This would necessitate a corresponding increase in other taxes, reducing the disparity between residential and commercial assessments. The disparity is furthermore subject to being outlawed by the courts.

The machine has certainly lost forever low taxes as a reason why many voters have supported it in the past. While no tax rebellion has yet shown up in Albany election returns, and loyalty to the O'Connell machine seems as widespread as ever, the depth of that loyalty may have been significantly reduced by the tax rises, leaving the machine more vulnerable to attack than ever before.

Assessments are the most legendary realm of political tax manipulation. They are not the only one.

Another is the handling of tax delinquent real estate. Attention was first drawn to this area by an audit report by State Comptroller Levitt in 1959. The report criticized an extraordinary accumulation of real estate tax delinquency in Albany, which was steadily increasing because available means of collecting the taxes were not employed. This was held inimical to the city's welfare in several respects: it increases the burden on those who do pay their taxes; removes urban land from the private real estate market, contributing to premature suburban development and inefficient deployment of utility and municipal services; and encourages neglect of properties and the consequent urban blight.

Acting on the Comptroller's Report, the New York State Investigation Commission held hearings in 1960. The S.I.C. graphically documented Albany's uniqueness by comparing it with four other

---

[*] The recent split-off of the school system from the city budget allowed Corning to greatly increase taxes for other municipal purposes. His administration also blames its fiscal difficulties on the proliferation of tax-exempt state properties in Albany, especially the gargantuan South Mall complex.

counties of similar population. Albany County's accumulated delinquency of nearly eight million dollars was 33 times greater than the average for the other counties; Albany was losing 14 times as much through compromising tax liens; and Albany's backlog of delinquencies was increasing ten times as fast. So large was the delinquency accumulation that if all of it were collected, the County could go without taxes for a year.

Not only did the County have a delinquency problem of its own, but it was taking on the City's problem as well. At the end of each year, the City of Albany turns all its delinquencies over to the County for collection. The County pays the City the full amount of the taxes due, and then theoretically tries to collect the money from those who owe it. Thus, to whatever extent the County fails to collect these bills, the County's taxpayers are bailing out the City's. And the 1960 investigation demonstrated shocking misfeasance on the part of the County in collecting the bills. Leo Quinn, Dan O'Connell's sidekick and Superintendent of the Board of Tax Delinquencies, admitted to laxities even in sending out tax bills, many of which would go to vacant lots instead of to the lots' owners. Quinn testified that he'd never used a telephone book to try to find any taxpayer. County Clerk Donald Lynch admitted that his office had no system for notifying Quinn's of changes in property ownership. County Treasurer Eugene Devine stated that except for forty foreclosures, no action whatsoever had been taken over the preceding four years to collect delinquent taxes. And those forty foreclosures had been commenced the very week of the hearings.

Besides its inaction on collecting back real estate taxes, the County has lost millions by compromising them. Tax compromises in Albany became a matter of course during the Depression, when many property owners could not keep up with their taxes—and foreclosures would have been pointless because most of the property was unsaleable at any price. However, the S.I.C. charged that Albany County had in effect frequently made gifts to delinquent taxpayers by compromising the amounts due, even when the Depression was long over, when the persons involved could afford to pay in full, and when the property, if foreclosed, would be readily saleable.

The procedure has been for the taxpayer to go to the Board of Tax Delinquencies and get a statement of what he owes. Then he proceeds to Mayor Corning, who decides on the figure to be offered as a compromise. The taxpayer accordingly makes the offer to the Board. Corning has said that he was unaware of a single instance in which his recommendation was not accepted by the County Board, even though he is not a county officer.

The Mayor has defended this practice by arguing that "the benefits derived from tax compromises since World War II enabled at least 90 per cent of the new homes to be built." In other words, land lying unused could be sold for development if the developers would be relieved of the tax burden being carried by the land. Especially if the developers are Democrats with good machine connections.

Obviously, the compromise of tax delinquencies is a fertile ground for political favoritism. It is not necessary to discover whether Democrats get better breaks than Republicans; in a machine-run town like Albany, anyone who receives such a break is bound to understand its political ramifications. He is expected to feel indebted to the machine, and knows it. Indeed, he is likely to feel a gratitude that is genuine. After all, the machine has put money in his pocket.

While everyone, Democrat or Republican, who asks for a compromise gets one, the favoritism comes in whether one is aware that he can get such a compromise at all. The availability of this procedure is not widely known—to those not loyal to the machine. In 1960, the S.I.C. was advised by its assistant counsel that "provided one knows *or is told* what Albany County's policy is on tax collections, one can be virtually exempt from taxes for an indefinite period."

Governor Rockefeller commented on the S.I.C. report that "it discloses shocking inequities in the treatment accorded local real property tax payers in the city and county of Albany." This was a reference to the county's taxpayers (about half Republican) picking up the delinquencies of the city (mostly Democrat), and to the fact that the honest citizens must make up whatever isn't paid by those who take advantage of the machine's lax procedures.

Only recently have more stringent tax collection procedures been inaugurated by the County Treasurer's office. It has now adopted an *in rem* foreclosure proceedings policy, in which all property more than four years delinquent is foreclosed. Moving against delinquent properties may be an effort to hold down the current wave of tax increases. In any event, a disproportionate amount of delinquencies still remains on the books.

Another facet of this situation is what happens when the taxes cannot, for some reason, be compromised, and the property must be seized and sold at auction. In the past, the County itself often bid in these auctions. When it takes title to the property, the County becomes its own creditor, discharging all tax liens automatically. The property itself can then be sold once more. The S.I.C.'s objection to this was that the county was selling the properties too cheaply, and that sales were apparently being made to favored individuals.

One such individual was Donald Lynch, then county clerk. The S.I.C. found that Lynch, in partnership with Albany State Senator Julian B. Erway, was garnering large profits on real estate deals involving delinquent properties. For example, in 1956, a large tract of land along Washington Avenue was carrying a tax lien of $8,200. Lynch bought the property at a total investment of $15,000, of which the county accepted only $3,850 in full settlement of the taxes. Immediately after buying the land, Lynch leased a portion of it to the Hellmann Theater interests at an annual rental of $25,000. The land now also holds the Thruway Hyatt House motel, a branch of the State Bank of Albany, and the main State University campus, all paying rent to Lynch.

When choice parcels of land were to be auctioned by the County, the auctions were scheduled at odd hours and locations, with minimal publicity. Another advantage held by machine intimates in dealing in such properties is that they could feel free to pay no taxes at all on them, waiting for the land to become productive. The County was not going to go after Donald Lynch for back taxes.

Lynch's activities in this realm attracted so much adverse publicity that he did not run for re-election as county clerk in 1962. However, almost a decade passed before County-conducted land auctions were taken out of the back room and into the light of day. Truly public auctions were a newsworthy "first" for Albany in 1972.

CHAPTER 14

Justice, Albany Style

IN THE American system, courts play a key role as the final arbiters of many types of disputes and grievances. In public affairs, the courts play a policy-making role rivalling that of the executive and legislative branches of government, and may make more far-reaching political decisions than the electorate. And of course, for particular individuals, judicial actions can alter their lives.

It is therefore important that the judiciary be independent of the other political branches. The courts provide citizens with protection against hostile and improper actions by the government—protection which is lost if the judiciary is not independent. When a political organization can control the judiciary, as well as the other arms of government, its sphere of action is greatly expanded, and the ability of opposing forces to combat it is greatly reduced.

In Albany, an important factor in the success of the O'Connell machine has been its domination of the judiciary and of all the machinery of justice. Through this control, the machine has been able to protect its friends, intimidate its rivals and stymie efforts calling it to account.

The machine has always controlled the police (covered in

Chapter 19). Until 1968, it had always elected the Albany County district attorney. It has controlled the appointment of the county attorney. It has elected all judges in the city—police court, city court and traffic court—and the county—family court, county court and surrogate. The machine has also managed to put a steady parade of its men onto the State Supreme Court bench, in addition to aiding the nomination and election of many others. O'Connell has even placed protégé Francis Bergan on the State Court of Appeals.

This does not mean that the district attorneys and judges in question have been incompetents, or even corrupt. But no one who runs on the Democratic ticket in Albany County does so as his own man. He knows that he is the machine's candidate, to be elected not on his own merits, but by machine resources. Furthermore, the machine will not place unknown quantities into sensitive posts. No one is nominated whose loyalty to O'Connell and the Democratic party is in doubt.

So it is not surprising if, in any case where the machine has an interest, the district attorney or judge bends over backward to protect it. They don't have to be ordered to do so by Dan O'Connell —they understand their duty without having it explained.

This pro-machine bias does not, of course, infect the entire administration of justice in Albany. The machine is interested in only a tiny fraction of the cases. But the impact of the bias in that fraction is tremendous.

In addition to the police, the prosecutors and the judges, the O'Connell organization has specialized in controlling both the grand and trial juries. For years, the machine had the lists of names from which jurors were picked screened for political reliability by Commissioner of Jurors Elizabeth Pinckney. This was made easy by keeping the lists small. The percentage of Albany's population on its jury list has been the smallest in the state.

A report to the Republican opposition by some of its lawyers in the mid-1960's probed the bias in jury selections. They found that despite Albany containing less than half the county's inhabitants, 77% of those on the jury list were from that city, and the percentage remained constant year after year. As for the political complexion of the lists, consistently more than 70% had been registered Democrats, with an unusually high proportion of party workers, committeemen and patronage employees. Furthermore, the balance of the jurors were mostly independents, leaving Republicans severely under-represented, averaging each year around 3%.

This would ensure that many 24-member grand juries would be completely free of Republicans.

The survey found not a single black grand juror in the three year period studied. Over half the grand jury panelists served more than once, indicating the lack of randomness of the selections. The study found bank and insurance company employees very prominent in selections, along with employees of certain firms, and that three wards in Albany had an extremely inflated representation on the jury lists. These wards were the machine's most stalwart bastions. Certain wards—those with concentrations of blacks—were systematically excluded.

Besides party hacks, the Albany grand jury panels have included some curious personalities. While the law requires grand jurors to be "of approved integrity, fair character, sound judgment and well informed," a member of the 1943 panel was a known slot machine operator; three were convicted black marketeers, and another was under indictment for receiving stolen goods. On the following year's panel, one member had had his beer license revoked for illegal activities, and another admitted he could not read or write.

In 1964, as a result of local reformers' agitation, the state courts ordered a change in the grand jury selection process, aimed at broadening the spectrum of jury members. The lists from which panels were drawn were required to be lengthened, and the actual selections to be made by lot. Yet the Democratic machine still had the allegiance of the majority of the county's voters, so even a fairly selected panel would still be sympathetic if not controlled by it. The machine thus substantially retained its grip on the grand jury despite the reform.

Control of the accusatory machinery—police, D.A., grand jury —has obvious advantages to any political machine. During the 1930's, the O'Connell organization was known to manufacture charges against obstreperous opponents, both in political and gambling spheres. They were told the charges would be dropped if they left town.

While the district attorney can be aggressive when wrongdoing by machine opponents is involved, he can take a more limited view of his powers when his political allies are being accused. Charges against them can be bottled up and prevented from ever reaching trial. John Garry, when he was D.A., sometimes used the excuse that he lacked jurisdiction to make any investigation unless a specific crime was reported to him.

But such notions are cast aside when the machine decides something needs investigating. Grand jury probes have been used to harass and discredit those who make the local powers look bad. On one occasion, a panel looking into an allegation of police brutality wound up indicting the newspaper reporter who covered it (detailed in Chapter 20).

A prime example of grand jury harassment was the 1963 Russell Broughton case. Broughton, a telephone company executive and pillar of the church, was walking to work one morning and noticed a policeman beating a young black. The cop asked Broughton what he was doing. "I'm just watching you manhandle that boy," said Broughton.

"You're just as bad as he is!" returned the officer, John Cody, and he arrested Broughton on the spot. Broughton was put through the police routine of fingerprinting, surrender of possessions, mug shots, handcuffing, and was marched into court under guard, charged with interfering with an officer. He was not permitted to call the police chief, a personal friend.

Broughton did call another friend who was a lawyer, John S. Bartlett, Jr., an unfortunate choice, since Bartlett was a machine wheelhorse, later to become county clerk. An alert lawyer might have brought suit for false arrest, but Bartlett advised Broughton to sign a release promising not to sue the City. Only after Broughton signed were the charges dropped.

When the incident became known, a public outcry condemned the policeman's high-handedness. Paradoxically, Mayor Corning's reaction was that "there is an organized and concerted effort to interfere with and destroy the effectiveness of the Police Department."

The grand jury was convened to investigate. Russell Broughton was interrogated at length on diverse subjects; a number of individuals including associates of Broughton were also subpoenaed, even though they had no role in the incident supposedly under investigation. Broughton was treated more like an accused than an accuser. At the same time, the machine conducted a whispering campaign to discredit him, which even included unfounded rumors of sexual deviation.

Nothing came of the investigation; except, perhaps, that Russell Broughton died a few years later of a heart condition undoubtedly aggravated by it. The policemen involved began a libel suit against the Albany newspapers, but it was never pressed. John Cody remains on the police force.

Another instructive case was that of Norman Early, an Albany black whose crime was to inquire why some people were being arrested. In Police Court, Judge Michael Tepedino convicted him of interfering with an officer, even though Early had done nothing physical, having used only words. The conviction vitiated the possibility of suing for false arrest. Perhaps that was all the machine cared about at that point, because no other penalty was imposed. The conviction was upheld by County Judge Martin Schenck. At the Court of Appeals, the case was assigned to Justice Bergan, who refused to allow the appeal to be heard. In an almost identical case, *People* v. *Adickes* (June 7, 1972), but arising out of an incident in New York City, Bergan held for the Court that free speech was involved and there was no interference with an officer.

So machine-elected judges do bend the law in political cases. This is especially true in Police Court, where the application of the law is a rough-and-tumble business; yet Police Court affects many people, and cases of political import often begin there. Of prime concern to the machine is that its police force be supported, with police repressions kept out of the glare of publicity. The Police Court judgeship is not an attractive position; the pay is low and the caseload is unappealing, involving the most sordid facets of modern life. These judges, installed by the machine, tend to be law-and-order oriented, with a strong bias in favor of the police. Once arrested by an Albany cop, it is no easy thing for a defendant to disprove guilt in Police Court.

The willingness of higher court judges to do right by Dan O'Connell was graphically illustrated during the Dewey investigation. Indeed, this was one of the main reasons for the investigation's failure.

Supreme Court Justice Gilbert V. Schenck, an old O'Connell crony, admitted that he had talked with the boss about a case. In fact, two telephone conversations between Schenck and O'Connell, over the latter's private unlisted wire, had been intercepted and tape-recorded. Schenck told O'Connell of the confidential deliberations of the Appellate Division on which he sat, and complained of his difficulty in getting one of his fellow judges to favor the machine: "I would have had three votes tonight, except your little boy out in Schoharie—even when I got him in his own room, and tried to pin him down, he wouldn't go with me." Schenck explained that

Right: County Judge Martin Schenck (*Courtesy of Capital Newspapers*)

Below Left: Justice Francis Bergan, New York Court of Appeals (*Gerber Collection*)

Below Right: Supreme Court Justice Russell G. Hunt (*Gerber Collection*)

the other judge wanted "that highbrow stuff"—a legal basis for the ruling. Subsequently, the court found for the prosecution (Schenck dissenting) and the Court of Appeals affirmed. Schenck told O'Connell he'd done the best he could.

Throughout the battle with Dewey, O'Connell enjoyed favorable rulings from the judges whom he had placed in office. In only two or three of their many decisions was the State supported.

As for Justice Schenck, the American Bar Association recommended his removal from the bench. His partisanship toward a political organization was held improper conduct for a judge. Schenck was not removed, however, only censured by a vote of the State Assembly, after Dan O'Connell testified on the matter before its judiciary committee.

Local Albany judges have also violated the canons of judicial ethics by holding political party positions while on the bench. Tepedino continued as a committeeman after becoming police judge, even after attracting public criticism for it. Finally, Tepedino resigned as committeeman and his wife took over the office—but he continued to do the legwork.

Gilbert Schenck's son, Martin, followed in his father's footsteps, becoming Albany County Judge. When reporter Edward Swietnicki was indicted for perjury (see Chapter 20), accused of lying to the grand jury, Schenck refused his lawyer's motion to inspect the very grand jury minutes in question, and upheld the flimsy indictment. (Also denied, by Justice Bergan, was the defense motion for a change of venue.)

County Judge Martin Schenck again proved his worth to the machine that elected him when a Republican district attorney tried to prosecute some of its members for bilking the city on snow removal contracts. In the trials of both Joseph Lynn and Alderman Marvin Tanksley, Schenck dismissed the indictments at the close of the prosecution's case. He attracted some bad publicity for his handling of these cases, and ultimately removed himself from them. It has been speculated that Schenck could no longer in conscience follow the demands of loyalty to O'Connell, and that this lies behind his decision to retire in 1972.

After Schenck removed himself from the snow fraud cases, they went to Judge John McCall, who had no qualms about doing his duty. He had earlier acted as attorney for the contractors indicted as a result of the 1961 S.I.C. probe into city purchasing practices, a very similar political case. In the snow cases, Judge McCall threw out some indictments on the ground that the grand jury had been improperly extended beyond its regular term, and dismissed the indictments of Frederick and Margaret Avant and Arnold, Richard and Ronald Leto on the ground that their waivers of immunity had been unconstitutional. These indictments were reinstated by the Appellate Division of the Supreme Court.

During the aforementioned S.I.C. investigation, the records of the Beatty Supply Company were seized by S.I.C. agents. Beatty had done business with the City for many years. An order was obtained from Supreme Court Justice Russell G. Hunt—another machine judge—forcing the return of the records. The S.I.C. was dragged into a lengthy court wrangle over the matter, and Hunt denied its motion to remove the case to another court. In July, 1962, Hunt quashed subpoenas that would have given the S.I.C. access to county jail records, on the ground that the O'Connellcrat Board of Supervisors had already designated someone to look into the same matter. Hunt's order was soon set aside by the Appellate Division. Litigation over the jail records meanwhile continued, and in November, the Appellate Division once more reinstated the S.I.C. subpoenas, sharply rebuking Judge Hunt's reason for decision on the matter. But Democratic attorneys continued to bombard the courts with appeals and petitions for stays, so that by early 1963, the S.I.C. still hadn't seen the records, and the county had utilized the time gained to clean things up, drawing the teeth of the investigators.

In the same manner, S.I.C. subpoenas of government officials to testify were repeatedly voided by Hunt and other machine judges. Of course, the subpoenas were reinstated by the Court of Appeals after lengthy delays—but by that time, the matter was moot. Some of the indictments in this decade-old case remain outstanding, with judges accepting the claims of the accused that their health is too poor for them to stand trial.

The story was repeated in a similar 1972 S.I.C. investigation. Hampering the commission this time was its inability to bring certain individuals, including City Purchasing Agent Mary Dollard, to the witness stand. Her claim of ill health found succor in the courts, even though she was healthy enough to remain at her desk. The machine also used the courts to resist the S.I.C. probe of the Albany Police Department, challenging the constitutionality of the S.I.C. itself. Supreme Court Justice A. Franklin Mahoney of Troy, an O'Connellcrat judge, issued an injunction forbidding the S.I.C. from doing anything until the constitutionality question was dragged through the courts. Mahoney's ruling was not only reversed by the Appellate Division, but was labelled an abuse of discretion. A similar rebuke was administered by the Appellate Division to Judge Hunt, for his reissuing an injunction that had already been vacated.°

Besides hampering anti-corruption efforts in Albany, judges have had occasion to make life difficult for machine opponents in other matters. An example is the experience of the Joint Action Force Community Organization (JAFCO), unfriendly to city hall, which sought incorporation for broad community purposes. Judge Hunt refused to allow the incorporation, claiming that approvals from the State Departments of Social Welfare and Education were required. Those agencies reported that no such consent was needed, but Judge Hunt persisted, and promulgated an order denying JAFCO's application, which prevented their going to another judge. Meanwhile, to satisfy Hunt, the state agencies both provided JAFCO with consent certificates. Yet Hunt still refused to grant the application, now on the ground that the wrong consent forms had been used. In the end, he was overruled by the Appellate Division, but JAFCO had been delayed for more than a year.

Finally on this subject, the role of the Albany bar must be borne in mind. Since the machine controls the courts, it is inevitable that it influences the lawyers who practice in them as well. Lawyers who are inclined to oppose the machine know what they can expect from local judges. (This has hurt the Republican party; see Chapter 18.)

However, the carrot is used much more than the stick. The lawyer friendly to the machine can benefit by having cases referred to him. Also, the courts appoint lawyers as guardians and referees in matters to be handled outside of trial, which can result in very large fees. It may be noted that lawyers appointed as guardians or trustees may sacrifice the interests of their clients rather than bring any lawsuits that might embarrass the city or the machine.

Control of the courts and the ability to benefit lawyers financially provides the machine with a cadre of loyal, talented and useful workers. Many lawyers serve as party committeemen, since they are in a better position than most to profit from political influence. They also serve, when called upon, as troubleshooters for the machine and city hall, in court battles and elsewhere. Because of its control of the courts, the machine never has to scrounge for legal talent to defend it.

° While city hall's lawyers kept the S.I.C. stalled in court, Mayor Corning accused the Commission of "dragging its feet" in the police probe!

CHAPTER 15

"The Miracle on North Pearl Street"

      "Every year in November a strange and miraculous thing happens on North Pearl Street and on dozens of other streets in the City of Albany. Men and women begin to receive unmarked envelopes containing five dollar bills. . . . There are two things all these people have in common. They are registered Democrats and they vote every year. The miraculous thing about all this is that the people who pass out these presents do not really exist. The five dollar bills are real, the people who receive them are real, but the donors are some kind of wraiths who appear and disappear each November . . . many people have seen these wraiths and received money from them; some of them even have names. Yet the Grand Jury is never able to discover their whereabouts or existence. It truly sounds miraculous." (From a 1967 sermon by the Reverend Nicholas Cardell)

      Vote buying in Albany? According to Dan O'Connell, the charges are "a lot of junk." Dan has said that he "worked in the poorest district in Albany for thirty years, and never knew a vote to be sold. During the year, if they were short of money, we'd give them a little help-out. That's what counts . . ."

Allegations of Democratic party vote frauds in Albany first received wide currency in 1938, following Governor Herbert Lehman's very close race for re-election. Lehman won by 67,000, with Albany providing its usual 20,000 votes of that plurality. Eight days after the election, the Governor launched an investigation of Albany's contribution to his own victory margin.

Wary of any involvement by Albany locals in this probe, Lehman kept it clear of their hands. Attorney General John Bennett brought up three members of his New York City rackets squad to run it, while the State Police, rather than the Albany department, conducted the field investigations. Tough Brooklyn Supreme Court Justice John McCrate was imported to sit at the trials. While sternly lecturing defendant after defendant, the judge suspended many sentences because he felt that five or ten year prison terms were too harsh for these election offenses. Yet McCrate was plainly outraged by what was revealed in his court room. He thundered at one black repeater, "Even the civil war didn't give you the right to vote twice."

174 convictions were obtained, mostly for registering more than once, sometimes as many as four times. One wag called this practice "seeing your duty and overdoing it." Many defendants were rooming house proprietors charged with failing to file certified lists of occupants before each election. Of course, in the absence of such a list for a building, anyone could freely vote from it. Of these small fry who served sentences, not one turned state's evidence against the machine—which supported their families or paid them off for the inconvenience while they were in jail.

This probe also delved into the subject of vote buying. The final report found "very definite indications that there exists a widespread practice of paying sums of money varying in amount up to $5 to voters on Election Day . . ." The report also indicated that the bribe was an incentive to illegal repeat voting. An election would certainly be profitable for anyone voting three or four times at $5 a throw.

On election day, a police sergeant had arrested a city water inspector, William F. Reilly, caught passing unmarked envelopes to people leaving the voting booths. A search of the man yielded 45 such envelopes containing $4 each.* He was released when he explained that he and others were contributing to a charity fund to

---

* An alternative to the envelope method was to fold a five dollar bill between two small squares of cardboard held together with rubber bands. This package could be slipped unnoticed into the voter's hand or pocket.

purchase shoes and food for the needy and that the polling place was the most convenient spot to do this systematically! Among other things, the incident pointed up a source of lucre for the machine's foot soldiers—the price for a vote was supposed to be $5, and any committeeman paying less was pocketing the difference.

During the 1940's, Governor Dewey launched the most extensive investigation ever into Albany affairs, including election abuses. This was regarded as a failure, as discussed in a previous chapter. The Dewey probe seems, however, to have brought about a temporary discontinuance of some of the machine's more brazen tactics, including vote buying. For a while, the politicians were careful. The ensuing election showed no decline in the Democratic vote on account of the lack of bribes. Dan O'Connell quipped, "Well, they never proved we were crooked, but they certainly proved what damn fools we've been."

Nevertheless, the purchase of votes was shortly resumed.

By 1965, the scandal of Albany elections was festering once more. The State Attorney General's office conducted an inquiry into that year's voting, and informed the Albany Board of Elections that "the evidence accumulated during the investigation reveals that there is a basic lack of understanding of, or in the alternative a widespread disregard of the Election Law on the part of many inspectors of election in Albany County." Particularly ridden with abuse was a paper ballot redistricting referendum held that year. Booths were not even provided, so that the ballots could not be marked in privacy—and in one instance, the inspector himself was seen marking and depositing ballots.

Election irregularities and vote buying were also the subject of a joint state legislative committee hearing in December, 1965. The following spring, the Albany County grand jury finally yielded to demands for an investigation, only to abort it suddenly after hearing just two witnesses. Several further witnesses were sent away unheard, with the jurors saying they'd heard enough. Some thought them afraid to hear more.

The issue was still hot as the 1966 elections approached. The reformist Albany Independent Movement asked the State to assign deputy attorneys general to the known contact places for payment for votes. At a highly publicized meeting of the Catholic Inter-Racial Council, attorney Walter Langley presented a resolution to condemn the $5 vote, deeming it a racial problem in that it chiefly affected the poor and the black. One member argued in opposition that while the sale of a vote was evil, consideration had to be given to taking $5 out of a poor man's pocket. The resolution was voted down.

The *Times-Union* editorialized that "if Albany's Democratic organization has been getting them for $5 each, they've found a way to really hoodwink the poor souls who've been selling . . . five dollars would be a cheap price indeed for something that ordinary people consider so valuable they wouldn't sell at any price."

On Election Day twenty picketers appeared in the South End carrying signs reading "Don't Sell Your Soul For $5." Most of them were from The Brothers, an activist black community organization, and all were arrested on charges of intimidating voters. Mayor Corning found it "interesting to note" that no precedent existed for such arrests. The charges were dismissed.

Near year-end, District Attorney John Garry revealed the issuance of a number of subpoenas, looking toward a grand jury probe of local election irregularities. But Garry also promised to prosecute sellers as well as buyers of votes, which would hardly be conducive to getting the testimony necessary to convict either party to a vote buying transaction. Whether immunity from prosecution would be granted to any witnesses thus became the key issue. Conviction in cases of this type is generally obtained by offering immunity to the party whose offense is considered the lesser. Here, plainly, the buyer of the vote is the principal offender, whose conviction would serve the public interest.

A large group of Albany clergymen urged that witnesses not be required to waive their immunity before testifying, and also that the grand jury be serious in its investigation. The ministers were convinced vote buying existed, and exhorted the grand jury to at least apprise citizens of that much. Community pressure on the issue mounted. James Gallagher, Chairman of the Albany Independent Movement, wrote to Governor Rockefeller urging a state takeover of the probe, a plea later reiterated by the aforementioned clerics. Rockefeller responded that he was closely watching the proceedings and would "take whatever action may become necessary."

By now, the investigation was under way. The first solid information came from Harry Vodery, regional NAACP director, who publicly stated that a "political figure" had offered him $5, which he had spurned, and that he had seen three others accept the bribes. Then Mrs. Mildred Collins stepped forward to declare that she had seen vote buying take place. The grand jury advanced the date of its next session to hear these witnesses. They were given immunity—a meaningless gesture since they had committed no crimes.

On Valentine's Day, 1967, Leon Van Dyke, a Brothers leader, offered to tell the grand jury the name of the Democratic committeeman who had given him $5 after voting in 1964. The committeeman, Van Dyke related, came to his home saying, "Oh, you probably voted Communist." Van Dyke explained that he took the money because he was broke and needed it.

The County Board of Elections did not delay in taking action on this story. The Board requested the grand jury to determine whether Van Dyke himself had violated the election law, since he had served a sentence for a felony in another state and had voted without having a governor's pardon. The Board made no mention of the vote-buying allegation, prosecution of which would have implicated a good Democrat along with Van Dyke. This was quite in keeping with the Albany tradition of more assiduously investigating accusers than accused.

On the first of March, Van Dyke appeared along with several fellow Brothers, but the grand jury refused to hear them after they declined to sign waivers of immunity. One of them, Peter Jones, complained that he had been barred from the stand despite his announced readiness to sign a waiver. He had earlier offered to name names and to go to jail if necessary. The grand jury's refusal to grant immunity sparked renewed charges that it was conducting a whitewash, and renewed pleas for further investigation under State auspices.

Finally on March 15, Peter Jones testified at length along with seventeen others. All signed waivers of immunity. Fifteen of them denied any vote buying in Albany. Although Jones' testimony was received behind closed doors and never made public, he told the author its substance: he disclaimed ever having personally received a $5 bribe, but described several such transactions which he had witnessed in his apartment building. Jones named Artie Green, a liquor store owner and Democratic ward leader, as the dispenser of the bribes. Green was alleged to have specifically said that the money was in return for votes. Present in the court room during Jones' testimony, Green was not called to the stand.*

---

* Jones also related that he was asked a large number of seemingly irrelevant questions about his personal history, the answers to which could have formed the basis of a perjury indictment had he made any slips. He spoke too of having been beaten up severely afterwards, suffering three cracked ribs and a dislocated shoulder. Jones viewed that aftermath with equanimity, taking satisfaction in its indicating the impact of what he had done.

The 1967 vote buying investigation then ended with a bang. On April 14, the grand jury called two surprise witnesses: Joseph Frangella, the Republican county chairman, and his Democratic counterpart, eighty-one year old Daniel P. O'Connell. Their testimony was not made public.

The denouement came the same day with the grand jury reporting that despite widespread allegations of vote buying, there was no proof to sustain an indictment. Nothing was mentioned of Peter Jones and Artie Green, and the grand jury did not even say that vote buying really existed. The panel was thereupon discharged by County Judge Martin Schenck.

Naturally this outcome was greeted with outraged cries of "Whitewash!" even without public knowledge of Peter Jones' testimony. State and federal investigations were demanded. But Governor Rockefeller responded that no action would be taken, because there was no evidence that the grand jury had failed or been unwilling to perform its duties.[*]

The vote buying issue persisted, with blacks concerned about its impact on their community. A colorful confession appeared (under a pseudonym) in the *Albany Liberator,* a black-directed publication, following the 1967 election. It is a document instructive on the workings of the practice.

"U. T. Hippie," the author, had voiced support for a candidate whom The Brothers were running against in the incumbent 7th Ward alderman. But on Election Day, the machine's committeeman paid a visit, offering to escort "Hippie" to the polls. "Wanted to kick the cracker clean out of my house, but 'spite myself I'm 'fraid won't have no more house, if'n I don't go along," he wrote. So he went with the committeeman, although still intending to vote independently. The committeeman, meanwhile, was making his "knowed we could count on you, you're a real loyal boy" speech.

The Alderman himself was at the polls, looking very much as though he knew this voter's intention. "That mean cat fixed me with his evil eye, an' I saw myself kissin' my job, my house, everything goodbye! Even maybe landin' in jail soon . . .

". . . So I'm standin' there, surrounded by whitey, cops an'

---

[*] The clergymen who had made the request charged that the Governor's stance was dictated by his dependency upon the good will of the local machine for the continued development of his South Mall project in Albany. Another possible reason for the Governor's refusal to forward the investigation, despite his generally helpful attitude toward G.O.P. leader Frangella, was the charge that Frangella himself bought votes in his home town. This allegation had been made by a Ravena minister.

Toms. Every one of 'em smilin', starin', and waitin', knowing just exactly how long it takes to pull them levers straight down 'Row B.' Well, all right—I did what I always done, what I got to do to survive 'round here, what the Man done ordered us all to do."

And after assuring the committeeman that he had voted straight Row B, "Hippie" was rewarded with "bread," evidently not the eating kind.

So, we return to the question, vote buying in Albany? The grand jury notwithstanding, the practice exists, if not rampantly. During the 1971 school board election campaign, it was reported by several ministers. Others had seen copies of a flyer promoting the Democratic slate distributed with five dollar bills folded inside.

"Sure, votes have had to be bought," a high-ranking Albany politician once told a church group. "The going rate is five dollars. But the bum whose vote we buy for five bucks is no different from the person whose assessment we lower $200 and who then votes our way." And he added: "we have had to put the peek on people occasionally." *

He was referring to violation of the secret ballot. For many years, the Albany machine resisted the introduction of voting booths; even today, in some measure the faithfulness of voters to the machine stems from their belief that their ballot is not secret, and that there can be reprisal for a vote against the machine. As in the case of "U. T. Hippie" quoted above, there is widespread fear that the machine can get a man fired through pressure on his employer; and certainly many local employers would be sensitive to such pressure. This is only one area in which retaliation is feared. Those who are paid for their votes understandably feel this pressure to vote "right" most keenly. Thus is the machine reasonably assured that what it buys will be delivered.

The organization calculatingly fosters these beliefs in Albany. One trick used, when The Brothers ran their insurgent candidate, was to accost all suspect voters as they left the booth and confront them with having voted for The Brothers' man. Some, of course, denied it. Others exclaimed, "How did you know?" These people not only revealed their votes, but they also went home and told family and friends that it is true that the machine knows how one votes.

How much is myth and how much reality? Some voters be-

---

* *Knickerbocker News*, September 28, 1967.

lieve that because they are given numbers by the inspectors, their votes can be revealed. This is not true—the numbers are used merely to keep track of the voters during the commotion usually permeating a polling place. The voting machine itself gives only totals, and does not record individual votes.

Likewise, paper ballots are truly secret. They have numbered stubs, but the stubs must be removed before the ballots are dropped in the boxes. Yet some Albany voters, long used to machine-style elections, have no conception of a secret ballot, and paper ballots regularly turn up on which voters have signed their names.* The machine, aware of voters' feeling less secure about the secrecy of paper ballots, uses them wherever possible. (Paper ballots are also more susceptible to tampering than is a voting machine.)

On the other hand, stories have been frequent in Albany of sandpapered and punctured curtains, booths set up so that they could be looked into, and even of the politician found belly-down on the floor above, looking through a knot-hole into a voting booth. Another method is to put an extremely bright light bulb in the booth—which casts a sharp, tell-tale shadow of the voter as he operates the levers. Albany has been required by law in recent years to reduce the wattage of the bulbs from 75 to 60. A man active in Albany politics points out that to vote a straight Republican ticket (the first row on the left) one is inclined to face at an angle into the corner of the booth, and this can be observed from the outside by an experienced shadow-reader. And finally, any voter who takes more than a few seconds to vote has probably split his ticket.

Overt peeking into voting booths is probably much less prevalent today than it was in the more rough-and-tumble past. The machine has found that it is not really necessary to know how each person voted—it does well enough if it is *believed* able to know. That way, voters intimidate themselves. Besides, any neighborhood committeeman who has worked an area for a number of years should instinctively know which way his people are going. The committeeman can learn a man's vote just by looking him in the

---

* The law requires such ballots to be voided, along with any others that have any marks on them other than votes for candidates. This seems harsh, but is vital to guarantee that voters are not intimidated into revealing their votes by coding their ballots. Of course, this gives the machine a chance to void many opponents' ballots by adding marks to them that voters didn't put there.

eye as he leaves the booth. Even an opposition candidate said she could tell everyone's vote by this method.

So much for peeking *qua* peeking. There is also peeking *qua* "voter assistance." Election inspectors are legally permitted to enter the booth and assist a voter who for some reason is unable to operate the machine unaided. Theoretically at least, inspectors of both parties must be present, and the voter must request the help. Yet Albany seems to have a vastly disproportionate handicapped population. In the 1971 elections, complaints were rife that Democratic election workers were insinuating themselves into the booths with voters. A person knows that refusing an offer of such "assistance" would be tantamount to confessing an intention to vote against the machine.

This practice seems even more insidious than peeking, going beyond a violation of the secrecy of the ballot. At least a voter who is peeked upon still has the personal liberty to vote as he chooses. But when a brawny Democratic worker gets into the booth with you and starts pulling the levers for you, your right to vote has been extinguished altogether. Under such intimidation, it would take a rare moxie to attempt to vote Republican. While election beatings have not been common in Albany, a machine of this type cannot help but have some in its ranks with a propensity toward ruffianism. Physical violence is always an implied threat—in the voters' minds, if not the politicians'—in such situations.

These types of abuses and violations of the election laws, and others such as handing out campaign literature in the polling places, go on despite the presence of Republican inspectors and poll watchers in many wards. The Republicans are undermanned and spread too thin to provide an effective psychological check on the practices of the Democrats. Although the election law gives Republicans an equal chance to elect board chairmen in all districts, the Democrats manage to get and keep this position in almost all of them, and then mis-use it to harass opposition workers. The machine's board chairmen do not readily allow opposing poll watchers to exercise their legal rights, and frequently throw such watchers out of the polling places.* Some chairmen refuse to follow the law, even when it is shown to them in black and white. In a 1973 aldermanic primary Jane Ramos, an apparently victorious insurgent, sought to have the ballots impounded—only to find that

---

* At this writing, warrants are out for the arrest of James Ryan II of the Ryan clan, for such violations. Chairman of a local board, Ryan physically ejected the poll watchers before counting the ballots.

some of the board chairmen, instead of properly turning them over to the court house, had given the ballots to Democratic committeemen!

Furthermore, some outwardly Republican election officials have in reality been machine hirelings. This was true until recently of the "Republican" members of the bipartisan Election Board. Even honest Republicans may be afraid to confront the intimidating Democrats.* Any attempt to have violators prosecuted would have been futile, at least until the election of a Republican district attorney in 1968. Even afterwards, there have been no significant prosecutions in this realm, despite a considerable outcry following the 1971 ballotting.** The D.A.'s office explained that the offenses observed were not readily susceptible to the identification and prosecution of the culprits.

The very atmosphere surrounding voting in Albany is intimidating. The polling places are always manned by a horde of Democratic ward workers, inspectors, poll watchers and "gophers" (whose function is to go for coffee or sandwiches). A voter cannot ignore their presence; one leading Republican calls the result "compulsive voting." Indeed, so aggressive are the Democratic workers that many voters, who would otherwise not bother, show up to vote just to avoid antagonizing them.

Democrat Donald Lynch has a different view of this situation. "The people we have around the polling places," he explains, "have been there for years and are part of the neighborhood. It's natural for voters to ask these people about the election. They're still perfectly free to do as they wish." It is true that Albanians are severely provincial, seeking comfort in the bosom of the neighborhood and resenting outsiders. This attitude on the part of voters is another handicap to anyone attempting to combat the abuses practiced by the Democrats.

Lynch denied that any widespread violations had occurred in the 1971 elections, and even if the law had not been followed to the letter, "the people waiting in line have some rights." If all the

---

* Republicans and other machine opponents are up against the police as well as the Democrats, since the policemen assigned to the polls are in league with the machine. Poll watchers who attempt to enforce the law may be thrown out by the police for "interfering." In one district in 1972, the Republican watcher was thrown out first thing in the morning by Officer John Cody (of Broughton case fame). The replacement watcher was expelled bodily twice, after which a G.O.P. Elections Commissioner ordered him reinstated.

** Many violations were reported in the 1973 primaries. As previously noted, one significant prosecution has been brought, that of James Ryan II.

technicalities of the law were observed, he said, it would take half an hour to vote. He felt that elections were being reasonably conducted in line with the "practicalities," and that the purpose of a party or candidate is to help people make their choices. However, other areas have experienced no difficulties in conducting elections strictly by the book.

One interesting example of official machine disregard of the election laws occurred in the 1970 primary. Leon Cohen, a leader in the New Democratic Coalition, sought a county committee seat, and the machine neglected to file for more than one of the two district posts. The election law clearly requires that in such a case the unopposed candidate be declared the winner with no primary being held, unless a petition to write-in is submitted. The Democrats did not realize their predicament until the time for filing the necessary petition was past. Heedless of this, the Election Board opened the ballot to write-ins. The machine's write-in candidate won, but when Cohen took the case to court, it was apparently decided by the Democrats that the one committee seat was not as important as the adverse publicity they were getting. They allowed Cohen to take his seat.

Most of the foregoing pertains to election abuses with regard to voters who are legally entitled to vote in the first place. But they have not been the only people voting in Albany.

One writer in a 1944 book flatly stated that "[f]raudulent voting by means of heavily padded registration lists and ballot-box stuffing is one of the methods by which the O'Connell machine has maintained its grip . . . For many years the number of persons registered and the number of votes cast in Albany in proportion to population has been the highest in the country. The explanation does not lie entirely in political awareness and civic-mindedness on the part of Albany's residents. The population of the city of Albany in 1940 was 130,577 and 79,821 votes were counted, an incredible figure mounting to more than 61 per cent of the entire population. The theoretical maximum would be about 66 per cent —if every resident over 21 years of age voted." * Thomas Dewey charged that more people were registered to vote in Albany than could be found in the city directory.

The vote in Albany has been augmented, as in other machine-run cities, by people voting more than once. They may register

---

* Charles W. VanDevander, *The Big Bosses*, Howell, Soskin, pp. 81–82.

more than once under their own or false names, or vote under the names of people who are dead or no longer resident.

It may be observed that Albany's fantastic vote turnouts have fallen off. In the 1949 mayoral race, the vote reached 77,000, and dropped steadily in subsequent mayoral elections. The vote was 53,000 in 1969, which is still quite a high figure for a city the size of Albany. Total registration also fell from a 1948 peak of 85,000 down to 58,000. Since the city's drop in population over the same period was only about 14,000, this is partly attributable to a decline in graveyard and repeat voting, a consequence of tighter registration and election procedures developing over the last twenty years, as well as of Republican state administrations occasionally interested in exposing the local Democratic machine.

» »

CHAPTER 16

The Gravy Train

GOVERNMENT spends public money. It is inevitable
that the money will be spent in such manner as to accrue political
advantage and perpetuate the leaders in power. Political advantage of those who govern may, of course, be consonant with the
common weal. Thus in Albany it was politic for the O'Connell regime to spend public funds to solve the water supply problem.

On the other hand, when a citizen asks his leaders, "What
have you done for me lately?" the emphasis may be more on the
me than on the *done*. It is good to make the public as a whole
happy, and better still to make individuals happy. When public
moneys are expended in order to accomplish the latter, the practice may be termed patronage. Whenever the government spends
money, someone comes out ahead. Patronage in essence is the political selection of those who come out ahead.

If there is one salient image conjured up at the thought of old
style machine politics, it is the clubhouse politician feeding at the
public trough—the government payroll. Yet any political outfit
holding the reins of government must fill a certain number of jobs;
and rarely if ever do the leaders, be they corrupt, honest or even
reformers, eschew the emplacement of their supporters into these
jobs.

Appointing the faithful to jobs is only one facet of the practice. The machine can use jobs to gain new adherents as well as to reward the old, and this is one of the prime uses to which patronage is put in Albany. The jobs are given to the doorbell ringers and political footmen as incentives for their labor, and also to others who have done no party work at all, in order to win their loyalty. The bond to the machine created in the latter case may be as strong as in the former. Indeed, while the man who gets a job after years of party service may feel that he is merely getting his due, the one put on the payroll with no such background should feel more gratitude.

A political group coming into power will generally sweep out most top officials, and then their underlings to a greater or lesser extent and down to a higher or lower level in the bureaucratic hierarchy. As for the high offices—the city commissioners, department heads, members of government boards, judges—they naturally go to top men in the party. But in terms of vote-getting power, these elite jobs mean little or nothing. The bread and butter of the machine is the welter of smaller jobs which it can control, to be doled out to its committeemen and ward workers and others. "I would rather have the charwomen and the janitors," Dan O'Connell has said. "They need the work and usually come from large families with a lot of votes and a lot of friends. The Commissioner has only his and his wife's votes."

And of course, there are many more janitorships than commissionerships. O'Connell has more jobs available per capita than most city bosses because Albany is the state capital. Republicans, in power in the state, would like to fill all the posts, but most of the lesser ones cannot attract people to move to Albany, and there are few suitable local Republicans. So Dan O'Connell is happy to fill these jobs as well as the city and county ones. To round out the picture, there are usually available to a political machine some patronage berths in the private sector. Businesses to whom the party has been good may be willing to put its wardheelers on the payroll.

As Dan O'Connell is fond of saying, his machine's emphasis is on the little jobs. During the Depression, when even the lowliest jobs were received with gratitude, it was upon the lowliest that the machine thrived. If it had a vacancy in an $8,000 a year position, it might be broken up into four $2,000 jobs. That way, the machine secured the loyalty of four families, not one.

The O'Connell organization, in this and other respects, regards patronage almost as much a social welfare device as a political tool. The boss seems to honestly feel that aside from garnering votes by his methods, he has done a lot of people a lot of good. And most voters in Albany seem to agree with him, approving of his patronage operation as being preferable to the alternative, ordinary welfare. Thus the machine gains support from the general public as well as from those to whom it gives jobs.

"The best patronage we ever had was to old people." O'Connell has said. He would always rather give a job to an old man than a young one, even though the youngster would be longer on the voting rolls. O'Connell gives the example of a man who retires after having worked all his life. He gets to be a nuisance around the house. The machine picks him up, puts him to work, gives him a measure of dignity and independence, and this increases as well as ennobles his lifespan. "I went out of my way looking for them," says O'Connell. "Did it all my life. It probably was the best thing we did."

Legendary in Albany are the park jobs given to retired oldsters. During the warm seasons, they can be seen mowing lawns, planting flowers, raking leaves, picking weeds and gathering trash. These men need have no prior connection to the machine. One of them, seventy-seven, retired after forty-nine years with a local stationery firm, and with no political background, got his job in Washington Park through his ward leader. He said that he wasn't aware of any of the other men working in the park having had a history of political involvement. He concurred with O'Connell's philosophy about these jobs: "It's something that keeps you busy, it's better than just sitting."

Many of these elderly park workers are retired railroad employees. O'Connell told the story of one man, a brakeman who used to let him ride home from school on the train. "When he retired, he came to me one day and said his pension wasn't enough to live on, so I got him a job weeding the flower gardens in the park." *

The ward leader doesn't have to tell a man, "We'll give you this job if you promise to vote our ticket from now on." The man will be grateful—it isn't easy for old men to get any kind of work —and will probably feel that the least he can do to repay the favor

---

* It should be noted that while the "welfare with dignity" aspect of park patronage has made it sacrosanct in voters' eyes, reform leader Theresa Cooke has attacked the usefulness to the city of the expenditures, and points out that many of the no-show park jobs are not in fact given to old men.

is to vote Democratic. So will his family and maybe his friends. And since many voters believe their ballot is not secret, they may feel their jobs implicitly require their voting Democratic.

Dan O'Connell has pointed out that he has given these jobs even to Republicans, however. Dan tells them to say they are Democrats, but that they can vote any way they like. While the boss avowed that he did this simply because he wanted to, aside from political considerations, he did agree that in the long run it made his organization stronger. Giving jobs to Republicans could have created more goodwill than those given to Democrats because people hearing of Republicans put on the payroll would tend to look less cynically askance upon the machine. And this weakened the Republican opposition by removing the antagonism of some of its members, and has even been used to seduce workers away from the G.O.P.

The concentration by the machine on smaller jobs as opposed to high-paying plums has resulted in Albany's employing a veritable army of workers, all of them at meagre salaries. A few years ago, one of Albany's newspapers noted the listing of 84 custodial workers in the budget under County Court House and Superintendent of County Buildings. "We hold to the belief that 84 is a lot of custodial workers," said the *Times-Union*, even while acknowledging that the jobs paid only $1,096 to $1,800 a year. Further, under "personal services" for the courthouse alone, in the categories of custodial workers and utilitymen, there were listed salaries for 131 people. There were 76 deputy sheriffs on the payroll for 1968. At the Ann Lee Home and Infirmary for the elderly, 149 custodial workers, laborers, utilitymen and watchmen were slated, not to mention 145 hospital attendants. Reminiscent of the very campaign that brought the machine to power, appropriations for the county jail and penitentiary were scrutinized, with a total of 69 persons found to be on the payroll. "County institutions are being used somewhat excessively to provide jobs for the politically faithful . . . One of these days, the local citizens are going to tire of paying not only the formal welfare costs but the informal ones . . ."

A look at the city payroll for January of 1972, published in its entirety over several weeks in the *Knickerbocker News*, showed little if any change in the situation. There were 37 custodial workers to clean city hall's four floors—while in the nearby Twin Towers building, 39 workers handled twenty floors. At city hall, each worker was assigned to 1,428 square feet of usable space, whereas a worker in a commercial building would take care of four to six times as much space. The payroll also showed 23 men on the job at Washington Park, 9 at Swinburne Park, 39 at Lincoln Park, plus 29 assigned to the Parks Department. There were 16 employees for the Swinburne skating rink, 17 at Bleecker Stadium, and 25 on the Municipal golf course. In *January*.

Part and parcel of this form of patronage employed in Albany is the city's miserable record in civil service administration. The city has been notorious for ignoring civil service procedures in putting people on its payroll. In New York State, the civil service law has applied to county government since 1943, and Albany has carried off the booby prize for being the worst in the state in compliance.

A report of the State Civil Service Commission pertaining to the County in 1971 found that its "administration of civil service was generally *unsatisfactory*" (emphasis in original). The County Commission had been cited for numerous deficiencies in two previous surveys, and this latest report found the problems to have been compounded even further. They consisted chiefly of delinquency in holding examinations, permitting illegal long-time provisional appointments to exist, and failing to enforce proper payroll certification procedures. In the realm of examinations, the County's program was labelled a mere token effort and the worst in the state. While some of the practices of Albany County may have allowed people to go on the payroll who ordinarily would not qualify, the report pointed out that the County's "gross negligence" resulted in many employees serving without the legal tenure and job security that would be theirs upon passing an examination.

A 1970 report covering the operations of the city government was similar, finding that the City's administration of civil service "continues to be extremely *poor*" (emphasis in original) and that most of the previously cited unsatisfactory conditions, far from being corrected, had increased in magnitude. The city's examination program was termed "decisively inadequate," preventing a large number of provisional employees from attaining permanent status.

In the wake of these reports, the County Civil Service Commission has inaugurated a long overdue effort to straighten out the deficiencies cited, and has been working with the state commission to resolve them. However, the City Civil Service Commission has taken no such action.

Besides facilitating favoritism toward the machine's people, the lax civil service compliance of Albany has helped it to keep salaries low. The level of municipal and county salaries is indicated by the fact that the Mayor earns only $12,000 a year.° While perhaps the organization would like to see the people to whom it has given jobs do better, the machine is also concerned about holding expenditures and taxes low, to keep the electorate happy. The machine would also rather give jobs to many at low salaries than to few at high salaries.

How can Albany pay such low wages? Many of the workers do not have to support themselves on these salaries—retirees, housewives, etc. They aren't expected to work very hard at their jobs, keeping rather leisurely hours, and so whatever they are paid is that much "pin money" for which they are grateful to the machine. For many, too, this is the only employment they can get. This is especially true of the elderly, in keeping with the welfare-oriented job philosophy of the machine. Meanwhile, as for breadwinners on the government payroll, they can make out despite the abysmal salaries by working overtime, or more commonly, by moonlighting. State Investigation Commission hearings in December, 1972, revealed that some employees of the City Bureau of Streets held full time jobs with the U.S. post office. One high-level Bureau employee admitted leaving work every day at noon; another, County Legislator John Furlong, was unclear about the hours he worked in the past, but produced hilarity by stating, "now I only get paid for the time I put in."

The face of public employment in Albany may be changing, though. Tightening civil service and attendance rules, the presence of the state government paying much higher salaries, and the rise in living costs without corresponding increases in Albany wages have made some of the machine's jobs more like peonage than patronage.

Giving out jobs is not the only form taken by political patronage. Most local businessmen have no interest in the public payroll, but for them there is an even richer source of lucre—government spending for contracted goods and services.

Distributing the favors of city and county spending to the businessmen is only tangentially intended to win their votes. A more immediate purpose is to bolster their financial contribution to

---

° Corning has a large outside income. His chief aide, Joseph Healy, draws a salary of $6,000, and his full-time secretary, $5,000.

the party. In addition to money for the party from the lucky entrepreneur who deals with the local government, another form of payoff is putting party hacks and others on the company's payroll. Finally, there may even be something for the pocket of the politician who arranged it all. This, classically, is "graft."

Of course, the influence at work may not be quite that crass. The businessman himself may double as a politician, in which case mere comradeship will cause commercial favors to be thrown his way (albeit not without his kicking back something to the party). Similarly, the businessman may be the backslapping friend of the politicians. This is called "having connections" or "pull."

Mayor Corning, when asked whether he saw any conflict of interest in contracting with friends and political allies to do city work, emphatically answered in the negative. Patronage? "Oh yes, there's no doubt about it," Corning said. "If you have friends in business, you're going to help them if you can . . . You do business with people you can trust, and I don't see anything wrong with that." * (Indeed, regarding city jobs, Corning unashamedly told the S.I.C. he believed that a man's political affiliation has a bearing on his ability to do a job.)

Dealing with the City may not turn out to be so lucrative to a businessman after all, when the payoffs and kickbacks and contributions are added to his normal operating expenses. This problem is easily solved, however, by padding the bill to the City.

Thus, for example, 1971 Purchase Order Number 11276 shows a payment by the City of $494.49 to Ninth Ward Leader William Carey's North End Contracting. This sum is not of Tweedian proportions; but the job involved was merely to move two three-by-four-foot boxes containing park swings.

On many of these contracts, the contractors are guaranteed a profit, since the City is billed on the basis of a fixed percentage above costs. Such a system is hardly an incentive to a contractor to keep his costs, and the City's, low. On the contrary, the more expenses a contractor incurs in doing a job, the larger his profit on it, and he can't lose by overspending.

In the above example, Carey, a ward leader, undoubtedly netted a handsome profit. On the other hand, for a contractor not so well situated politically, it has been speculated that even where

---

* *The Washington Park Spirit*, January 13, 1972. Corning has personally profited on some of the City's contracts by insuring the contractors, including Carey's North End firm.

the contract price to the City has been vastly inflated, the contractor must pass so much of it back to politicians that he would be
better off with a straightforward deal in the first place.

A slight obstacle to all this is the State's Second Class Cities
Law, which generally requires competitive bidding for the letting
of contracts over $500. But there is a loophole: bidding can be
waived if 80% of the aldermen vote to deem it impracticable. For-
tunately for the O'Connell machine, it elects 100% of the aldermen.*

Albany has taken full advantage of this exemption from the
bidding requirement. Mayor Corning contends that competitive
bidding is not a purchasing panacea—"often guaranteeing not only
the cheapest price but very often the cheapest product." Of course,
everyone knows that Republican firms put out shoddier products
than Democratic firms.

Thus, another example: in 1970 the City awarded a contract
for 750 folding chairs to Albany Supply and Equipment, Inc., even
though two lower bids had been submitted by other firms. It was
natural that the city fathers turned to this company despite its
higher bid. The firm had been embroiled in a dispute with the City
of Cohoes government, after the O'Connell satellite regime there
was replaced by a reform group. They contended that the company had charged Cohoes excessively on purchases, and that the
purchases had been illegal. Even the firm's own bookkeeper admitted that much lower mark-ups would have been fair. The company
wound up suing to get payment from Cohoes, and the suit was dismissed by the Court of Appeals.

This now-defunct company did $500,000 worth of business a
year with Albany. It was not, however, supplying the City with its
own wares at all, but was acting as a middleman. Each order from
the City would simply be filled on the open market by telephone,
with the company reaping a fat profit for this service.**

Albany has evaded state law in order to deal with firms like

---

* Even after the City adopted a redistricting plan proposed by the
League of Women Voters and drawn up by machine nemesis Victor Lord. Albany has a nineteen-member council of yes-men; for decades, no negative
votes were cast there at all.

** The S.I.C., in its 1972 investigation, seized a "little black book" which
evidently listed, in code, payoffs by Albany Supply & Equipment to various
city officials. The firm's head, William Graulty, on separate occasions described the book as one listing wholesale prices of inventory or as meaningless
and made up for the amusement of his grandchildren. (Graulty also sketched
his personal pantheon: "Here's God—and just under him, on his own pedestal,
is Dan O'Connell.")

this without public bidding by declaring bidding for most contracts to be impracticable. For a long time, there were almost no
contracts for which bidding was deemed practicable. However, the
S.I.C. pressure caused the City to reassess some of these contracts.
On some jobs, bidding turned out to be practicable after all—and
money-saving besides.

Another way of getting around the competitive bidding requirement is to take advantage of its application only to jobs over
$500. A contract can simply be split up so that each piece of it is
less than that amount. Indeed, City books show an almost endless
profusion of such small jobs. The S.I.C. hearings elicited testimony
from an official of Albany Dodge, Inc., that he was directed to
keep all repair bills to the City under $500. Many of these pay-
ments under $500 are still illegal, since state law requires that
where a number of identical jobs aggregate more than $500 in a
year, they must be put out for bids.

The law can also be evaded by printing the bid offering in the
little-read City Record. Favored contractors can be cued in to the
published offers by their political contacts, while potential competitors remain unapprised.

Failing every other gimmick, there can always be resort to the
specifications for a City contract. The City can simply stipulate that
the trucks it wants to buy must have a certain type of ornament on
their hoods. If your trucks don't have it, don't bother bidding. Thus
in 1970, City Purchasing Agent George Farley threw out Interna-
tional Harvester's low bid for dump trucks by rewriting the specifications to favor Ford. The Ford dealer who had been outbid on
the first go-around happened to be a Democratic town leader.*
The S.I.C. revealed that the sergeant who had written the specifications for police cars *got them from Albany Dodge*. (The hearings
also indicated that aside from any profits on the sale of cars, Albany Dodge was doing spectacular business repairing them. The
cars sold to the City by that firm seemed to need expensive repairs
incessantly.)

In addition to Graulty's Albany Supply & Equipment firm,
the S.I.C. in 1972 focused upon two others. It was revealed that the
City's street sweeping contract was granted by Mayor Corning to a
firm with virtually no capital, William Clark's Municipal Sales &
Service. The City itself financed that company's leasing of equipment to do the job, and furthermore paid Clark a mark-up profit

---

* *Times-Union*, May 10, 1970.

on the cost of that financing. For the mere use of equipment that cost $290,000, the City paid Clark $400,000 in a three-year period; he even charged for its use during winter months when snow halted street sweeping.

The other firm investigated was Carey's North End Contracting, with a $900,000 no-bid contract to operate the city's sanitary landfill. S.I.C. accountants accused the company of overcharging the City by $450,000. One 1947 jeep that cost $800 was rented by the hour, for a total bill of $23,208. When it became known that the investigation was underway, the firm returned $88,000 to the City. City Comptroller Frank Hoffman testified that he had accepted the refund without knowing why it was offered, and that he had never audited the firm's bills because he "trusted them implicitly." A state law prohibiting continuation of a contract where the contractor refuses to answer questions about it was afterwards invoked against Carey, he has also been indicted for cheating the City.

Mayor Corning admitted playing a large role in the awarding of these contracts, but denied all knowledge of any overbilling. He would not even concede that someone was doing a poor job for the City, or that it could have saved money by doing things differently. (Dan O'Connell disagreed. Carey, he said, "took too much.") However, just before mounting the witness stand, the Mayor ordered an audit of all accounts in question.*

After the hearings, the S.I.C.'s Deputy Commissioner stated they established "that the City of Albany has been had."

"The question," said Commission Chairman Paul Curran, "is, was it rape or something else?"

The answer seemed obvious. Albany was not being fleeced by the contractors because of stupidity on the part of the city officials. The city officials knew exactly what they were doing. They, joining with the contractors, fleeced the taxpayers.

One need not go beyond the city budget to appraise the cost of this corruption to the taxpayers. Albany's 1973 budget is some $40 million, the same as Syracuse's, while Syracuse has a population half again as large as Albany. Nearby Schenectady, whose population is about two-thirds that of Albany, has a $17 million budget.

The overexpenditure becomes even more apparent when one examines individual items. Street cleaning, contracted by William Clark, cost Albany $848,199 for 235 miles of streets in 1971. Syra-

---

* The firm selected to do the audit was an annual $1,000 contributor to the machine.

cuse, with more than 300 miles of streets, spent only $308,372; Schenectady, with 176 miles, spent $146,245. Albany's cost per mile was more than twice that of Syracuse and more than three times Schenectady's. Albany's cost per capita was also three times that in the other two cities. It has never been said that the people of Albany put more dirt into their streets than do those of other cities; nor are its streets cleaner than elsewhere. On another item, schools, Albany spent more per pupil than any other big city in the state in 1971; yet the quality of education in Albany is so low that half the city's school age children are in Catholic schools.

Entwined with patronage is the question of how the O'Connell machine finances its own political operations.

"Graft, shakedown, extortion, gambling, prostitution, theft, embezzlement . . . and voluntary contributions" was the somewhat facetious answer given to the question by one machine opponent. While all of the above sources provided funds in past years, modern fundraising is somewhat more tame.

Albany Democrats have not been waging lavish campaigns for their candidates. On the other hand, the machine's election expenses are considerable. The party committeemen are paid what amounts to an annual salary, and they as well as runners and inspectors receive "expense money" on election day. One of the machine's largest annual expenditures has been its traditional policy of rewarding voters, both through the five dollar bribes and its general welfare operation including Christmas turkeys and the like. The machine's expenses in this latter realm were much greater during the Depression, when government welfare was just beginning and many people depended on O'Connell largesse to keep their heads above water. Money for this was probably derived from such machine enterprises as the baseball pools, other forms of gambling, protection of prostitution, etc. Much of the money, from these sources and others, must have reached the needy after a sojourn in the O'Connell's own pockets. Their benevolence was strongly personal in character.

The baseball pool was broken by federal prosecution, gambling in Albany has been toned down, and the more open whorehouses were closed in the 1940's. While the latter resulted from church pressure, it may have been eased by a declining need by the machine for money for its welfare operations.

The discussion earlier in this chapter of City contracting practices should indicate a fertile source of political money. In addition to the moneys actually expended by local government, a political machine and all of the people in it control the disposition of considerable wealth. For the County of Albany, the total amount so controlled was estimated in 1965 at fifty million dollars a year. Obviously, this much money is not susceptible to winding up in any politician's pocket, nor even in all of the pockets of all of the politicians in the county. But whenever money goes from one place to another, there are questions of how much and to whom that must be decided, and *other* money may be brought into play for the purpose of conducing advantageous answers to those questions.

Part of the amount by which the City is overcharged by its contractors finds its way into the coffers of the Democratic organization. Some of the contractors, like John Martin, openly contribute large amounts. In other instances, such as that of Carey's North End Contracting, the S.I.C. found withdrawals of thousands of dollars being made every October. The explanation for these mysterious withdrawals was never forthcoming, but it may be assumed the money was used on election day.

Another source of money financing the machine is the assessment of the salaries of City and County employees. This annual campaign shakedown of employees at one time took as much as 10% of their yearly earnings, but usually the assessment levied is less devastating. These contributions to the party are ostensibly voluntary, but no one is fooled. "This is my pay envelope," a city foreman once said. "Today I must turn this over to hold my job."

During the 1972 S.I.C. hearings, the paymaster at the Bureau of Streets garage testified that each October, Thomas Donahue, deputy public works commissioner, would visit. Donahue told the workers how much each was expected to contribute, and set up shop right in the garage to take payments. Paymaster Cresswell himself contributed $500 at Donahue's suggestion.

State law prohibits such assessments, or even soliciting political contributions in public buildings. Mayor Corning, under questioning, saw nothing intrinsically wrong with the practice. His only concession was that the transactions should not take place "on city time."

Nothing discussed in this chapter—or indeed, in this book—was invented by the O'Connells. The book is not about Albany as a paragon of iniquity, but rather about Albany as a uniquely instructive example of the iniquities practiced almost anywhere. Politicians in city after city have operated in a similar manner. Barring some epochal change in human nature, this is how it will always be. The only question is the extent of the abuses. And that depends on who is caught, and how smart the voters are, and how much exploitation they will tolerate.

Dan O'Connell thinks he knows how much, and has yet to be proven wrong.

CHAPTER 17

Confession Booth, Voting Booth

"You mean there's a difference?"

That is the answer once given by Albany newsman Doc Rivett to a question about the relationship between the city's administration and its Roman Catholic diocese. In Albany, the wall of separation between church and state has had some large chinks in it.

The first amendment to the United States Constitution prohibits Congress from making any "law respecting an establishment of religion." This was intended as a ban on an established church, supported by the power of the state, such as was typical in Europe centuries ago. With the government prevented from compelling worship, freedom of religion was secured. To be sure, Albany has not violated the Constitution by "establishing" the Catholic church. Nor are we concerned here that almost all important government officials save the Mayor happen to be Catholics. That is to be expected in any predominantly Catholic community.

Nor, even, is it improper that the church has influence in secular matters. The leaders of the church are community opinion leaders at the same time. Their influence upon the political powers is direct, as well as indirect through their influence on parishioners, who are voters. And the church itself is a major interest group spokesman in the community, with a stake in its progress and entitled to a voice in its government. It has such a voice, and while the voice is often soft, it is powerful.

The City of Albany is today about half Catholic. Most residents seem to think the proportion is greater, and indeed, it used to be. The Catholic strength has declined over the years, partly due to the exodus to the suburbs. Albany's Catholics had been established in the city long enough to have become well-represented in the middle and upper classes, and thereby mobile to the suburbs. Another factor has been the influx of blacks and others, many of them state workers, most of them non-Catholic. The Catholic proportion of the white population still approaches two-thirds—a significant datum in that the political rulers pay minimal attention to the black community as part of their constituency.° Republicans constitute another segment of the electorate that the machine can ignore, further enhancing the importance of the Catholic Church.

Albanians are strongly Catholic in belief as well as in numbers. This is reflected in the fact that the overwhelming majority of Catholic children are in parochial schools, so that almost half of the city's elementary and secondary school students are outside of the public school system. The high Catholic school enrollment is also due to the abysmally low regard in which are held the city's public schools, and the reluctance of parents to send children to schools with substantial black enrollments. And the more students in the Catholic schools—the higher the percentage of blacks in the public schools.

That half the youngsters go to Catholic schools has kept down the cost of education to the city. Every child in parochial school is one whom the taxpayers don't have to educate. To the extent that Catholics are paying tuition to educate their own children, whereas they would be placed in free public schools in almost any other city, the tax rate in Albany has been artificially and deceptively low. Parochial school tuition should be added to taxes to give a realistic picture of their level. The Catholics are in effect

---

° The machine has continued to do well in black areas using basically the same techniques employed elsewhere, if only cruder, and because of the overwhelming black preference for the national Democratic party. Nonetheless, the Albany machine seems to fear black votes, and hence has mounted no registration drives. And of course, with the blacks under-registered, the machine is inevitably under-sensitive to their aspirations.

Governor Herbert H. Lehman with Bishop Gibbons, 1936
(*Gerber Collection*)

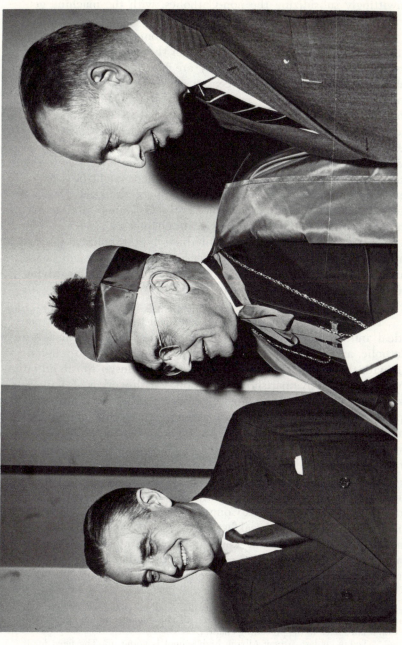

Governor W. Averell Harriman, Bishop William A. Scully, Mayor Erastus Corning (*Gerber Collection*)

unwittingly subsidizing the non-Catholics, with the machine getting the advantage.*

To complete the circle, this situation ironically also allows the city to get away with the poor quality of the public schools in the first place. Most schools in the city are hopelessly outdated, and school construction virtually ceased for most of the machine's era.** Relegated to these public schools are the blacks and the poorer, mostly non-Catholic whites. They have the least political clout to stir up the issue. They are also the least likely to stir it up because family vaunting of education and college ambitions are less endemic to them. If Catholic schools were not available to the great preponderance of Catholic students, there might be a major revolt over the quality of education in the public schools. This can become a devastating political issue, as the O'Connell satellite machine in Cohoes found out (discussed in chapter 22).

The upshot of all this is indebtedness by the political powers toward the church for helping to keep education costs and hence taxes low, while the churchmen are indebted to the city for driving students into church-run schools, so they can be inculcated with religious orthodoxy. The interests of both are served.

There is another, natural bond between the religious and political infrastructures. Most of the machine's committeemen are Catholic, and they find it advantageous not only to be co-religionists with their constituents, but for the church's luster to rub off on them through active parish participation. Parish work is also an excellent way of maintaining ongoing contacts with a neighborhood's voters. This is nothing more than a consequence of the church and the party sharing a mutual constituency. Undoubtedly parish priests would find it useful in their work to also serve as Democratic committeemen.

Thus, County Treasurer Eugene Devine is on the board of directors of a diocesan publication, *The Evangelist;* local Democratic dignitaries such as ex-Congressman Leo O'Brien frequently turn up as communion breakfast speakers; and District Attorneys show responsiveness to the church by mounting anti-smut campaigns now and again. It would make scant difference were the priests and the pols to suddenly exchange roles.

---

* Despite the poor quality of education and the low overall cost, Albany's cost of education *per pupil* is one of the highest in the State. The reason relates back to the preceding chapter.
** Today, at last, a new Albany high school is going up. The need for it was declared critical in 1930.

In past years, the church's link to the political machine was partly biological, too. The local parish priests would come out of the same families as the Democratic neighborhood committeemen. They would have been boyhood chums. These were clannish people, and they were that first and priests or politicians second.

The church-city concordance over the schools is not the only area in which the church gains from friendship with the political powers. The city gives the churches a break on water supply, plows snow from their parking lots, cuts their lawns, and has even provided the land on which many of them were built (for which the city was paid, but at bargain prices). Also congenial to church interests is the conservatism of the machine as reflected in its principle of deferring to private enterprise many aspects of community development such as hospitals and parks. The church is pleased to have the freedom to move into these concerns. Finally, many of the church's biggest contributors are the biggest political wheels.

Church coziness with machine politicians, then, is merely the derivative of their ability to give the church things it wants and needs. This relationship has endured for fifty years, and has comprehended not only the Roman Catholic church but others as well. "We trust them," one black minister, his church built on tax-delinquent land, told a reformer. "You get in power, and we'll trust you."

In 1965, Bishop William A. Scully took pains to make clear that "the Catholic diocese of Albany is not now, never has been and never will be in alliance with or dominated by either a political organization or its enemies." The statement is true, yet it does not negative the obvious fact that no dominant community church can seal itself off from the local political environment, any more than the political powers can ignore the church. Priests can hardly expel Catholic wardheelers from their parishes.

Despite all the foregoing, the church and the city administration have occasionally found themselves at odds. One noteworthy instance occurred during the Depression, when it was proposed to license movie theatres to open on Sundays. The church fought the idea and lost, which may have contributed to then-Bishop Joseph Gibbons' aloofness toward all secular affairs of the community. The latter manifested a fortress mentality that has affected Catholic church thinking in the past. In the mid-1940's, Bishop Scully took over from the aging Gibbons, and Scully was regarded as being closer to the machine. But even during Gibbons' reign, coolness at the top of the church hierarchy could not have purged away the natural bonds between church and party discussed earlier. They were inextricably linked at the grass-roots level.

While the Catholic diocese has generally refrained from opposing the machine on policy questions, nor has it blessed the machine with open support. There is still some feeling that the church should stay out of such matters, at least publicly. As for taking positions on city affairs, the church need not do so for public consumption, but can make its views, and its weight, felt privately. The example may be cited of the clean-up of the open and notorious brothels that flourished in Albany until the 1940's. It is said that Dan O'Connell was not disposed to do anything about the problem until Bishop Gibbons, feeling pressure from within the church, made known his intense concern.*

The above paragraph applied to the leaders of the church; there have been many instances in which its underlings did skirt the boundaries of improper political involvement. In 1962, when reformer George Harder was waging a primary fight against the machine, Monsignor Norbert Kelly refused to allow a group of Harder supporters to appear at his communion rail. Then, just a few days before the primary, the same cleric issued a church bulletin announcing fruition of its efforts to get a traffic light installed at a nearby intersection—as well as noting and decrying the criticism then being levelled against the O'Connell machine.

A more overt incident occurred a few years later, and involving the hierarchy this time. Reverend Bonaventure O'Brien was a young Franciscan theology teacher stationed at nearby Siena College. His social conscience had pointed him toward Albany's South End, to work with a number of secular and interfaith organizations for the betterment of slum conditions. In November, 1965, Father Bonaventure received instructions from his Franciscan superiors to discontinue such activities completely. The Franciscans acted at the express request of the Albany Catholic diocese. This occurred immediately after Father Bonaventure had shown up at the polls on Election Day, offering moral support to South End poll watchers organized to check violations of the election laws. Father Bonaventure in so doing became embroiled in an argument with a Democratic worker. He had previously been heard to criticize the city administration for its failure to do anything about the slums, and to inveigh against the machine. There was a considerable pub-

---

* Paul B. Simmons, *Preacher And Patroon*, SUNY Graduate School of Public Affairs, unpublished paper (1966).

lic outcry at the sudden muzzling of Father Bonaventure; the president of the Catholic Inter-Racial Council assailed the move as contravening the teachings of the Church itself.

Bishop Scully described the action as "an administrative decision, not one of policy. Such decisions are the responsibility of the Bishop alone, and the reasons for such decisions must be left to God and the conscience of the Bishop." Scully specifically disclaimed any political reason for the move.

If the removal of Father Bonaventure from the South End is ascribed to a general social conservatism in the Catholic Church, rather than directly to political reasons, it is curious that the diocese in defending itself pointed to other South End social work being freely done by other priests. The church did not explain why Father Bonaventure had been singled out—immediately after a political expression on his part.

This is not to imply that Dan O'Connell telephoned the Bishop and asked him to pull Father Bonaventure out of the South End. The point is that he didn't have to telephone. The incident is indicative merely of the unwillingness of the church to rock the boat. The elders didn't need any political advisers to tell them that Father Bonaventure was rocking the boat. The church did not want the boat rocked, not because it feared to do the rocking, but because it felt comfortable in the boat as it was. The church and the political machine both shepherded the same flock, and both had conservative outlooks. And both were made up of human beings.

Today, the church is still made up of human beings, but of a somewhat different sort, and this has had an impact on its relations with the political machine in Albany. The Catholic church as a whole is shedding the fortress mentality that had characterized such men as Bishop Gibbons and had stayed the church from any real grappling with social issues. In Albany, the old pastors with strong local roots and personal bonds to machine politicians are being replaced with newer, younger men. Often from the outside, they come to the city with if anything a distaste for the machine's style of politics. Even Bishop Edwin Broderick, the new head of the diocese, is from New York.

This latent potential for a break between church and machine was activated early in 1972 by the City's contract dispute with its firemen's union. Mayor Corning, with the eventual backing of O'Connell, took the position that the firemen did not deserve any pay raise, deeming higher salaries paid to policemen merited by the job. The church evidently became involved in the negotiations, and Bishop Broderick met with Dan O'Connell (which fact was at first denied by the latter, ultimately to be admitted). The Bishop felt that he had received some promises, it is said, and that those promises were not kept when the machine opted against any raise at all for the firemen.*

While Bishop Broderick felt that he could not come out publicly on the firemen's side, others in the church, including Bishop McGinn, were not so recalcitrant. Of the 72 parish priests in Albany, 56 signed petitions backing the firemen. With Bishop Broderick antagonized, and the politicians distrusting him as an outsider, there was no pressure from the hierarchy to squelch this anti-machine agitation by priests. The touchy relations between the church and the machine could not have been improved when Dan O'Connell, in a radio interview, invited Bishop Broderick to keep his nose out of the contract dispute.

The parishioners harbor apposite feelings of loyalty toward both the Catholic church and the machine. In a political contest, the church could presumably take no stand. Silence, though, can speak loudly, and in Albany a clear-cut withdrawal of the heretofore tacit church approbation of the machine could be a thunderbolt.

---

* Interview with Father Joseph Romano, February 1972.

» »

CHAPTER 18

The Opposition

ONCE during the Barnes era, Packy McCabe asked
Colonel William Gorham Rice to run for mayor on the Democratic
ticket.

"That's very nice, Mr. McCabe," the Colonel replied, "but I
don't want to be mayor of Albany."

"Who the hell said you were going to be mayor?" shot back
McCabe. "I just asked you to *run.*"

At that time, the Republicans were in and the Democrats were
out, and it didn't seem as though things would ever change. Now it
is the other way around. Albany is a solidly Democratic town. It is
Irish, Catholic, beholden to and shepherded by an efficient Democratic machine, developed down through the years, which the Republicans could not match even if the complexion of the electorate
were not so stacked against them. As Republican County Chairman Joseph Frangella described the difference between the two
party organizations, "We take our politics lightly, but with the
Democrats it's a way of life. To some of them, it's more important
than religion." Republicans tend to dilettantism in their politics,
making it a hobby, or a means to some end, and at that, a largely

disagreeable chore. Democrats practice the art with a zest, they have it in their blood.

As the Democrats in Albany began rolling up one victory after another in the 1920's the two-party system weakened. The verve went out of the Republican opposition. Whether by collusion, apathy, despair, pragmatics or a combination of all these, the G.O.P. lapsed into ineffectuality, and this in turn discouraged people from enrolling in the party or running for office under its banner. The party suffered a reverse bandwagon effect. In later years, a cliquish attitude at the top also served to disenchant would-be Republican activists—much in the same manner as the Democratic party has been inhospitable to potential comers who might rock the boat. Places on the Republican county committee languished unfilled, with no one willing to serve or even to recruit committeemen.

Dan O'Connell has said that the Republicans always lost because they never fielded really strong candidates. He missed the point: Republicans never fielded really strong candidates because they always lost. Those nominated have usually been mediocrities or worse because of the hopelessness of winning. Men of ability had better things to do. And further, the candidates were forced to raise their own campaign funds because the county organization was unwilling to waste money on them.

Another aspect of the problem is that as in the case of the American Labor Party and later the Liberal and Conservative parties, O'Connell has found it easy to place his own henchmen into the Republican party. Some ostensibly Republican election officials have actually been Democrats in disguise, and the undermanned Republicans could not effectively combat the practice, since anyone is free to enroll in the party of his choice. Others, true Republicans at heart, are neutralized by the machine through favors and patronage. Until recently, the County Legislature, required to put two Republicans on the Board of Elections, used two men whose enrollment was in that party but whose real loyalties were to Dan O'Connell. After a lengthy battle, Frangella gained the right to have real Republicans on the Election Board.

O'Connell has been on good terms with some of the Republican county leaders and has controlled some Republican officials. Many believe that he long controlled the whole party outright, on the basis of appearances which will be detailed herein. It is doubtful that he ever had such full control; he didn't need it.

Most Albanians have an honest preference for the Democratic party. This grows from ancestral and personal ties, and the feeling that the machine has given Albany fairly good government and low taxes, at least in the past. Also, many are literally afraid to be Republicans. They fear that the machine will harass them, raise their tax assessments, even get them fired from their jobs, in retaliation for any manifestation of Republicanism. This atmosphere of repression, even if it is mostly in the voters' imaginings nowadays, gravely demoralizes the G.O.P. Of course, the machine astutely nurtures these lurid imaginings—without giving them a substance that can be proven.

Even those who should be expected to support the Republican party—the establishment, the business elite—do not. Albany's upper crust is embodied in the Fort Orange Club, several hundred prominent old families liberally laced with bankers. These people are nominally Republicans, they are philosophically Republicans, but they won't often be found rolling up their sleeves or rolling out their money for the party. They have been thriving comfortably under Dan O'Connell's status quo, their banks bolstered with vast State deposits, under Republican and Democratic state administrations alike. While it has been said that O'Connell is the front man for the Fort Orange Club, the relationship seems more symbiotic than parasitic. It has also been said that the Fort Orangers have the wherewithal to get rid of O'Connell if they really want to. Perhaps—but it would not be easy—and query precisely what advantages they would have under a Republican or reform local regime. So, they live with Dan.

All of this leaves the Republican party in the hands of its hard core of steadfast leaders, who have their own little world to safekeep. "Our people," complained one Republican leader, "have been too concerned about preserving the party organization, about making sure that power was retained. The first thing was always to retain power, and the second was to win elections. You keep hearing it said: 'The day after you get the drubbing you still have to have a Republican party.'" But the logic becomes less convincing with each successive drubbing.

While the power husbanded by Republican party chieftains would be vastly enlarged if they could supplant Dan O'Connell, they may have felt in the past that it could be cut down if, more likely, they tried such a leap and failed. There was some feeling that they existed at all by virtue of O'Connell's benevolent tolerance.

It was not really patronage that was on their minds. For all but four years of the last thirty, they have benefitted from a Re-

publican state administration. Albany Republicans are in a unique
position to sup from this trough, being based right in the capital itself. But on the other hand, so feeble has the Albany G.O.P. been
that it has not been able to use all the patronage available. "It was
more difficult to find people to fill the vacancies," said one county
chairman, Edward Conway, "than to find the vacancies." *

The crux of it is that just like the Catholic Church, the Republican party is to an extent forced to coexist with the machine. Dan
O'Connell controls the judges and the grand juries, and with the
G.O.P. having a large lawyers' contingent, a live-and-let-live spirit
is inevitable. The Republican attorneys have to practice before
Dan's judges and grand juries; they have clients with political
connections and susceptibilities; they are conscious of the realities
and naturally reluctant to antagonize the boss.

Furthermore, most of the suburban and rural townships in the
county are Republican-dominated, which means that local Republican officials must deal with the O'Connellcrat county officials.
Many local projects and programs require the approval of the
County Legislature. If the Democrats were so inclined, they could
go far toward destroying the Republican leaders and damaging
the party's support in the towns by stymieing the local programs.
But this would not serve the Democratic machine, since it would
thrust up a more combative breed of Republicans in place of the
ruined amiable ones.

So the Democrats have not warred against the town Republicans, and vice versa. And as one influential Republican put it further, "What do Bethlehem and Colonie and Guilderland stand to
gain if Republicans get control of the county? Only more responsibility. They never did want the headache and heartache of running
the county. If you've already got two steaks to eat, who needs a
third?" As has been mentioned, the suburban G.O.P. is not starving
for patronage.

The above attitude has been denied by the leading voice of
town Republicanism, J. Palmer Harcourt, former Colonie boss. "To
say we lie down and trade olive branches with the Democrats is
absolutely absurd," he has avowed. He has simply despaired of
winning. "You could run FDR at the height of his popularity in the

---

* Yet, patronage has been a sore point between the city and county organizations. The G.O.P. is controlled by the suburbanites, because of a law that
allocates county committee voting strength on the basis of Republican election
returns. The suburbanites are contemptuous of the city Republicans because of
their defeats, and do not always cooperate with them on patronage. City ward
leaders have had difficulty even in getting State jobs for their workers.

City of Albany on the Republican ticket and he'd do about as well as the ash tray on my desk."

But it has seemed to many that the opposition provided by the Republicans has not been as vigorous as it could be. The factors discussed above are both reasons for it and results of it. The appearance has been that of a Republican party controlled by Dan O'Connell, while the reality is probably closer to that of human Republicans attuned to pragmatism.

The most visible—indeed, the notorious—evidence of an accommodation between the machine and its Republican friends was for years the bipartisan nomination of State Supreme Court judges. "As far as I know," an Albany Republican attorney has said, "except for the judgeships there are no deals. Maybe I'm naive, or very dumb. But where there's one deal apparent, the people feel there must be fifteen not apparent. And here they have proof positive of one deal."

Thus, the judgeship arrangement—which is practiced elsewhere and often regarded as a salutary means of relieving judges from political campaigning and saving party funds—has had the effect of cynicizing the electorate toward the Albany Republicans.

The arrangement supposedly arose out of the fact that the third judicial district, which consists of the counties of Albany, Rensselaer, Columbia, Sullivan, Greene, Schoharie and Ulster, has been closely divided between the parties. In 1935, the district first went Democratic, electing Francis Bergan over Judge Ellis J. Staley. After that, the parties compromised in most judicial elections, by either cross-endorsing each others' nominees, or by taking turns putting men on the bench without opposition. Sometimes though, the parties fought it out.

The theory of the deal has it that the Republicans originally feared the loss of patronage available through the judiciary, or worse, that the party would be shorn of its protection from the machine if it had no sympathetic judges on the bench. However, history indicates that the third judicial district is not as inhospitable to the Republican party as some of its apologists have intimated. In one contested election, in 1946 (admittedly a good year for any Republican candidate) John Boyd Thacher, the machine's all-time best vote getter, lost the district to Isadore Bookstein. Republicans also won contests in 1952 and 1958, and in 1971, County Attorney John Clyne of Albany was beaten for the Supreme Court. The current G.O.P. Chairman believes that no Democrat could be elected in the district without Republican help.

A reprehensible political deal will be envisioned by the public whenever the Republican party endorses a Democratic judicial candidate. The Republicans are presumably not fools and must be getting something in return. Often, that *quid pro quo* is another judgeship. And often, that judgeship goes to the Republican leader who arranged the deal in the first place. This self-dealing by G.O.P. county leaders has not contributed to a favorable image for the party. It cannot have failed to dampen the enthusiasm of Republicans in the rank-and-file, who are led to suspect that their leaders are selling out the party for their own gain.

In 1966, the Republican county chairman, Edward S. Conway, was nominated by both parties for the State Supreme Court. He had no compunction about his route to this lawyer's Valhalla. "I made a good study of it to get there myself," he later said. "I never hid it. I figured if that's the system then you have to use it. If there was some other way I would have tried that. You go to law school and you take the bar, and I don't know how you can criticize the guy who does it." * So Conway's main purpose in assuming his political chairmanship was to use it to attain a judgeship. In order to get that judgeship, he needed the support of Dan O'Connell. What effect this must have had on his stewardship as leader of the opposition party seems obvious.

Certainly Dan O'Connell never said to Conway, "if you see to it that your Republicans don't give my Democrats any trouble, you'll get that judicial robe." Dan didn't have to. Conway would have known where his judicial prospects would stand if he gave Dan a hard time.

Conway and other Republican leaders have been criticized within the party for this and other sins. Every so often, some Republicans have rankled at ineffectual leadership. Kenneth MacAffer was accused of letting the G.O.P. degenerate into "a pink tea party" that couldn't win. MacAffer was soon afterwards elected to the State Supreme Court. A few years later, U.S. Senator Irving Ives went on record publicly as being "greatly disturbed" over the limp condition of the party in Albany. There followed an unsuccessful movement to oust Walter Wertime, MacAffer's successor. Wertime's eventual successor, Charles Curlette, was likewise accused of letting the party sink "further into oblivion."

In 1963, the entire Watervliet G.O.P. Committee resigned in protest against "indifferent performance and implied collusion" between the county leadership of their party and the Democratic ma-

---

* *Times-Union*, January 10, 1967.

chine. The following year, Thomas Mulligan, a former mayoral nominee, wanted to form a party committee to examine the reasons for its constant defeats. Conway was made a member of the committee, but obstructed it. The Republican state chairman at the time happened to be Fred Young, a native of the Albany area and a friend of O'Connell. Mulligan's attempt to interest Young in his effort to revitalize the Albany party met with failure.

At the 1964 county committee meeting, Mulligan challenged Conway for the chairmanship and lost. He then launched a new "Republican Information Service" that would try to force the regular organization to battle the Democrats more vigorously. In October, Mulligan was fired from his $12,000 state job, at the insistence of Edward Conway.

Joseph C. Frangella is a successful mushroom entrepreneur from Ravena in the southeast corner of Albany County. His family, long resident in the area, were old-time acquaintances of the O'Connells. Frangella began his political career as a Young Republican in 1948, and two years later won a primary fight for a committee post in the town of Coeymans. By 1960, he was town Republican chairman. While holding that post, he upset the reigning Democrats and brought the G.O.P. to power. In 1966, after Conway got his coveted Supreme Court nomination, Frangella went after the county chairmanship.

His chief opponent was the powerful Bethlehem party leader, Bertram Kohinke. The even more powerful G.O.P. leader of Colonie, J. Palmer Harcourt, supported Frangella. This was possibly because Harcourt thought Frangella the weaker alternative, hence more easily controlled. He may also have feared that Kohinke would grab an undue share of the boodle for his own town, and eclipse Harcourt.

Frangella was elected Republican county chairman, and immediately denounced the long history of bipartisan agreement on judicial nominations. Frangella noted that he is not a lawyer, nor is anyone in his family, so he could not be led astray by this temptation.

This was an attempt to set a different tone for Frangella's chairmanship than his predecessors'. On another field, Daniel E. Button, executive editor of the *Times-Union*, was seeking nomination to Congress, and Frangella supported him strongly. Kohinke backed the man who had lost the same office by 88,000 votes two years before.

Button won the primary. In this campaign, Frangella put a

Opposition party leaders. Right: Joseph C. Frangella (*Courtesy of Capital Newspapers*)

Below Left: Harold E. Blodgett (*Author's Collection*)

Below Right: Morris Zuckman in 1958. (*Courtesy of Knickerbocker News*)

new emphasis on fundraising, and was able to finance Button with more money than had been raised by the party all year. Aside from that, he turned Button loose to run his own hard-hitting campaign. The new Republican strategy, replacing the defeatism of old, was to fight as though victory were possible.

It seemed almost as though wishing made it so. Button was elected. Frangella had achieved a major breakthrough within months of his accession to leadership. In the 1967 local battles, the G.O.P. made gains in the county legislature, strengthened its hold on the suburban towns and cities, and gave the Democrats a good scare in the county clerk race. In 1968, Button was re-elected, and the Republicans won two Assembly seats, the state senatorship and the district attorney's office (see chapter 23.)

Frangella's successes in Albany had gained the notice of a resident there named Nelson Rockefeller. The Governor assigned one of his chief political aides to work with the new county chairman on the 1967 drive. Frangella was also boosted into the position of secretary of the State Committee. It is reported that Rockefeller had been interested in aiding the Albany G.O.P. ever since his election as governor in 1958, but that the local climate was inhospitable. Now, Republicans credit the Governor with a large responsibility for their revitalization.

The Albany Republican party has come a long way under Joseph Frangella. It has shed the stigma of collusion with Dan O'Connell and has elected some important officials. The county as a whole is no longer to be regarded as Democratic turf, and Dan O'Connell himself has acknowledged that any countywide race nowadays starts out as an even proposition.

The Republican party has been the O'Connell machine's chief nexus of opposition, but minor parties have also played a role on the Albany political scene. The story of the American Labor Party is instructive on the ways of the machine.

The ALP was formed in New York State in 1935 by a group of socialist union leaders. An Albany chapter was organized about 1937, with one of its leaders Morris Zuckman. He ran for mayor on its ticket in 1941, garnering 168 votes.

During the early 1940's, the ALP was rent throughout the state by the issue of Communist control. Communists, their own party legally defunct by virtue of federal legislation, moved into the ALP and dominated it in many areas. This prompted Alex Rose and David Dubinsky to split away and form the Liberal Party in 1944. Meanwhile in the Albany ALP, the split culminated in a primary fight which was won by Zuckman's faction, allied with the Communists, and with strong aid from the local Democrats. Many Democrats, on instructions from their party leaders, had changed their registration to American Labor in order vote in the primary.

While the ALP was not a significant factor in local elections, its importance was greater in the third judicial district, where Republicans and Democrats were evenly matched. The Democrats, when they had to fight Republicans for the Supreme Court judgeships, were anxious to add any votes they could. Yet despite O'Connell's wooing of Zuckman by helping him win the primary, the local ALP remained hostile to the machine, and spurned O'Connell's efforts to reach an accommodation. Eventually, the machine lost its patience, and set about enrolling enough of its own stalwarts into the ALP to take it over completely. Orchestrating this were a labor leader named Jack Kiley and Frank Cox, later assemblyman. Zuckman vigorously resisted, fighting in the courts to purge his party of its fifth column.

In 1946, with postwar Republicanism running at high tide and the ALP still rambunctiously independent, the Democrats were scared enough to offer Zuckman a city court judgeship in return for ALP support in the Supreme Court race.* Zuckman held out for nothing less than an Assembly seat, which the Democrats were unwilling to yield. No deal was made, and the Republicans won the Supreme Court race. They also won the Assembly seat, which would have gone Democratic but for the ALP vote, which was the balance of power.

Thus the tussle came to a head. In 1947, the ALP enrollment zoomed from 798 to 1443 in the county and from 526 to 1234 in the city, its ranks swelled by O'Connell's followers. Zuckman went to court in an effort to have these newcomers banished from the ALP. By this time, the true believers were a small minority of the American Labor enrollees. Supreme Court Justice Bookstein (elected the year before) ordered the Democrats expelled en masse, which would have put the Zuckman faction back in control. But when the case reached the Appellate Division, about five hundred Democrats were allowed to return.

At the 1948 primary, the Democrats poured out of their

---

* One of the city court positions was a "Jewish seat" then held by Sol Rubenstein. He was asked by O'Connell to leave the bench to make room for Zuckman, and was offered a job in the sheriff's office if he would go along. Rubenstein refused to submit to this, and was not renominated when his term ended.

"wooden horse" and wrote-in the names of their own local candidates in place of the regular ALP slate. The write-in vote overwhelmed Zuckman's regulars. Then the Democratic nominees formally declined the ALP nominations they had thusly won, wiping the ALP off the ballot. This left a blank space next to the Democratic column; the machine had thought that at least half of the ALP vote was being accidentally cast by Democrats. In 1949, no ALP candidates at all were filed except for coroner. Zuckman ran that year for mayor on the "Unity Party" ticket, at the far end of the voting machine, and polled 177 votes. That was the end of Albany's American Labor Party.

By similar means, O'Connell was able to control the Liberal Party for many years. The Liberals eventually managed to break away, and then O'Connell took over the Conservative Party. This story is told in chapter 23.

Finally on the subject of opposition parties, we turn briefly to the City of Schenectady. For several decades, the *éminence gris* of the Republican party there has been Harold E. Blodgett—the senior partner of an Albany law firm that includes Donald Lynch. Blodgett is a curious link between the two parties and cities, and his role may be evidence of a general bipartisan "understanding" concerning the tri-city metropolitan area of Albany, Schenectady and Troy.

The nominal "boss" of Schenectady from the 1930's until recently was James E. "Ed" Cushing, a road and building materials contractor who died in 1971. Despite being a Republican, Cushing maintained amiable political—and business—relations with Dan O'Connell. The two party leaders would agree, for example, on the make of trucks to be patronized by their government and private enterprises. O'Connell was in the brewery business, Cushing was a contractor, and both had a large need for trucks. Of course, it may be assumed that the fortunate truck seller reciprocated for this patronage in some suitable way, probably money. It was also noticeable that while Republicans in Albany were dormant, Democrats in Schenectady would be equally quiescent.

Cushing's chief helpmate and/or nemesis was Harold E. Blodgett. A graduate of Union College and Albany Law School and classmate of Edward O'Connell at both places, Blodgett has become a successful criminal lawyer with a practice straddling the two cities of Albany and Schenectady. Now in his eighties, he is still active. Early political experience included stints in the State

Assembly in 1920–21 and as district attorney. Since then, Blodgett has acted as a puller of strings.

Despite this prominent role in the Republican party, he maintained a close friendship with Ed O'Connell and his brother Dan. Blodgett professes great pride in this friendship, which has extended to his frequent legal representation of Democratic Albany. He maintains that he is not concerned with politics in Albany, and that there is no conflict between his roles in the two cities and two parties.

Blodgett was set to become Schenectady G.O.P. chairman when in the late 1940's Cushing temporarily stepped out of the titular leadership. The story is told that Governor Dewey interceded, rousting Cushing out of bed before breakfast to threaten patronage disaster to Schenectady should Blodgett become chairman. Dewey's animus was Blodgett's having acted as one of the attorneys employed by the Albany machine in the Governor's battle against it.*

While Cushing interposed a succession of acknowledged figureheads, Blodgett's influence was unimpaired by this fiasco, nor was it impaired by his association with O'Connell. Blodgett, seemingly as Cushing's opponent, has backed a series of "insurgents" in primaries since that time—and has always won. While he acknowledges that this was the case, Blodgett demurs to the suggestion that he should therefore be regarded as the real power in the Schenectady G.O.P. On the other hand, it has been suggested that the ostensible split between Blodgett and Cushing was an illusion deliberately contrived by the two men. Indeed, Cushing was never ousted from his nominal bossdom.

---

* Blodgett himself attributes his sidetracking to the opposition of Schenectadian Oswald Heck, speaker of the State Assembly, who was personally antagonistic. Heck is said to have threatened to hold up Dewey's legislative program in the event of Blodgett's accession.

» »

CHAPTER 19

Politicians, Policemen,
Pushers and Pimps

IN 1972 a Republican committeeman knocked on a
voter's door and introduced himself. "I am a former Albany cop,"
the voter told the committeeman with a grim smile, "so you know
what that means."

James Q. Wilson wrote in his 1968 book, *Varieties of Police
Behavior,* that the political system and the operation of the police
department are "congruent" in any city. We have already examined the impact upon such institutions as the Catholic Church and
even the opposition party of having to live in a city controlled by a
political machine. So too does the Albany Police Department have
to live with the machine. And unlike the Church and the G.O.P.,
the police department is directly controlled by the political powers. In fact, the police constitute an arm of the organization.

Police department jobs in Albany are political patronage. Both
entry into and promotion within the department are controlled by
the O'Connell machine, and neither can be obtained without the
approval of one's ward leader. In 1972, with a *New York Times* reporter present, Mayor Corning rejected a telephoned request for a
police appointment with remarks such as "Who the hell is what's-

his-name?" This sort of political control of the police has long been facilitated by the lax manner of civil service administration in Albany, discussed in an earlier chapter. The city is one of the few in the state to use a local rather than a state civil service examination.

Appointments to the Albany Police Department are not run-of-the-mill, but rather highly desirable patronage berths. Although police salaries may be low in comparison with those elsewhere, they are high for municipal salaries in Albany. Furthermore, the police can do well for themselves with overtime pay. Sergeant Robert Westervelt of Castleton made $21,645 in 1971, a salary topped only by that of Police Court Judge Tepedino. By comparison, Mayor Corning made $12,000, and Police Chief Edward McArdle $13,780. In 1971, 26 policemen grossed more than the chief, 18 of them making over $15,000. Of course, these figures do not include such graft as may be available.

The patronage situation ensures the loyalty of the police to the party and its needs. No challenges to that loyalty are permitted. In 1961, a group of cops attempted to organize a Patrolmen's Benevolent Association, Albany being the only large city without one. The Police Chief squelched the movement, and its instigators resigned from the force. The chief later crowed, "They wanted to break up the political organization and get [me] out of office, but I'm still here and the organization is still here. But they're not."

Like others on the patronage payroll, policemen are required to kick back part of their salaries to the machine. The amount is determined on the basis of rank and years of service. The base rate for patrolmen is $30 apiece, while sergeants are expected to cough up $40. A few weeks before an election, each policeman is shown a card that tells him where to deliver his "donation," usually a downtown hotel, as well as exactly when he is expected to do so.

The advantage to the party in controlling the police is simply that the police do things the party's way. What the machine basically wants is for the voters to be happy, and this means that the police must keep a lid on things, and avoid bad publicity. Wilson characterizes the Albany Police Department as a "watchman" type of operation, whose primary thrust is the maintenance of public order, as distinguished from a more rigid law enforcement style. Thus does the Albany department, for example, compile a high record of drunk-and-disorderly arrests.

Yet, there has been dissatisfaction with the force's performance of its watchmanlike functions. In Albany, if anything, the reputation of the police encourages crime. As one policeman explained: "It's a proven fact that most crimes—especially drug crimes—are never reported to police. By running things the way they do here, the department has turned people off even more, so that most of them won't even bother to report being ripped off or seeing someone selling dope. When the stuff is reported, the department breaks down a lot of it to 'yellow' or 'blotter' offenses that'll never end up in FBI figures. All they want to do here is look good." (FBI crime rate reports are compiled from data supplied by local police, for the accuracy of which the FBI does not vouch.)

Knickerbocker News investigative reporter K. Scott Christianson is even more emphatic: "dishonesty, greed and ruthlessness in the Albany Police Department are fostering deep distrust and disgust. The result: Many residents have simply given up trying to help police catch criminals."

The corruption engendering such attitudes is discussed later herein. But even as a general matter, the machine does not want citizens to be "over-policed." For example, people should be allowed to double park outside of stores. Maintaining such a policy is agreeable to the police as well as to the party, since many merchants happily pay the cop on the beat a monthly or weekly stipend to allow patrons to double park.

The police can also help the machine by creating the sort of obligations on which it thrives. Fixing parking tickets, for example, is a way of life in Albany. Tickets are taken to the ward leader, who passes them on to party headquarters for fixing *en masse*. Parking tickets received by newsmen have a habit of finding their way onto the Mayor's desk at his weekly press conferences.

The police can also protect the machine. Nonresident businessmen seeking to trade in Albany have on occasion been checked out by the Police Department so that the party could have a better idea of with whom it was dealing. The policemen are also charged with keeping order at the polls on Election Day, and given the amount of chicanery that goes on in Albany, it is indispensable that the police be allied to the machine.

The police force can be utilized by the machine to ride herd on its antagonists. Such an incident was the 1966 arrest of Election Day picketers exhorting citizens against selling their votes, mentioned earlier. The *Times-Union* editorialized that "this latest episode is only one of several that have caused considerable comment about a police state atmosphere which appears to prevail under certain conditions in Albany. All of us recall the arrest and imprisonment of a responsible and mild-mannered citizen [Russell Broughton] who had the temerity to question the actions of the police as they made an arrest in downtown Albany some years ago. All of us recall the more recent misdemeanor arrest, holding without bail, and ordering of a psychiatric examination of an administration opponent following a conference between the mayor and the judge involved." (The latter incident is discussed in chapter 20.)

The Albany police have also been charged with particular brutality against blacks. A former officer has said that "in the old days, any Negro who talked back was hammered on the head, right, wrong or indifferent, and nobody thought twice about it." The police had the backing of the community in thusly dealing with blacks. Grand jury investigations of several such incidents in the 1960's did more to intimidate the accusers than to get the facts. Wilson suggests that increasing organization of the black community by groups like The Brothers has contributed to a slightly more humane handling of blacks by the police, with the political machine becoming more sensitive to the matter. On the other hand, blacks have not been the only victims of police brutality in Albany. The officer quoted above in this paragraph was once himself charged with assaulting a white man. He told the complainant, "You know how the juries are picked in this county. You don't stand a chance. If you take this to court, I will be acquitted and then I'll slap a law suit on you." The complaint was withdrawn.

Wilson suggested a few years ago that the political machine of Albany does not in fact tolerate large scale police corruption and organized crime. The latter was said to have been kept out of the area, with the police tough on major criminals. One tangential reason for the machine's longtime hostility toward organized crime may have been the kidnapping by some racketeers of the O'Connells' nephew in 1933. But as Wilson pointed out, the real reason for the machine's stance is "a love, not of purity, but of monopoly."

It must be understood that the O'Connell operation has been more than a simple political one. It does more than win offices, more than run the politics of the county—it has run just about everything. The machine is the county's number one economic fact of life. Thus, much of the dirty money that in other cities would go to crooks or the police has in Albany wound up in the hands of the politicians. As an example, during Prohibition, a major part of Albany's beer supply came not from gangster bootleggers, but from the O'Connells. Wilson quoted one police officer: "This is a city in which everybody at the top has their huckle, but not the cop on the beat. Everything goes to the top."

The machine has tolerated gambling and vice, as long as it was conducted under local auspices, with no outsiders trying to muscle in. Locals could more easily be kept under the thumb of the machine, which takes a cut of the profits from these enterprises. But in 1971, reporter Christianson found that the mob had finally infiltrated Albany's prostitution, narcotics, stolen goods and other rackets. He also re-examined the proposition that there is no widespread police corruption in Albany. It seems now to be rampant, and the S.I.C. is investigating.

Prostitution has long flourished in Albany. It was concentrated in an area called "the Gut," centering around downtown Green Street, packed with brothels, gin mills, honky-tonks, clip-joints and streetwalkers. A state legislative committee exposed this condition in 1911, but nothing was done about it. Down through the years, the political powers defended the existence of the Gut on the notion that it served to keep the riff-raff all in one place and out of the way of respectable citizens. Pressure from the Catholic Church caused some of the more obtrusive establishments to be phased out in the 1940's, but the real end for the Gut did not come until the 1960's, when it was simply torn down to make way for the South Mall project. Many of the dislocated enterprises never reopened. One reason for that was a dwindling market. As Wilson observed, "Albany was once a working-class city with factory workers, railroad and river boat men, and lumber jacks from the north looking for a good time. Now it is a city of civil servants, and elderly, and Negroes."

When the Gut was in its heyday, prostitutes paid off directly to Democratic Headquarters at 75 State Street, at the rate of $20 each per week. During this era, the machine hogged all the takings for itself; patrolmen were forbidden to receive anything but "small favors."

Today, prostitution still exists in Albany, and there even remain some brothels. In fact, spurred by its profitability to the police, prostitution is now seen as becoming wide open once again. Heavy police involvement in prostitution dates only from the late 1960's. One patrolman told of being taken by his partner into a brothel to collect a payoff, while still a rookie. The madam became indignant, and threw the veteran out. "How dare you," she said, "corrupting young cops too." Another officer recalled his participation in a rare event—a raid on three brothels—and said that "The bust wasn't popular with some guys on the Albany force. No vice raid was. They lost a good source of income because of it."

That income takes two forms. The traditional method is for the cops to shake down the girls and the houses for protection money. The bolder, modern method is for the cops to go into business for themselves, as pimps. Some cops have more than one girl on the streets. Such an enterprise would be very profitable for both parties—since unlike the competition, neither prostitute nor pimp has to pay protection money to the police.

When a prostitute does get busted, she is then at the mercy of the courts. They can be merciful indeed if she hires the right lawyer—one well-known Albany attorney with strong courtroom pull in particular. He has enjoyed a near monopoly of such cases. His minimum fee for getting the charges dropped is $250—which is more than the normal fine levied upon a convicted prostitute.

And then there is the realm of drugs.

It is one in which Albany law enforcement is scandalous. Reporter Christianson concentrated on hard drugs in his series of articles on police corruption, published in the *Knickerbocker News* in October, 1971. Albany was identified as a major central receiving depot for hard drug importations. One black man was quoted as asking, "Why is it? A two-bit junkie comes here from Memphis or Kalamazoo and buys heroin in half an hour. But the cops can't get to the same pusher—even though he's been the biggest dealer here for years." The answer seems evident. As Albany black leader Leon Van Dyke put it, "Either the cops are the most ineffective bunch of idiots that ever were assembled, or they're crooked as hell."

Narcotics enforcement ties in closely with prostitution. This is because half of the city's several hundred prostitutes are addicts. As one patrolman has cogently explained, "The pushers have the girls and the girls are paying the cops. If the cops bust the pushers, they take money out of their own pockets."

An intensive study of Albany's recent drug arrests revealed that while small fry, typically pathetic addicts who do a little selling to support their habits, are being busted on misdemeanor charges, the big pushers are untouchable. And the big pushers are also the biggest pimps as well, having found that prostitutes are a good shield, by virtue of being a gold mine for crooked policemen. Pushers have also insinuated themselves into friendships and business relationships with policemen, influential politicians, attorneys and respectable businessmen. Some mob-controlled night clubs, havens for the dope and skin trades, have Democratic politicians as part owners. This renders them immune to trouble with the law.

Receiving a cut of the profits from dope peddling naturally makes the Albany police unenthusiastic about enforcement in this area. A problem for them is that others have different ideas. One white collar worker who secretly supplied detectives with tips about pushers voiced fears for his own life. "The cops are out to get me," he said, "I know too much." An experienced undercover agent quickly left town after discovering that city narcotics detectives had deliberately placed him in a situation endangering his life. "I've worked all over," he blurted incredulously, "but Albany is the worst, most unbelievable operation I've ever seen." Other undercover agents told similar tales: the police had deliberately blown their covers, failed to protect them from pushers, and generally conspired to get them killed.

Is this another case of a few rotten apples spoiling the barrel? Are the higher-ups working to root out this corruption? According to Christianson, it is more realistic to talk of a rotten barrel. "Cops who are on report for shaking down some prostitutes and hiring some of their own; for fencing; for brutally beating and framing suspects; and even tipping off pushers and pimps about scheduled raids, not only remain on the force—they have been promoted or assigned to choice details."

One honest narcotics detective brought to Chief McArdle's attention that a leak in his division had enabled major pushers and pimps to escape arrest. "I said it's either him (the corrupt detective) or me. Chief McArdle said I could quit if that's the way I felt about it . . . So I did."

One might expect a machine like O'Connell's not to tolerate such corruption—as was the case for many years. But the problem has gotten out of hand, and other considerations come into play. A major factor staying the authorities from combatting police corruption is that the crooked cops have powerful political connections. For the machine to crack down on its own cronies would wreak havoc with the sense of loyalties it has so carefully nurtured. Thus a policeman with a "rabbi" or "hook"—a political friend who may have gotten him his job in the first place—simply cannot be disciplined. And of course, those cops who are secure in this manner feel the freest to engage in corruption. Thus, the political system prevailing in Albany for appointing and promoting police officers has an effect just the opposite of weeding out the rotten apples.

The honest cops who won't play ball are weeded out, and the rotten ones rise to the top. In fact, as one veteran policeman explained, "The men are afraid to talk. It's because the party plays so dirty—they let the men become corrupt and actually want them to, so they can keep them under their thumb. The men are scared to move as a result—they've got too much to hide." Another observed, "It's harder for a cop to keep clean here than it is for him to turn crooked." (All of this does not mean that every policeman in Albany is corrupt. Indeed, some of the more encouraging responses to Christianson's articles were those of honest cops who expressed a determination to stay on the job.)

When the foregoing story of Albany Police Department corruption unfolded in the pages of the *Knickerbocker News*, the response of Mayor Corning was to publicly challenge the accuracy and intentions of the series. He called the articles "trash" and "completely irresponsible," and invoked the traditional machine incantation that they were printed for partisan political reasons. Nevertheless, he was soon calling for a full investigation. A probe was begun by the State Investigation Commission; however, Corning has attempted to thwart it, fighting the S.I.C.'s efforts to bring members of the Albany police force to New York to testify, and even obtaining an injunction from a machine judge against the Commission acting at all.

CHAPTER 20

Zenger Redivivus:
Politics and Press in Albany

A STRONG political machine does not need a sympathetic press. People do not vote for machine candidates because
they believe them to be embodiments of civic virtue; they support
the machine because it has done them favors, or because they
think it can do them harm if they balk, or because its nearest arm
is someone in their own neighborhood whom they know and trust.
As long as taxes are reasonable and the city is not going to pot, the
newspapers can scream for reform until blue in the face without
result.

Of course, that does not mean the machine wouldn't prefer to
control the press and escape criticism. It does not mean that the
machine won't fight back, if it is attacked by the press.

In 1960, Albany had two daily newspapers. One was the old
Times-Union, now owned by the Hearst Chain; the paper still professed an affection for the Democratic party, despite a national
Hearst conservative bent. The other was the Gannett-owned
Knickerbocker News, a declared Republican paper. Both enjoyed
the patronage of government legal notices, which law requires to
be divided between two papers.

The *Knickerbocker News*, floundering, was purchased by the Hearst Corporation in October of 1960. The two papers were now produced in the same plant while maintaining separate staffs; but they soon united in an anti-O'Connell editorial stance. When in 1961, the reformist CURE campaign was launched for the mayoralty election (see Chapter 21), the two papers looked with favor on the movement and its candidate.

Mayor Corning, after the election, openly assailed the papers for their coverage of the CURE campaign, charging them with flagrant inaccuracies. The legal advertising was thereupon withdrawn from both papers by the city and county governments. The revenues from this advertising were estimated at $250,000 to $300,000 a year, a serious financial loss to the papers. This business was now given to two small-town papers.

Albany Democrats have since that time remained hostile to the publisher, editors and many of the reporters of the *Times-Union* and *Knickerbocker News*, for what they feel is the publication of distorted stories. They complain that the papers have broken the canons of journalism by publishing what amounts to editorial comment in the news columns.

A painstaking statistical analysis of the *Times-Union* for the campaign periods of 1963–67, to probe its partisan bias, concluded that the Republican party did receive more extensive and more favorable coverage than the Democrats.[*] The Republicans had a heavy advantage in the number and size of stories, but only a small advantage in their slant. The author of this study acknowledged as a qualifying factor that, because of their feud with the papers, the Democrats have shown less interest than the Republicans in soliciting coverage in the *Times-Union*. The Democrats distrust the paper because of its anti-machine stance, and do not cooperate with it. (Here is another evidence that the machine does not feel threatened by unfavorable press treatment. It has reacted more with the stick than the carrot, punishing the papers without any real intent of winning them over.)

It was felt by the analyst that the G.O.P.'s advantage is so

---

[*] David A. Nathan, *Analysis of Political Coverage in the Albany Times-Union: 1963–1967*, unpublished paper, SUNY Graduate School of Public Affairs, Fall, 1967.

There have been instances of apparent pro-machine bias in the Albany papers. More than one *Times-Union* story in 1973 implied that Alderwoman Gloria Ballien was investigating forged signatures on her opponent's nominating petitions; in fact, the forgeries were on her own petitions.

great that it cannot be attributed wholly to Democratic uncooperativeness. But he did not determine whether developments in the
Republican party during the period studied were inherently more
newsworthy than those in Democratic ranks. During this period,
the G.O.P. underwent a significant change in leadership, while for
the Democrats, it was O'Connell's "same as usual."

The Democrats have not limited themselves to financial reprisals and uncooperativeness in their feud with the papers. Once the
legal advertising was taken away, the chief vehicle used for harassing the press was the grand jury.

Gene Robb, publisher of both papers, openly protested to a
grand jury in 1963 that newspapermen had been called on the car-
pet three times in less than a year, and that eight staff members
had made a total of nineteen appearances. "Within my thirty-five
years as a newspaperman," said Robb, "I have never heard of a
comparable situation anywhere in the United States."

It was not only that newsmen had been called to testify. 1962
saw a startling instance of the grand jury being used to intimidate
the press. The case began when Samuel Clark, a post office worker,
publicly charged that he had been beaten in an Albany police
station—an altogether credible allegation, since Clark was black.
The black community became incensed, since the evidence
strongly corroborated Clark's claims, and Mayor Corning called for
an investigation. But the grand jury, instead of focusing on what
happened inside the police station, concentrated on the press handling of the affair. The only indictment to come out of this investigation was that of Edward Swietnicki, a *Knickerbocker News* reporter, for second degree perjury.

What was the evidence supporting this charge? Swietnicki
had testified to having told his editor that he had been waiting for
years to get a good story on police brutality. The editor did not remember his having said that. For this discrepancy, Swietnicki was
indicted for perjury. He speculates that the machine lodged this
flimsy charge in hopes of making a deal: Swietnicki would tarnish
the papers by pleading guilty, and they would get back the legal
advertising. But when Swietnicki instead fought the charge,° the
machine's lawyers set out to convict him. Even though it was only

---

° The newspaper had hired Samuel Aronowitz (Ed O'Connell's old law
partner) to represent him, but Swietnicki did not feel he was receiving an aggressive defense. He fired Aronowitz and engaged his own counsel, M. Andrew Dwyer of Troy, who would not be subject to any local pressures.

a misdemeanor case, two assistant district attorneys prosecuted, at
a trial lasting days. Nevertheless, Swietnicki was acquitted by the
jury.

Knickerbocker News Executive Editor Robert G. Fichenberg
discussed Swietnicki's case in a column. "The basic issue is this,"
he said: "The attempt by a powerful, entrenched political machine
to harass and intimidate a newspaper and its reporters in an effort
to discourage public disclosure of any story that might not reflect
favorably on the machine. Any newspaper that caves in under this
type of threat betrays its public trust."

History repeated itself in another major clash between the
newspapers and the grand jury in 1966. This followed an October
14 *Knickerbocker News* editorial written by Fichenberg calling for
a state investigation into the arrest of a young black civil rights
worker, George Bunch. State investigation was urged as opposed
to "the usual whitewash by Albany officials or by an Albany
County grand jury."

Bunch had been arrested for slapping a girl after she called
him "Blackie," thereby causing a disturbance. He had apologized
to the girl's father and was arrested belatedly, after a conference
over the matter between Mayor Corning and Police Court Justice
Michael V. Tepedino, who was to preside at the arraignment. The
newspapers noted the impropriety of a magistrate's consulting with
anyone, especially a political official, on how to handle a case before a warrant had even been issued.

Bunch turned himself in, and Tepedino ordered him held
without bail for psychiatric examination. He was released three
days later by the grace of a writ of habeas corpus issued by State
Supreme Court Justice T. Paul Kane, who decried the custody without bail on a misdemeanor charge. (The Bill of Rights protects citizens against excessive bail.) Shortly thereafter, the controversial
Knickerbocker News editorial appeared, opining that "the handling
of the case of George Bunch . . . raises some disturbing questions
that are so serious they deserve a public airing by the highest
qualified public agencies . . . Not only George Bunch's constitutional rights are at stake. Yours are, too." °

The grand jury took action one month later. But instead of

° Bunch was black, and most whites are not upset by a denial of constitutional rights to blacks. The paper was saying that if they can do it to
Bunch, they can do it to anybody. Judge Tepedino has in fact been accused
by some of the lawyers appearing before him of venting his prejudices not
only against blacks but against anyone not an Italian or a white Democrat.

probing the Bunch incident itself, once again, it set about investigating the papers' handling of that incident. Summoned to appear were Publisher Robb, Editor Fichenberg, and four other editorial executives. The grand jurors wanted to know why the term "whitewash" had been applied to their mode of investigation. Fichenberg answered simply by pointing to the Clark-Swietnicki case of a few years before.

On December 21, the grand jury issued its report on the Bunch case. "The citizens of Albany County," it said, "have a right to know that the editorial of October 14, 1966, published in the *Knickerbocker News*, which castigated the officers of Albany County and the grand jurors of this county, was written without any basis of fact or evidence and was completely false . . . Such forms of journalism are a threat to one of our basic constitutional rights . . . The grand jury system is a proven, basic protection afforded to citizens and we uphold the system at all times."

The report was formally called a "presentment," which is generally issued against public officials, with instructions to the prosecutor to indict. No case was known of a presentment against a private organization. The grand jury defended its action on the ground that a newspaper is a public service, a justification many lawyers found dubious. In any event, no indictments were suggested or made.

Finally, when Bunch appeared on January 19 before Albany County Court Judge Martin Schenck, the charge was reduced to disorderly conduct and the plea was guilty. Schenck suspended the sentence. Bunch was later quoted as saying, "As far as I'm concerned, the grand jury that called Fichenberg and the others certainly whitewashed my case. They should have called the Mayor and Judge Tepedino. Those papers saved my career."

As for Tepedino's conduct in the case, he cites a letter he received afterwards from the Appellate Division of the Supreme Court absolving him of any breach of propriety, or other mishandling. He is critical of the newspapers for failing to play up this exoneration he received.

Today, Executive Editor Fichenberg characterizes relations between the papers and such public officials as the Mayor as "correct and civil." Human nature being what it is, he says, "they wish we'd go away, I'm sure." While he notes that the papers have endorsed some local Democrats, he views the relationship between government and press as inherently adversary, with the newspapers obligated to criticize where appropriate. And while the Democratic organization has not altered its opinion of the Albany press, the election of a Republican district attorney in 1968 has taken from Democratic hands the means for grand jury harassment of the papers.

Part Four:

LOSING POWER?

» »

CHAPTER 21

The Attack of the Goo-Goos

IN 1961, there came to Albany what sooner or later comes to all cities governed by a political machine: a reform movement. Albany's was the model urban reform crusade—launched by clean cut young men and political independents, the quintessential "goo-goos" or "good-government" seekers.

It was embodied in a new political party called Citizens United Reform Effort, known by its felicitous acronym, CURE. The leading organizer and spokesman was the Reverend Robert K. Hudnut. Of the cosmetics Hudnuts, he was born in Cincinnati, attended Princeton University and Union Theological Seminary, and was in Albany on his first ministerial assignment as assistant pastor of the Westminster Presbyterian Church. He was twenty-seven years old.

As Hudnut later reflected in a book, *Surprised By God,* published in 1967 after he had moved on to a Minnesota congregation, he "was the young idealist, a Protestant minister shocked after two years in Albany by the tales of votes being bought, and voting booths being peered into; by reading in the paper about the 90-year-old fire chief . . . by seeing policemen ignoring triple-parked

CURE mayoral candidate Robert K. Hudnut (right) and running mate Charles Liddle campaigning in a 1921 Buick. (*Courtesy of Capital Newspapers*)

cars and stalled traffic and driving through pot-holed streets in Buicks.

"I spoke out about the obvious political and physical deterioration.

"People contacted me, and I listened and learned about the power beneath the surface—about 'Uncle Dan's' carrot and stick, the carrots being city jobs, of which Albany has more proportionately than any other city in New York State, and the sticks being property tax manipulations, the surest guarantee of a vote because they ally your politics with your pocketbook; about the annual pre-election 'contributions' to the party by the city employes, many of whom work for 85 cents an hour; about the 4,500 declared Republicans in a city of 130,000 who had not elected anyone to anything in the memory of a generation, about the thousands of other Republicans who were registered as Democrats.

"A woman called me to tell of the $10 bill slapped down on her mantle before the last election by a Democratic politician. A prominent businessman told me of the Democrat who offered to 'fix up' his assessment. A clergyman wrote me about a man who had been stood up against a wall by the police and worked over so thoroughly he couldn't stand."

Hudnut's indictment of the machine points up some of the difficulty he faced in his reform effort. There is a difference between something that is merely wrong, and something shocking. Hudnut saw a great deal wrong with Albany, but all of it had been quite familiar to Albanians since before he was born. He had no great new scandal to present to the people. Hudnut was posing issues they had decided—for better or worse—long before.

Unaware of this, or undaunted by it, Hudnut organized a reformist party. The independent route was chosen because efforts within either major party seemed doomed—the Democrats appeared impregnable to assault in the party primary, and the Republicans were dismissed as hopeless defeatists who could not possibly provide enough votes to win an election. Large numbers of Democratic votes would have to be garnered, and the G.O.P. was incapable of attracting them to its line even temporarily, because of the traditional pro-Democratic and anti-Republican bias of most local voters, who felt that Republicans had a condescending attitude. They, it was said, seem to regard all Democrats as social inferiors.

Reverend Hudnut was the CURE candidate for mayor in the 1961 election, with running mates Charles Liddle for council president and Stanley Ringel for treasurer. All three were almost too young and clean-cut looking to be true. The Republicans, having nothing better in mind that year, endorsed the entire CURE city-wide slate. Actually, throughout CURE's presence on the political scene, there was tension between the independents and the Republican organization, exacerbated in some of the ward races, with a constant fear in CURE ranks that the Republicans were trying to swallow them up and make them an adjunct.

Getting enough signatures on petitions to put CURE on the ballot was no easy task. The petition process is always a roadblock to such reform efforts because of the natural hesitancy of the American voter to put his name on anything, heightened where he is asked to put his name down as an opponent of the local powers. As Hudnut tells the story, "Oh, no, I couldn't do that" was a typically fearful reply to a solicitation to sign a petition. One man said, "You think I'm crazy? I sign your petition and my taxes go up like that"—a snap of his fingers. There were especially slim pickings when Hudnut personally canvassed the ward in which Dan O'Connell grew up.

As he left one house, he heard a voice calling from the shadows, that of a young teenager.

"My dad didn't sign, did he?" asked the boy.

"No."

"Well, I would if I could, and all my buddies would, too." *

The voters' fears that the machine would take an interest in whose petitions they signed was not chimerical. While the organization cannot tell how one voted, the nominating petitions, once filed, are public record. In 1967, a Democratic candidate actually collected the names of those who had signed the petitions for his opponent, and sent each of them a letter telling them he had noticed their signatures. The message that the machine had "noticed" their indiscretion could not have been lost on these voters, quite possibly inhibiting their enthusiasm for the opposition campaign.

Hudnut did manage to file enough signatures to deter any attempt by the Democrats to get him off the ballot by challenging

---

* The younger generation turning against the machine? If that was beginning to happen in 1961, the machine would be a memory now. But youngsters have a habit of growing up, with relatives on the city payroll, and caution over their own jobs, and over the assessments on their homes. In a city like Albany, pinning all one's hopes on the next generation of independent thinkers is bound to be forlorn.

their validity.° The Reverend's name appeared on the ballot both under CURE's crescent and the Republican eagle.

CURE presented for that 1961 campaign a detailed platform and an 8-point "Bill of Rights for Albanians," most of which is still apropos a decade later.

"We are disgusted," began the platform, "by the spectacle of citizens obliged to beg as special favors the rights and services which in other cities are provided as an accepted responsibility of local government.

"We are dismayed by the evident hostility to new business and industry, and by the resulting reluctance of many of our most promising young people to make their homes here.

"We are appalled that local officials have scarcely opened their eyes to available and tested ways of turning urban decay into urban growth.

"We are indignant that so many public services are slovenly; so many public facilities are dingy and inadequate; and that law enforcement is whimsical at best . . .

"We believe that control by fear, control by favor, control by boss are a continuing insult to our dignity as human beings."

After this preamble, CURE offered ten "prescriptions" for Albany. Number one was that city services could be well financed if tax delinquents were properly assessed. Mayor Corning was singled out for criticism on account of his allegedly illegal compromising of tax disputes (see chapter 13). Also suggested were more businesslike (and implicitly, less corrupt) purchasing practices.

Other platform planks called for an end to political use of tax assessments, snow-free streets (a recurring political football in recent years in Albany), trash collection (Albanians must still sort their refuse and arrange privately to have part of it carted away), a representative and independent school board, consultation by the government with the people of the city, and the charting of efforts toward civic improvement in place of "piecemeal planning and spasmodic starts."

Among the items in the Bill of Rights for Albanians was the

° Challengers should always try to file many more signatures than the minimum required, because flyspecking election boards can easily find fault with and disqualify petitions for candidates they don't like. The Chicago board of elections chief explained his method of determining the validity of opposition candidacies: "We throw their petitions up to the ceiling, and those that stick are good." (Mike Royko, *Boss*, Dutton, New York, 1971.)

secret ballot, "the right to differ with the government in power without fear of reprisal," the right to a tax assessment based on property value and not political affiliation, and the right to do business with the government without paying a kickback, or to work for the government without having to finance a political party.

Reverend Hudnut and his CURE running-mates campaigned in a 1921 Buick to remind the voters of the year in which the Democrats took over and of the expensive cars being used by the police (since replaced with Dodges). Into factories the campaigners went armed with literature, coffee and doughnuts. In one factory they were thrown out, and in another, they drank the coffee themselves. Hudnut's explanation for this was simple—no one wanted to be seen with an anti-O'Connell candidate.

The CURE candidate was accepting all invitations to speak or debate, Mayor Corning none. But the Kiwanis Club found it necessary to rescind its invitation to Hudnut. A high school civics teacher told Hudnut that a visit to the class would have to be cancelled. The reporters for a parochial high school student newspaper told him that they couldn't print their interview with him. The editor of the College of St. Rose's paper reported the same thing; she had also sat for hours in the Mayor's office in an unsuccessful attempt to get an interview.

On election day, November 7, 1961, Mayor Erastus Corning received 49,406 votes while Hudnut got 15,756. Corning's vote had declined about 8,000 since the previous mayoral election, while the opposition total had climbed by a like number. Hudnut received almost 1,000 more votes on the CURE ticket than he did on the Republican line.

But this was not quite the end of CURE. After the election, the group reorganized into a regular party complete with a county committee, Gren Rand replacing Hudnut as chairman. Hudnut continued, however, as the guiding spirit. In March, 1962, there appeared the first issue of CURE's monthly newsletter, *The Independent*, a slick printed four page document mailed to about 1,400 homes.

The party was faced with a dilemma as the 1962 campaign approached. Obviously, they could not endorse any Democratic aspirants for office, even though CURE's members were predominantly Democrats. Democrats of the regular stripe were still lepers because of the very presence of Dan O'Connell as their leader. As for the Republicans with whom there had been coalition in the past, this time the GOP refused in advance to accept anything short of a blanket CURE endorsement of its whole ticket. CURE blanched at this on the basis of its fusionist ideals. Plainly the Republicans, chagrined at CURE's having outshone them in the 1961 voting, had handed down this ultimatum as a means of either absorbing or killing the new party. As for running its own third party slate, CURE decided against it, on the ground that such a move would simply dilute whatever opposition some of the Republicans might have been capable of offering the O'Connellcrats. Thus the new party wound up not participating in the election at all.

There have since been other attempts at establishing a reformist political party in Albany. 1966 saw the creation of AIM, the Albany Independent Movement, headed by James Gallagher; and in 1969 there was the Action Party headed by newspaperman Edward DeCosmo, which couldn't even get on the ballot. In 1971, however, the Citizens Convention for an Elected School Board ran well in the school board race, electing Gallagher to a seat on it. The Citizens Convention has shown no interest in the more political elections.

As for CURE itself, once the young Reverend Hudnut moved on to other if not greener pastures, the organization's spirit languished.

Like MacArthur's old soldier, CURE did not die; it just faded away.

» »

CHAPTER 22

The Cohoes Secession

ALBANY COUNTY contains three cities: Albany, Cohoes and Watervliet. Cohoes has a population over 20,000 and was for many years a loyal province of the O'Connell empire. In 1963, the city virtually seceded from the rest of the county—removing itself from under the O'Connell thumb, yet not aligning with the Republican areas with which O'Connell was usually able to make an accommodation. In so doing, Cohoes became a unique enclave of political independence within the county.

It was originally a knitting mill town—almost everyone worked in the mills, and the mill owners reigned supreme. This meant Republican political domination. Active support of the Democratic party was simply not tolerated by the employers. This state of affairs was undermined by an advancing labor unionism, safeguarding dissident employees from being fired. Then, after World War I, disaster overtook the entire mill industry; unemployment gripped the town and the hold of the mill owners was broken. By 1923, the Democrats out-enrolled the Republicans, and an O'Connell client machine was on its way to being formed in Cohoes.

Its boss was Michael Tecumseh "Big Mike" Smith, a stereotype of the old-time politician if there ever was one. He could not read or write, wore a ten gallon hat, smoked fat cigars and was chauffeured around the town in a black Rolls Royce. Smith was perhaps more a partner of O'Connell's than just a crony. Dan O'Connell has said, referring to his entire county organization, "Mike Smith and I put this thing together."

Smith's techniques were fairly typical, and he was known for the standard largesse of leaving coal in the doorways of poor families and the like. "Many people in Cohoes still think he was a God," says his descendant and namesake, Mike Smith. As Paul Van Buskirk, leader of the local reformers, puts it, "He was a latter day Robin Hood who took from the taxpayer and maybe split 50-50 with the poor." Big Mike was also linked time and again with false voter registration and property assessment conspiracies. In 1944, during Governor Dewey's attempted crackdown on O'Connell, the Cohoes boss was indicted on fourteen counts related to such hijinks. He was, of course, acquitted.

Big Mike Smith died in 1949, and the Cohoes leadership was inherited by his nephew, Warren Smith. He was ousted as leader in 1958 in favor of William J. Dawson, but O'Connell's overlordship remained intact. Dawson later weathered a challenge from another Mike Smith, this one the son of Warren. (Dawson took the trouble to learn Japanese in order to make his account books incomprehensible. Nevertheless, he eventually went to prison for income tax evasion.)

Meanwhile, the Democratic ascendancy in Cohoes reached dizzying heights. The 1930's brought Franklin Roosevelt and a great national tide in favor of his party. Locally, the hard times of the Depression did not operate to dislodge the incumbent Democrat regime from city hall—quite the contrary, its welfare system ingratiated the machine even more deeply with the electorate. While the Republicans received the blame for the bad times, the Democrats took advantage of them, in some cases literally saving people from starving or freezing to death. Then too, Cohoes received a major influx of immigrants who were, as usual, easily absorbed by the glad-handing Democrats.

It is the thesis of one observer that although the voting trends do not so indicate, the Democratic party subtly weakened in Cohoes during the subsequent years. It is even suggested that the Depression itself bore the seeds of Democratic disaster, since the final demise of the last knitting mills sent the people elsewhere for employment, diversifying the town, with many of its citizens now

Edward J. O'Connell (left) conferring with Cohoes Democratic Leader Michael T. "Big Mike" Smith. (*Courtesy of Capital Newspapers*)

commuting to work. This would have broadened their horizons and outlooks. And of course, while the dole by the Democrats in the past was still remembered with gratitude, people no longer depended upon it. Furthermore, the proportion of newly arrived immigrants in the population declined sharply, and the second generation became more idealistic and more politically aware.*

Then too, the regard in which the political leaders were held changed over time. Those of the Mike Smith genre were respected as "local boys who made good," and the voters winkingly identified with or envied Smith's peccadillos, rather than condemning him. But Smith's heirs were regarded more as dreary party hacks than as charming rogues.

In 1959, the Democrats yet again won the mayoralty of Cohoes, by a record margin of 7,160 to 3,126. But trouble was roiling just beneath the surface. Within a short time, several civic organizations set about stirring things up. A group of discontented homeowners of Manor Heights, a newly developed area, got together to press for an improvement in the abysmal level of municipal attention given their community. There was also the Cohoes School Improvement Committee, which began inveighing against the political patronage system of teacher appointments and the extravagant mismanagement of school funds and construction. The fires of this controversy flared up when it was revealed that Cohoes' city hall had thwarted a proposal for an elected school board. Voters will tolerate much in the way of machine shenanigans, but not being short-changed in the education of their children. (How Albany has gotten away with poor schools has been considered in a previous chapter.)

The most important group was the Cohoes Citizens' Committee, which was formed in 1960 in the aftermath of the Republican vote perigee experienced the year before. The Citizens group was founded on the notion that the Republicans were incapable of providing a check upon or alternative to the Democrats, and was first conceived as an independent fiscal watchdog. The chief organizer was a civil engineer still in his twenties named Paul Van Buskirk.

The earliest forum for the Citizens group was the municipal budget hearing, which Van Buskirk and his supporters would prepare for and attend. An obviously inflated appropriation would be singled out and publicly drawn into question. The officials in-

---

* Winifred Nazarko, *Politics in a Changing City Or The Death of a Machine, Cohoes, New York, 1913 to 1963*, unpublished paper, SUNY Graduate School of Public Affairs, April 1971.

volved were nonplussed by this unexpected stream of inquiries, and were often left speechless, unable to articulate any rationale for their handiwork. This, and the resultant publicity, put the Democrats in a very bad light. The machine started dragooning out its committeemen to attend the budget hearings, as though to submerge the opposition by weight of numbers. But all this accomplished was to widen the audience before which the city officials were pilloried.

The Democrats responded to this new type of challenge obliquely, and in a way that may have done them more harm than good. They simply turned on the screws for support, tossing veiled threats around with reckless abandon. Probably as many people bridled against such tactics as knuckled under. The Democrats succeeded in alienating many who would otherwise have gone along with them. As will be seen later, this sort of tactic was typical for Cohoes in the 1960's.

The Citizens group began organizing politically at a grass roots level, girding to battle the machine at the polls. The first clash came when the Democrats put a proposal on the ballot to specifically assess the beneficiaries of street improvements. The Citizens opposed it, and won the issue.

The last straw came, in the most classic fashion, in 1963. The Citizens tried to see Cohoes' financial records, and were repulsed at the doors of city hall. They took the issue to court and won. Now the spotlight of publicity had been focused on the affair, so that when the books finally were laid open, the public was ready and waiting for the dramatic denouement. It was revealed—of course—that corruption had been rife.

To the Citizens group, rather than to the Republicans, the people of Cohoes turned for salvation. The Citizens were better able to capitalize upon the exposure because of the probity and public-mindedness of their membership and their nonpolitical stance. The climate in Cohoes was one of disgust toward the established political parties; but the Citizens, it seemed, were not in this battle to get anything out of it except better government.

Thus in 1963 the Citizens, now themselves a political party, joined the field, running Dr. James McDonald for mayor. McDonald was an old-time country doctor with one of the largest practices in Cohoes. Against this articulate, ideal candidate, the Democrats renominated the inept incumbent, Andrew H. Santspree. It was apparently felt that to dump Santspree would have given credence to the charges of corruption. The machine decided to stand or fall on its record—bad as it was.

While the Citizens Party hammered away on that record, the Democrats scarcely bothered to deny the allegations, and instead resorted to deprecating their opponents as outsiders (which they weren't) and even as political machinists in their own right. Van Buskirk was labelled "Boss Paul." [*]

On Election Day, Citizens' candidate McDonald swept the field, defeating Santspree by 5,857 to 4,443 (the Republican candidate placing a distant third). The first and second of the city's wards, home of the old residents, the poorer, the more ethnically attuned voters, were carried by the machine, but the other four wards all went to the reformers.

Four years later, the Democrats changed their formula. They tried to entice Mayor James McDonald into joining them, offering him the Democratic nomination for a second term, in return for letting the machine name the candidates for aldermen and supervisors. McDonald had been a successful enough mayor to be a favorite for re-election. The offer had been relayed by an attorney in the role of emissary from Dan O'Connell, according to an affidavit filed in Supreme Court by McDonald, laying bare the ploy. The Mayor reported having been told, "it will be a lot easier for you, your administration, and the people of the Cohoes Citizens Party if you go along with us." McDonald branded the offer as coercive, and the Albany *Knickerbocker News* editorialized about the Democratic organization's cultivating the veiled threat as a favorite political device. "If you know what is good for you," the line goes, "you'll do things our way," and the warning doesn't even have to be express. It is inevitably present in this type of situation, in Albany County.

Crude threatmongering has been frequent in Cohoes politics, not to mention those of Albany. The Citizens Party elected several of its number to the County Board of Supervisors, who, much more so than the Republicans, comprised a vocal dissident minority. On one occasion, Ralph Robinson was planning to introduce before the County Board a resolution to investigate the activities of Purchasing Agent James Ryan. Robinson reported receiving a telephone call from an anonymous but obviously savvy individual sug-

---

[*] Many feel Van Buskirk earned that sobriquet in his eventual role as executive secretary to the Mayor. This has caused dissension within Citizens' party ranks.

gesting that Cohoes' application for federal aid of $75,000 to build a new firehouse would be found to have some flaws in it, if Robinson didn't "get sick" on the night of the Board meeting. This would have been a black eye to Robinson as a Cohoes official who was promoting the firehouse. Robinson coddled his health, but his resolution was defeated anyway, 22 to 7.

During the reform administration ushered in by Dr. McDonald and continued after his death by his widow and successor as mayor, Virginia McDonald, Cohoes has seen a veritable rebirth. It has garnered All-American City honors, and a considerable federal investment through the Model Cities program. This has been termed "the most significant thing happening now in Cohoes." Underway are a number of major projects, including a new $1 million community center, a $1.8 million high rise apartment building designed for the elderly, and a comparable low-income housing project. Other projects on the drawing boards include an extensive expansion of Cohoes Memorial Hospital, restoration of a downtown music hall, a large industrial tract and renovation and rehabilitation of homes in an 80-acre area. As the *Knickerbocker News* has put it, "virtually everything in Cohoes is being somehow updated, or being changed in the process" of this rejuvenation program.

CHAPTER 23

"Try Harder"

IN A POLITICAL structure based upon parties, there are two avenues of opposition to an incumbent regime. One of these is the other party. However entrenched a machine becomes, it is not generally possible in America to eradicate the other party entirely.° In Albany, there have always been Republican candidates, even though they rarely posed any threat to O'Connell.

The alternative avenue of opposition is within the dominant party itself. Since the beginning of this century, the nomination process has been shifted to primaries. But the machine can control votes there just as it does in a general election, rendering the primary route of opposition no more effectual than the second party route. Indeed, disgruntled members of the dominant party should form a smaller proportion of the primary electorate than the total pool of opposition forms of the general electorate. While the disgruntled may be a minority within the dominant party, it is conceivable for them to combine strength with the second party and form a general election majority. Thus, where machines have been

---

° Even in true one-party areas like the old south, factionalization within the one party often tended to approximate a two-party state of affairs.

Insurgent George W. Harder tries to make a point of order at a County Committee meeting. (*Courtesy of Capital Newspapers*)

toppled at the polls, it has usually occurred in general elections rather than in primaries.

For the first forty years of its history, the O'Connell machine, while enjoying ineffectual Republican opposition, also enjoyed freedom from dissension within the Democratic party. Almost everyone was happy, and for the few who weren't, challenging the machine seemed so hopeless that no primary was contested throughout the entire period.

In 1962, for the first time, the Albany machine finally did experience a challenge by an insurgent Democrat in a party primary.

George W. Harder's father had been secretary to Lieutenant Governor Edwin Corning and to the Democratic State Committee. Now 36, a lawyer and former FBI agent, Harder quit a state job investigating labor rackets to join the political lists, opposing Assemblyman Frank P. Cox, an old machine stalwart, for renomination. "I had thought about it for a number of years," Harder explained, "and it bothered me to study about government . . . to understand the democratic process, only to realize that in Albany we have prostituted the tradition of our forefathers."

Harder's prospects for success were foreshadowed when he attended the county committee meeting that endorsed his opponent for renomination. Just as the meeting was closing, Harder jumped up and asked if he could say a word.

"No," answered John T. Delaney, the party's secretary, who then scooted off the podium.

Harder dashed to the front of the hall and pleaded, "Will anyone listen to me?" But the party regulars filed out past him, scarcely according him a glance. Dan O'Connell, from his back of the hall vantage point, appeared not to notice the minor commotion raised by the lonesome rebel.

"There is a wealth of talent" among Albany Democrats, Harder nevertheless contended, but "this awakened element . . . is shackled by a few old-timers who have lost their zeal." At that, he may have been generous to the machine, since there is evidence that it is wont to purge itself of such "awakened" elements altogether. A number of years ago, one of its brightest young men was Lawrence Kahn, unlike most of the machine's attorneys a graduate of an ivy league law school, and employed in the City Corporation Counsel's office. One day, Kahn walked into the office and found that his name had been removed from the door. And that was that. Today, Kahn is an active local Republican. Anyone interested in advancing in the Albany Democratic party is well advised not to appear too bright a young man or woman.

George Harder campaigned vigorously, attacking Democratic bossism, Republican complacency, and the city administration's opposition to the South Mall project. The challenger was initially dismissed by the machine as the merest nuisance, and was not expected to last a week in the race or even to get his name on the ballot. But Harder gained public attention with his energetic electioneering, while Assemblyman Cox continued the silence that had marked his legislative career, refusing to campaign or to meet Harder in debate. The organization, concerned lest Harder make a decent showing, undertook a quiet campaign of telephone calls and letter writing, to make sure that the committeemen did not lay down on the job and that their vote materialized in full at the polls. The insurgent may have doubly nettled the machine because of the honors it had bestowed upon his father. Harder was thus held to have violated the machine's canons of gratitude.

In the September primary, Harder polled 4,296 votes to Cox' 10,960. What might in other circumstances have been assessed as a sound drubbing looked like a moral victory in light of the earlier downmouthing of Harder's prospects. The candidate himself labelled this as merely the first round of a ten round fight, and recognized that the machine would have to be destroyed from the grass roots up. "We've got to start knocking them over at the alderman level," he said, scrutinizing the returns for weak spots in the machine's sphere of control.

In April, 1964, the undaunted rebel showed up again at the Democratic conclave, this time with about thirty supporters, mostly young people wearing "We Try Harder" buttons. Hopelessly outnumbered, of course, these dissidents chorused, "No, try Harder," when the chair called for the ayes for the slate. Mayor Corning was given a button, and took it gallantly, putting it in his pocket. Harder then went over to shake hands with Dan O'Connell himself, whom he likes to call "Saint Daniel." When asked if he would accept a button, Dan blinked a little in surprise and smiled.

Once more, Harder waged a vigorous campaign against Assemblyman Cox, this time putting out a newspaper, *The Albany Democrat,* highlighting State Investigation Commission probes of Albany corruption. Once more, Harder was overwhelmingly defeated—11,876 to 4,330. He was not even making progress, and attributed this to a special effort to beat him soundly, replete with widespread election violations. Fighting the Albany Democrats, he said, was the classic example of beating your head against the wall, and he also charged his defeat in part to the stay-at-home voters, whom he believed were for him.

As a small consolation, Harder and two supporters managed to capture seats on the County Committee. The post-primary committee meeting proved to be something distinctly out of the ordinary, when Joseph McCormick, a Harderite, placed in nomination an insurgent slate of candidates for the leadership posts. Nothing of the sort had been heard of before. Oddly enough, the slate consisted of old-line Democrats and was headed by Congressman Leo O'Brien, who was not present. It was explained by its proponents that their slate was intended merely to indicate the kind of leaders the Democrats should consider having.

When a reporter asked Dan O'Connell for a statement, the boss flashed a broad smile and said, "I'm too busy right now trying to get elected." But in the vote on the "leadership struggle," there was a resounding chorus of ayes and a few lonesome nays. So Uncle Dan remained as chairman.

Harder now rose to a point of order, challenging the election of Donald Lynch as second vice chairman, on the grounds that Lynch was not a member of the county committee and hence ineligible to the position under the party's own 1920 rules. This was met with booing and cries of "Sit down, you bum." Assemblyman Cox, who happened to be presiding, pointed a finger at Harder and warned, "If anyone came here to make trouble, let me tell you that we have been doing this the same way for the past forty-four years." Harder's point of order was dismissed out of hand.

In 1965, he was back in the race again, this time challenging the machine's other assemblyman, Ways and Means Committee Chairman Harvey Lifset. The organization drummed up a heavy vote to show its mettle, burying Harder once and for all by a 6-1 margin. The insurgent leader's ally, Joseph McCormick, was beaten by an 8-1 margin in his primary race against State Senator Julian Erway. These results belied Harder's earlier claims that he was losing because of the stay-at-homes, and were an impressive demonstration of the machine's vote-getting power. This was contrary to the usual experience wherein a heavy primary vote favors a dissident candidate (since the marginal voters who usually don't show up at the polls are typically those least subject to machine influence).

On that primary day in 1965, candidate George Harder himself was arrested and imprisoned.

He had been present as a legal observer at the polling place where Mrs. Kathryn (Kitty) O'Connell, Dan's sister-in-law, came in to vote, and Harder disputed the legality of a Democratic worker "assisting" her inside the booth. The worker in question was Francis Schreck, who has since become Albany County Welfare Commissioner. The election board chairman directed a policeman to expel the "trouble-maker," but Harder resisted, protesting that he was within his rights. A scuffle ensued, and Harder wound up in jail charged with assault and various other offenses. The State Election Frauds Bureau entered the case, and got it transferred from police court to the grand jury, which eventually exonerated Harder.

Between 1965 and 1973, although the New Democratic Coalition, a statewide organization formed in the course of the McCarthy presidential campaign, waged some primary contests, there was no frontal attack upon the machine such as that levelled by Harder.°

When the fight against the machine from within Democratic ranks languished from lack of support, it was picked up by the Republican party. In 1966, a new order was decreed in the G.O.P. with the election of Joseph Frangella as county chairman.

Congressman Leo W. O'Brien, who had represented Albany for sixteen years, was retiring. Selected by the organization to succeed him was the president of the Common Council, Richard J. Conners, another of its stalwarts. Meanwhile, on the Republican side, Daniel E. Button, executive editor of the *Times-Union,* announced his first race for public office. Button was obviously not the usual sacrificial lamb offered by the G.O.P., and his high caliber candidacy promised to make the contest an interesting one.

Further interest was contributed by the turmoil within Albany's tiny Liberal party. Long the captive of Dan O'Connell, the Albany Liberals were at last breaking free. The local party officers had endorsed the Conners candidacy, but the state leadership repudiated this stance, thereby intimating that it would no longer tolerate its Albany arm being the handmaiden of Dan O'Connell. The local party leaders, headed by Patrick Cox, decided not to send delegates to the Liberal state convention, expecting their

---

° He popped up again in 1971 as a Democratic nominee for Bethlehem town supervisor, supported by Kenelm Thacher, the former Mayor's nephew and Bethlehem party leader. Although Thacher is in the good graces of the countywide machine, he has been one of its more progressive leaders. Harder was defeated in that race by Bertram Kohinke, the town's Republican chief.

party loyalty to come under challenge if they went. In their place the convention welcomed an insurgent group from Albany County, seated as "fraternal delegates." There followed a court battle in which the insurgent group's attempt to nominate Republican Button was upheld. This marked the end of O'Connell's control of the Liberal party. His henchmen who had been enrolled in it withdrew—many of them changing their enrollment to the Conservative party, which the Democrats now moved in upon to replace the lost Liberals.

Unlike previous Republican candidates, Button campaigned as though he intended to win. He even made a trip to Viet Nam. His lavish campaign included extensive utilization of television. Conners was not using television, Dan O'Connell having told him not to worry, since he was a shoo-in. But the candidate grew concerned, pointed to his opponent's wide television exposure, and pleaded to be put on television too. The boss relented.

When Conners got to the television studio, Leo O'Brien was already there. The candidate wanted to talk in his own behalf, but was told, "Leo O'Brien is more popular than you'll ever be. Let him do the talking." So the commercial showed a silent Conners listening to the voice of O'Brien. There was no way for Conners to appear statesmanlike under these conditions, and the commercial was a pernicious one. It ruined him.[*] Daniel Button piled up 106,691 votes to only 89,327 for Conners.

This was widely taken as the first evidence of the organization's decay. Seemingly in response to the new threat, the party's slate of candidates in the 1967 local elections featured a number of new young faces. Yet there was still no major overhaul of the party, nor any change in its outlook. This year's election provided another jolt when the Democratic County Clerk, John Bartlett, won re-election by a bare few thousand votes over Rena Posner, a Republican-AIM candidate.

By now, the Democrats had bidden their long-time allies, the Liberals, adieu. No effort was made to recapture that splinter party, and indeed, many Democratic candidates were instructed to turn down Liberal endorsement. They were endorsed instead by the Conservative party, whose local contingent had come under O'Connell domination. The Conservatives were ripe for this, since they had been antagonized by the recent link-up between Republi-

---

[*] As noted earlier, it is possible that the machine deliberately sunk Conners in connection with a deal with Rockefeller.

cans and Liberals. Albany County Conservative Chairman William Farley charged that the local G.O.P. had been captured by "liberal elements from New York City." *

The endorsement of the Democrats by the Albany Conservatives would be repudiated by the latter party's state leadership. Contention, in and out of the courts, between the pro- and anti-O'Connell Conservative factions continues into the present.

In 1968, Frangella was promising a real fight for the legislative seats theretofore controlled by the Albany machine. One observer sees as the essence of the Frangella-wrought change his "unleashing" of the Republican candidates to campaign in whatever manner they thought necessary to win. In earlier times, Republicans had ignored their strongest issues, concentrating instead on tangential and even unpopular issues such as closing the after-hours gin mills. Those days were over.

Very slowly, but very definitely, things were changing in Albany. The complexion of the area was metamorphosing, with the great expansion of the state university and the hordes of state workers in the mushrooming bureaucracy of the Rockefeller administration. These newcomers to the area were frequently liberal-minded, frequently Republicans, and their educational level was high. At the same time the support given the machine by the city's homeowners and merchants was weakening. While the low tax rate was still appreciated, the atrocious level of public services was beginning to rankle. Some of the merchants are new, young, and even reform-minded; others represent national chains without local loyalties, and still others are growing resentful of the decay of downtown Albany and the party's callousness toward the problem. The South Mall project displaced thousands of the machine's most dependable voters, and removed some of the districts where floater and repeat voting was most easily accomplished. The suburbs were filling up, while Albany was beginning to acquire a substantial black population. The machine, made up in its grass roots with a large contingent of bigots, has been insensitive to the blacks and fearful of their potential power at the polls.

---

* Republican leader Frangella averred that he wasn't surprised by the Conservatives' switch in allegiance, "since the Democratic organization in this county is the epitome of conservatism." Congressman Button commented that "the party of FDR, JFK and LBJ lies traduced by its Albany County leadership in this unholy wedlock."

Despite this erosion of its base of support, the machine remained about the only thing in Albany County that was undergoing no change.*

District Attorney John Garry was leaving office in 1968, and the nominee to succeed him was Joseph Scully, of a family long prominent in the party's affairs. The Republican candidate was a thirty year old nonentity named Arnold Proskin. "Scully had one set speech he repeated everywhere," said an Albany politician afterwards. "And that points up the trouble with the machine: their candidates have traditionally 'stood' for office rather than run for it. Some of them never campaigned at all."

For the legislative seats, the machine renominated its old standbys, Senator Erway and Assemblymen Cox and Lifset. Against Congressman Daniel Button, they nominated Jacob Herzog, a lawyer locally prominent with a good political name, but a colorless candidate.

The heart of the matter is that the Democrats did not yet feel seriously challenged. They expected their candidates to win handily as always. Thus they campaigned casually if at all. Television invitations to debate were refused, and the fact of their refusal was broadcast frequently. Voters may well have begun to resent being taken for granted in this manner.

Despite a solid Albany County majority in the presidential race for Humphrey, Republican Button was an overwhelming winner for Congress, and helped carry in the rest of the ticket. Proskin was elected district attorney by some 6,000 votes. Republican Walter B. Langley defeated Senator Erway by 5,000. Republican Raymond Skuse nosed out Assemblyman Cox by 2,000, and Republican Fred Field trounced Assemblyman Lifset by 7,000.

It was a stunning sweep. If the legislative losses did not affect the organization in its breadbasket, the loss of the district attorney's office surely did. This, in one blow, struck from the machine's hands one of its most potent weapons and put it in the hands of the opposition.

Despite this defeat, by far its worst in the half century history

---

* Its xenophobia was as strong as ever; the County Board of Supervisors delayed for two years the receipt of federal anti-poverty funds out of fear of losing its authority to suspect outsiders. It delayed other federal programs because the required local matching funds would have meant increasing taxes. Thus until 1967 Albany was the largest metropolitan area in the nation not getting a slice of this great federal pie. The situation was ended only after the Office of Economic Opportunity decided to bypass the local authorities.

Republican winners, from left to right: Congressman Daniel E. Button, State Senator Walter B. Langley, District Attorney Arnold W. Proskin, campaigning on State Street. (*Courtesy of Times-Union*)

of the O'Connell machine, no flowers were being laid upon its grave. "Dead? The machine dead?" commented Albany G.O.P. Counsel John Tabner. "They lost an election, that's all."

And even if this Republican victory were to be the beginning of the end of the machine, Dan O'Connell was seen as going down with it, still at the helm. The election brought forth no proposal from within the Democratic party that the 83 year old leader step down or be replaced. Albany political reporter Arvis Chalmers noted that despite sharp differences among such major party figures as Erastus Corning, Donald Lynch, Eugene Devine and the Ryan brothers, there was unanimity on O'Connell's remaining chairman. This was shrewd politics on their part. The Albany Democratic party was loping along with its deeply felt loyalty and affection for Uncle Dan as the glue holding it together. As one prominent Democrat put it, "1969 is going to be a crucial year for us. No one is better equipped to unite or re-unite the party than Dan. It would be a mistake if he decided to step aside. It would hurt our chances next year. He's the leader."

There was, however, some feeling that many of the committee-men, the grass-roots contacts between the machine and its voters, were going slack. Defeated congressional candidate Herzog, in a bitter concession speech, indicted the party for not giving him enough help. Grown accustomed to winning elections, some committeemen sat back complacently and expected to win this one, without bothering to hustle up the vote, or even to pass along to the leaders intimations that all was not well. Shortly after the election, a re-evaluation of the list of committeemen was promised, to check which were producing and which ones were falling down on the job, along with a rejuvenation of the party through the promotion of younger candidates. As a further seeming reaction, Dan O'Connell named a five-member executive committee to administer the party. With himself as chairman of the committee, the others were his octogenarian vice chairman Mary Marcy, Mayor Corning, Donald Lynch and James Ryan. This was far from a revolutionary development.

Nor was the 1969 slate revolutionary. Renominated were Mayor Corning, Council President Conners, and most of the other familiar faces.

On the Republican side, the only man who wanted the nomination for mayor was Albert Hartheimer, a former campaign aide of Congressman Button. While county leader Frangella was cool toward Hartheimer's candidacy, he was unable to come up with anyone else, and so the Republicans were stuck with an admittedly unsatisfactory candidate.

Corning waltzed to his eighth term, 37,896 to 15,215. However, some comfort for Republicans could ironically be distilled from the fact of Corning's personal popularity, then still intact, as against the mediocrity of their own candidate. Furthermore, this 70% victory was Corning's smallest ever.

Since its longtime legislators had all been defeated, the machine was forced to come up with a completely new ticket in 1970. And the Republican state legislature gave O'Connell some help by providing him with the most popular man in the area to head his slate. That was Congressman Samuel S. Stratton of Schenectady, thrown by a redistricting into a race against Button.

Stratton had been a reform mayor of Schenectady and had been on the outs with the regulars in his early years as congressman. This relationship had warmed, however. The machine was happy to have a Democratic congressman with Stratton's conservative views, and Stratton had to be thankful for the machine's votes in the face of a legislative attempt to gerrymander him out of office. Thus, while the machine had given the cold shoulder to Stratton's 1962 gubernatorial aspirations, the Mayor specifically mentioned Stratton for the office in a 1971 interview. Dan O'Connell now calls him "phenomenal. Terrific."

The Stratton-Button race offered a clear choice between philosophies, muddled however by the fact that Democrat Stratton was a conservative very much in tune with President Nixon's policies, while Button was a liberal Republican—who nevertheless ran television commercials in which the President endorsed him.

Button had proved himself as a vote-getter in his two previous races, but he was no match for Sam Stratton, who demolished him. Despite this, Senator Langley easily bested his Democratic challenger, a former county sheriff, and Assemblyman Field retained his seat over former District Attorney John Garry, certainly a powerful Democratic opponent. The only recoupment registered by the machine was the narrow defeat of the city's Assemblyman, Raymond Skuse, by Thomas Brown, a young county legislator.

It must have been a frustrated O'Connell machine that faced 1971—and further frustration. For the old days were gone forever.

CHAPTER 24

The Seventies

THE 1971 election was not one in which any major office in Albany changed hands. Yet it was in several respects a key test of the machine's power over the electorate. The results defined the limits of that power, showing both what the machine could do and what it could not.

The organization was determined to recapture the district attorney's office, which had fallen into G.O.P. hands in 1968. District Attorney Arnold Proskin, although possibly giving the Albany administration a few uncomfortable moments over a snow removal contracting scandal, was hampered by Democratic control of the other governmental arms. He had not been able to tear the doors off any closets containing skeletons, over which there had been some Republican grumbling. But the D.A. was still a threat to the machine, even if more *in posse* than *in esse*. Its control of grand juries was neutralized by a Republican D.A. And of course, a machine always feels safer when it has a D.A. who can bear down upon its opponents and other malcontents.

Against Proskin the Democrats nominated Thomas W. Keegan, a thirty year old assistant city corporation counsel (now police court judge). He was the grandson of an old-time Democratic sheriff who had been a faithful cog in the O'Connell machine of the early days. As Keegan tells the story of his nomination, he had previously been known to but not intimate with Dan O'Connell, having met the leader only twice. He was offered the nomination, unsolicited, by Donald Lynch. Only thereafter did he confer with O'Connell. Keegan was plainly picked not for his ability to attract votes, but rather because he would be suitable to the machine as D.A. if he won.

Keegan's closeness to the organization prevented his gaining the support of many of the newer voters. Most of the candidate's campaign workers were older than he was. The main thrust of his campaign was that Proskin had been an ineffective district attorney, and that Keegan could do better. But his own qualifications were less than incandescent and there was some feeling that Proskin was handicapped not by incompetence, but by being a Republican trying to do his job in a Democratic town.

The Liberal Party endorsed Proskin. The Conservatives turned in dual sets of nominating petitions, one endorsing Keegan, and the other, Proskin. In the courts, it was the Keegan designation, by the O'Connell-dominated faction, that stood up. The Conservative Party also endorsed the balance of the Democratic ticket.

Another intriguing contest was afoot this year, Albany's first for a school board. The board had always been appointive and hence the province of the organization; for a quarter century it had been headed by Neile Towner, Edward O'Connell's old law partner, and in recent years, by Judge John E. Holt-Harris. The board, and Holt-Harris himself, were coming under increasing fire; the most persistent critic on the scene, Theresa Cooke, in fact charged that Holt-Harris was ineligible to serve on the board, and he resigned. Meanwhile, Albany's new Republican assemblyman, Raymond Skuse, shepherded through the legislature a bill aimed at an elected school board in the city, which set in motion a referendum on the question. Corning and the Democrats opposed the referendum, but in November, 1970, with—and probably because of—minimal fanfare given to the issue, Albanians voted overwhelmingly in favor of electing their school board.

After considerable further tribulation in the courts at the instance of Mayor Corning and the city fathers, the seven seat board did come up for election in 1971. It was to be a nonpartisan election, conducted at-large, citywide. The first slate was nominated by a Citizens' Convention, spearheaded by the League of

Women Voters, at which some seventy local organizations were represented with delegates. The Convention was independent of any organized political groups in the city, and prominent in its councils were many who had been identified with earlier reform efforts. The Convention slate included, for example, James Gallagher of the defunct Albany Independent Movement, and longtime machine opponent Victor Lord. The slate was not, as Mayor Corning predictably tagged it, a Republican one in camouflage; independents and independent Democrats predominated.

In due course, the machine's candidates joined the field. The ensuing campaign was surprising for its quietude, if nothing else. While the Citizens' ticket was able to mount a creditable effort, the paucity of available human and financial resources caused it to be something short of a blitz. At no time did the Citizens' Convention have more than forty people working for its slate. As for the Democrats, their energies were being channelled single-mindedly toward the district attorney race. Not until the late stages of the contest was any campaign made on behalf of their school board slate.

This is not to imply that the Democrats considered the matter unimportant. They were not about to allow a citizen takeover of the school board, and once they started working, they did so with a will. In fact, on Election Day itself, since everyone so inclined already knew how to vote Row B, it was the school board slate that the organization pushed. Numerous complaints were lodged that the Democrats were violating the election law by distributing leaflets showing how to vote their slate, within one hundred feet of the polls, and often inside the polling places themselves. The leaflets expressly identified the candidates as Democrats and even placed the Democratic star symbol next to each name, despite the nonpartisan nature of the election. Resentment against this might have contributed to the large vote polled by the Citizens' slate.*

Election Day of 1971 demonstrated that the organization could still turn out the vote within the city of Albany—but only there, and not as well as in its heyday. The county is becoming closely divided in elections between the two parties; although as of

---

* Donald Lynch of Democratic Headquarters labelled the controversial leaflets for "educational and identification purposes." As for distributing such material inside the polling places ("strictly illegal" according to the D.A.'s office), Lynch pointed out that people are permitted to bring any papers with them into the booths, and that the items in question were handed out "in good faith to assist the voters."

1972 the Democrats had a registration edge of 71,916 to 46,034, this does not reflect attitudinal shifts of long-registered people, and the balance of power is held by 39,747 independents.

The O'Connell machine would seem, then, to be almost quarantined to the city, where out of 61,394 voters as of 1972, 43,755 were Democrats and only 4,106 were Republicans. The Republicans are up from their abysmal 1965 total of 3,135, but more significant is the Democratic decline. In 1956, there were 54,419 Democrats in the city, and the total registration peak occurred even further in the past—1948, with 85,072.

So in 1971, it was more the fall-off in the Democratic vote in the city than suburban Republican gains that shaped the outcome. Even the ten-to-one Democratic advantage in the city was not enough to swing the county. Keegan carried the city in the D.A. race by a pale 7,000, a margin which Proskin overcame in suburban Colonie alone. The Republican won his county-wide race by more than 12,000.

The G.O.P. nearly also pulled in its candidate for county treasurer over Eugene Devine, a major figure in the machine hierarchy who had held the post for eighteen years. A recount showed that Devine had survived by a mere 317 votes, another indication of an essential partisan equipoise in the county.

It should be noted that Keegan's poor city plurality was due to a good deal of ticket-splitting against him, as the Democratic vote for other offices was closer to normal proportions. There was sympathy for Proskin as a man honestly trying to work despite political obstacles, but more importantly, a feeling that the machine was pushing too hard for Keegan, and that he was being oversold.*

Keegan himself attributes his defeat to a general feeling of dissatisfaction with the status quo, affecting not just Albany but the entire nation, and points to the election of Democratic County legislators in Colonie, which is normally Republican. This malaise, Keegan believes, included a growing antipathy toward the machine, a sentiment for which his candidacy became a "lightning rod." He sees many as having voted not so much for Proskin as against the machine which Keegan represented. Interestingly, Keegan regards such an attitude as a "valid" one, even while disagreeing with it.

---

* One young girl confessed to her Democratic committeeman that she had voted a straight ticket except for Keegan. The man was later heard to say, "Her mother would kill her for that, but I won't tell. We don't really try to hurt people who vote against us."

Despite the factors which defeated Keegan, the Democrats made their usual sweep of all nineteen county legislative seats from the city, and even increased their control of that body by virtue of a few upsets in the suburbs, apparently attributable to local issues. The legislature was crucial because of the large number of jobs that it controls.

The outcome of the city school board election was of particular interest. The Democrats' slate captured all but one of the seven seats, the exception going to James Gallagher of the Citizens' Convention. Some took this as a sign that the machine is still purring smoothly, and indeed, it may be thought an enviable achievement that the organization could turn out a vote on an ostensibly nonpartisan election with a complicated ballot arrangement.*

On the other hand, the Democrats may be regarded as having done surprisingly poorly in the school board election. Their slate polled less than 20,000 votes, a figure usually associated in Albany with Republican returns. And while the Democrats did win all but one seat, this should not obscure the narrow margin by which the Citizens' Convention ticket trailed. They came in right up behind the Democrats, so closely that their top runner managed to nudge out the Democrats' last runner. The identity of that lone Democratic loser, incidentally, points up at least some ability to discriminate by the Albany electorate. It was Alice Jackson, the sole black being supported by the machine.

While subject to varying appraisals, the 1971 election outcome was revealing of the machine's condition. Some labelled it as dead or in its last gasps; they ignored that despite some deterioration, the machine's web of active committeemen still pre-empts the city's politics. It is still one of the best of its kind in the country, and no opposing group could dream of matching it. A sizable segment of the electorate remains beholden to the machine for the favors given through the years. Many in Albany have a relative on the public payroll.

These ongoing machine strengths were evident in the following year's election results, in which normalcy prevailed. The machine defeated a McGovern slate in the delegate primary, and then in November, despite Albany's conservative character, the

---

* Many votes were probably lost to the Democrats because their stalwarts felt they had done their duty by voting Row B, and couldn't be bothered to fool with the separate and difficult school board section on the machine. The total board vote was markedly lower than for the other offices.

O'Connell organization produced a three-to-two edge for George McGovern in the city. Nixon barely carried the county. And although Republican State Senator Langley's personal popularity was sufficient to give him a large majority over a well financed challenger, Democratic Assemblyman Brown swept every city ward, burying Thomas Conole, who had campaigned tirelessly. The Democrats also managed to win all three county races by thin margins, electing Michael Tepedino to family court and John Clyne to succeed County Judge Schenck.

All this does not mean that the machine cannot lose. It does mean that voters in Albany will not oust it with the casual fickleness that people sometimes display in politics. It will take a deep and pointed voter dissatisfaction to override the countervailing tugs and install a new mayor at city hall. That the contest for mayor is of surpassing urgency to the machine will help it to win, because voters will feel more pressed to be loyal than they did in 1971.

Developments subsequent to that election may have laid the groundwork for the kind of dissatisfaction that could topple the machine. An earlier chapter has discussed the recent jarring tax rises. This will affect everyone, since those not owning homes should experience rent hikes. Low taxes have in the past been important to the machine—many forgave what they knew to be its deficiencies, in return for the low taxes.

The City also went through a nasty scrape with its firemen's union. The affair's antecedents go back several years, with Donald Lynch having spearheaded a futile battle to block unionization of the Fire Department. The machine's concern was that until recently, jobs and promotions in the department could not be had without a ward leader's say-so, and the firemen were milked for annual $35 campaign contributions. Unionization would end these political advantages. Lynch's inside lever in fighting it off was Deputy Chief Thomas Wink, who doubled as an Arbor Hill section Democratic leader. Several firemen were told point blank by Lynch, "You get out of that damned union and we'll make you a lieutenant!" But Wink's death was followed by unionization of most of the firemen, and the present bad blood between them and the Democratic political powers.

Mayor Corning plumped down publicly against any pay increase for the firemen. Meanwhile, union spokesmen claimed that in 1971, County Treasurer Devine as negotiator offered a $600 pay rise. But Corning secured Dan O'Connell's backing for his stand, and the Common Council rejected the pay increase.

The firemen thereupon collected enough signatures on petitions to put the matter on the ballot in the 1972 election. Their position had attracted considerable public sympathy and support from the Catholic diocese. Corning and O'Connell, sensing the public mood, first backtracked to the point of supporting the holding of a referendum. O'Connell even signed the petition. Then, the city settled with the firemen. It was during this imbroglio that Dan O'Connell incurred the ire of the city's Italian community by publicly calling the firemen's chaplain, a Catholic priest, "that Dago son of a bitch." O'Connell expressly refused to apologize for the remark, while Mayor Corning averred that the boss had "intended no disrespect" by it.

The City eventually reached a settlement with the firemen's union, but many of the firemen were dissatisfied with it and retained a resentment against the machine over the affair.

While all this was happening, Theresa Cooke and Robert Stein formed the Albany Taxpayers' Association as a watchdog over the city budget. They held their own hearings on the subject, Mrs. Cooke contending that a large part of the budget is waste. Her efforts to uncover skulduggery and waste led to the State Investigation Commission sessions of December 1972, covered earlier.

These revelations and the indictments in 1973 of some of its leading figures have been a source of embarrassment to the machine. Many Albanians, however, still distrust outsiders and are defensive about local officials. Some feel that the investigation is being pursued for partisan reasons; as for Mayor Corning's unresponsive and sometimes ludicrous performance under questioning, some Albanians seem proud of him for being able to stymie his accusers. Whether the ongoing probe of the Albany Police Department by the S.I.C. will spark indignation remains to be seen.

Then came the 1973 primaries, and the machine received a stiff challenge. Theresa Cooke entered the lists as a candidate for city comptroller, and Green Island Mayor John McNulty, denied the nomination for county sheriff by the committeemen, decided to seek it in the primary. This race seemed a continuation of a feud between McNulty's father and Dan O'Connell, but many reform-minded Democrats rallied to McNulty's campaign.

For comptroller, the machine put up the present Deputy, Lyle Hoffer, who campaigned on the idea that the investigations of corruption sparked by Mrs. Cooke were somehow bad for the city.

Right: Republican Mayoral candidate Carl E. Touhey (*Courtesy of C. Touhey*)

Left: Reform leader Theresa B. Cooke (*Courtesy of T. Cooke*)

Cooke pointed out how much taxpayers' money had already been saved as a result of her work, and stressed the need for an independent fiscal watchdog. Hoffer also attempted to paint a picture of Mrs. Cooke and her supporters as some sort of evil combine, but this tactic may have backfired.

For the aldermanic races, the city was redistricted, and a state law provided that a primary could be dispensed with if the new lines were not ready by a certain date. The machine tried to take advantage of this by delaying the reapportionment, but insurgent candidate Jane Ramos went to the courts seeking a primary, and won. During the court fight, the regulars had neglected to circulate nominating petitions for most of their aldermanic candidates; and when the decision came down, James Ryan tried to solve this problem by simply writing in the names of the aldermen on the petitions already filed for the rest of the slate.° This illegal procedure resulted in a ruling by Supreme Court Justice Edward Conway that threw all of the machine's aldermanic candidates off the ballot, except for those in two wards where, faced with challengers, the regulars had circulated additional petitions. But these extra petitions as well came under attack and were found not in compliance with the election law.

Despite their patent illegality, Judge Russell Hunt upheld the petitions. The Court of Appeals reversed him, but allowed a write-in vote in the primary, and extended this ruling to all of the wards. Only by grace of this last-minute decision were the Democrats able to get their aldermanic candidates nominated.

On primary day, June 4, 1973, the O'Connell machine suffered its first defeat at the hands of its own party members. John McNulty won the sheriff's race by about four hundred votes, in spite of a much more visible campaign waged by his opponent. Theresa Cooke lost the comptrollership nomination by four thousand, but surprised some observers by polling 38% of the vote. Mrs. Cooke won the Republican nomination by a write-in, and so the contest will be repeated in November.

In the closely-watched seventh ward aldermanic race, Jane Ramos apparently defeated the machine's incumbent by nine votes. Ramos' victory is being challenged in court. This situation, and the challenge to the apparent victory of insurgent David Sawyer in the twelfth ward, have not been resolved as we go to press.

These primary results give some indication that many of Albany's voters are at long last getting fed up with the machine. And if the time is ripe in 1973 for an all-out assault, the Republican

---

° Ryan has been indicted for tampering with the petitions.

party is preparing to mount one. In February, Carl E. Touhey, one of the city's most prominent business leaders and a former chamber of commerce president, declared his candidacy for mayor. An independent who never ran for office before, Touhey is an attractive, articulate contender, able to run a well-financed campaign and to garner the support of much of the establishment that was until now comfortable with O'Connell and Corning.

Touhey won the Republican nomination by a 15-1 margin, and his campaign presents the strongest threat in the machine's history. Even if they fall short of electing him mayor, the Republicans will substantially improve upon their usual city showing, which will help them elect Lawrence Kahn, John Graziano and Donald Lang in the county surrogate, clerk and sheriff races respectively. This would seriously damage the machine because of the large number of patronage jobs involved. A further prime Republican target is the county legislature, of similar importance.

In the midst of these tribulations, the machine has undergone some measure of internal transition.

While Dan O'Connell and Mayor Corning have always been on good terms, the same has not been true of their respective camps. The old-line O'Connell gang, consisting of people like Lynch, Clyne, Devine and the Ryans have long been antagonistic toward the Mayor, and the feeling seems to be mutual. It was exacerbated by the firemen's dispute, among other things. Among the rank-and-file party workers, while Corning is respected, he is not loved like Dan O'Connell, and he inspires no personal loyalty.

Yet none of the Irishmen could be effective as leader because in-fighting would surely break out among them. Thus while Corning has little true support other than what he commands by virtue of his patronage power, he is the only logical heir to O'Connell. For years, he was O'Connell's close partner—reporting to the boss, but actually making the decisions himself. That originally applied to governmental policy, but in recent times, Corning has in effect exercised almost the full measure of O'Connell's authority.

In 1972, Dan O'Connell, 86 and in frail health, considered himself "about through." He said that Erastus Corning is the chairman of the party in all but title.

We have seen how the O'Connell machine first came to power in a basically Democratic city disgusted with Republican tyranny and corruption; and how the O'Connell machine carried tyranny and corruption to new heights in Albany. We have seen how a party that started out giving the city honest and progressive government went slack once it stopped receiving vigorous opposition.

We have seen how the machine perpetuated itself in power through a tightly disciplined structure of hard working neighborhood committeemen and ward leaders;

Through a patronage system that has larded Albany's payroll with hundreds of low-paid workers;

Through manipulating tax assessments and tax delinquent properties;

Through judges willing to sacrifice their honor to help the machine that elected them;

Through vote bribery, peeking, intimidation and fraud;

Through control of gambling and vice;

Through corrupt and illegal self-dealing on city contracts, and budgetary trickery;

Through demoralizing the opposition by fostering myths of retaliation for those who support it;

Through a politically controlled and corrupt police department;

Through harassing its critics by improper use of the grand jury;

Through giving citizens as political favors what should be theirs by right;

And through persuading them to overlook all this in return for low taxes, with business taxed heavily to make up the difference, impairing the city's financial health and speeding its decay.

And we have seen how some things have been changing in Albany, threatening the machine.

It has lost some elections in recent years; it may even be driven from city hall. But if that happens, it will not be the final chapter. The machine won't vanish overnight. It is made up of a lot of people who have committed their lives to it, and who have carved out for themselves little niches of power and participation. Many of them will not cease to function politically until they cease to function as living beings.

As a tyrannical machine or as a tame organization, it will survive in some form. But the Corning machine can never be another O'Connell machine. The city is different, the times are different, and the people, both inside the machine and outside, are different too. The old personal magic is dying with Dan, and we will not see its like again. Dan O'Connell is the last of the breed.

With him passes a part of America.